Fifth Edition

Spanish for Law Enforcement

Ana C. Jarvis
Chandler-Gilbert Community College

Luis Lebredo

Walter Oliver
California State University, San Bernardino

D. C. Heath and Company
Lexington, Massachusetts   Toronto

Address editorial correspondence to:

D. C. Heath and Company
125 Spring Street
Lexington, MA 02173

Acquisitions: Denise St. Jean
Development: Sheila McIntosh
Editorial Production: Julie Lane/Helen Bronk
Design: Alwyn R. Velásquez
Production Coordination: Lisa Merrill

Published simultaneously in Canada.

Printed in the United States of America.

International Standard Book Number: 0–669–35461–9

10 9 8 7 6 5 4 3 2 1

Substantially revised in the Fifth Edition, *Spanish for Law Enforcement* presents realistic situations and the specialized vocabulary that law enforcement professionals need in the course of their daily work in order to communicate with Spanish-speaking people. Personalized questions, grammar exercises, dialogue completions, roleplays, and realia-based activities provide students with numerous opportunities to apply, in a wide variety of practical contexts, the grammatical structures introduced in the corresponding lessons of the *Basic Spanish Grammar*, Fifth Edition, core text. In this Fifth Edition, *Spanish for Law Enforcement* contains a preliminary lesson, twenty regular lessons, and four review sections.

New to the Fifth Edition

In preparing the Fifth Edition, we have kept in mind suggestions from reviewers and from users of the previous editions along with the need to develop students' ability to communicate effectively in Spanish. The following list highlights the major changes in the manual and its components designed to respond to those needs.

- A new *Lección preliminar* reflects the key communicative and structural elements introduced in the preliminary lessons of *Basic Spanish Grammar*, and focuses on high-frequency, practical vocabulary. The lesson is designed to foster students' confidence in their ability to learn Spanish and to encourage them to use the language actively from the very first day of class.
- The fine-tuned grammatical sequence parallels all changes made in *Basic Spanish Grammar*, Fifth Edition.
- The lesson framework has been reorganized to accommodate new features and to provide instructors and students with a more effective learning tool.
- The dialogues have been revised throughout to reflect current practices and situations encountered in law enforcement. To encourage students to derive meaning from context, the dialogue translations now appear in an appendix.
- To facilitate students' access to useful words and expressions, the optional vocabulary list that formerly appeared toward the end of each lesson now occurs in a new, thematically-organized *Vocabulario adicional* subsection that follows the lesson's main vocabulary. The lists have been updated and, where appropriate, expanded to reflect current practices and concerns in law enforcement.
- New *Notas culturales* highlight Hispanic customs and traditions, as well as background information on behaviors and values, to assist law enforcement personnel in their interactions with the Spanish speakers with whom they come in contact.
- For immediate reinforcement of new vocabulary and the dialogue's content, *¿Recuerdan ustedes?* and *Para conversar* sections follow the cultural notes.
- The grammar exercises have been revised and new exercises have been added to increase their contextualization and communicative thrust and to reflect the revised vocabulary load.
- New *Un paso más* sections provide supplemental practice of the *Vocabulario adicional*. Where pertinent, realia-based activities engage students in reading and using information from authentic documents.
- Each *Repaso* now features a *Práctica oral* section that is recorded on the cassette program. Throughout the manual, cassette icons signal additional recorded material.
- The appendixes feature a revised, more efficient reference tool for Spanish sounds and pronunciation, as well as a new appendix with useful listings of conversion formulas for the metric system and the Celsius scale.

Organization of the Lessons

- Realistic dialogues model typical conversations in Spanish, using key vocabulary and grammatical structures that law enforcement professionals need in their daily work.

- The *Vocabulario* section summarizes the new, active words and expressions presented in the dialogue and categorizes them by part of speech. A special subsection of cognates heads up the vocabulary list so students can readily identify these terms, and, where applicable, special notations identify useful regionalisms. The optional *Vocabulario adicional* subsection supplies supplementary vocabulary related to the lesson theme.
- *Notas culturales* equip students with practical insights into culturally determined behavior patterns and other pertinent information regarding Hispanics in North America.
- The *¿Recuerdan ustedes?* questions check students' comprehension of the dialogue.
- The *Para conversar* section provides personalized questions spun off from the lesson theme. Students are encouraged to work in pairs, asking and answering each of the questions.
- The *Vamos a practicar* section reinforces essential grammar points and the new vocabulary through a variety of structured and communicative activities.
- *Conversaciones breves* encourages students to use their own imaginations, experiences, and the new vocabulary to complete each conversation.
- The *En estas situaciones* section develops students' communication skills through guided roleplay situations related to the lesson theme.
- Open-ended *Casos* offer additional opportunities for improving oral proficiency as students interact in situations they might encounter in their law enforcement work. These roleplays require spontaneous use of Spanish and are intended to underscore the usefulness of language study.
- The optional *Un paso más* section features one or two activities to practice the supplementary words and expressions in the *Vocabulario adicional* section. In pertinent lessons, authentic documents expand upon the lesson theme and expose students to comprehensible input as they draw upon the use of cognates to assist them in developing their reading skills in Spanish. Comprehension activities guide students through the documents.

Repasos

A comprehensive review section, containing the following materials, appears after every five lessons. Upon completion of each section, students will know precisely what material they have mastered.
- *Práctica de vocabulario* exercises check students' cumulative knowledge and use of active vocabulary in a variety of formats: matching, true/false statements, identifying related words, sentence completion, and crossword puzzles. Solutions to the crossword puzzles appear in Appendix D so students can verify their responses independently.
- The *Práctica oral* section features questions that review key vocabulary and grammatical structures presented in the preceding five lessons. To develop students' aural and oral skills, the questions are also recorded on the cassette program.

Appendixes

- Appendix A, "Introduction to Spanish Sounds and the Alphabet," explains vowel sounds, consonant sounds, linking, rhythm, intonation, syllable formation, accentuation, and the Spanish alphabet.
- Appendix B, "English Translations of Dialogues," contains the translations of all dialogues in the preliminary lesson and the twenty regular lessons.
- Appendix C, "Metric System," features conversion formulas for temperature and metric weights and measures, as well as Spanish terms for U.S. weights and measures.
- Appendix D, "Answer Key to the *Crucigramas*," allows students to check their work on the crossword puzzles in the *Repaso* sections.

End Vocabularies

Completely revised, the comprehensive Spanish-English and English-Spanish vocabularies contain all words and expressions from the *Vocabulario* sections followed by the lesson number in which this active vocabulary is introduced. All passive vocabulary items in the *Vocabulario adicional* lists and the English glosses in the exercises and activities are also included.

Cassette Program and Tapescript

The *Spanish for Law Enforcement*, Fifth Edition, Cassette Program opens with a recording of the vowels, consonants, and linking sections in the "Introduction to Spanish Sounds and the Alphabet," that appears as Appendix A of the manual. The five mini-dialogues and the main vocabulary list of the preliminary lesson are also recorded. For the twenty regular lessons, the cassette program contains recordings of the lesson dialogues (paused and unpaused versions), the active vocabulary list, and the supplementary words and expressions in the *Vocabulario adicional* section. The recordings of the *Práctica oral* sections of the *Repasos* appear on the cassettes following Lessons 5, 10, 15, and 20 in accordance with their order in *Spanish for Law Enforcement*. For students' and instructors' convenience, a cassette icon in the manual signals materials recorded on the Cassette Program.

The complete tapescript for the *Spanish for Law Enforcement* Cassette Program is now available in a separate booklet that contains the tapescripts for the *Basic Spanish Grammar* program.

Testing

The *Testing Program/Transparency Masters* booklet for the *Basic Spanish Grammar* program includes a sample vocabulary quiz and two sample final exams for *Spanish for Law Enforcement*, Fifth Edition. For instructors' convenience, answer keys for the tests and suggestions for scheduling and grading the quiz and exams are also supplied.

A Final Word

The many students who have used the previous editions of *Spanish for Law Enforcement* have enjoyed learning and practicing a new language in realistic contexts. We hope that the Fifth Edition will prepare today's students to communicate better with the Spanish-speaking people whom they encounter in the course of their work as law enforcement professionals.

We would like to hear your comments on and reactions to *Spanish for Law Enforcement* and to the *Basic Spanish Grammar* program in general. Reports of your experience using this program would be of great interest and value to us. Please write to us care of D. C. Heath and Company, Modern Languages Editorial, College Division, 125 Spring Street, Lexington, MA 02173.

Acknowledgments

We wish to thank our colleagues who have used previous editions of *Spanish for Law Enforcement* for their constructive comments and suggestions. We also appreciate the valuable input of the following law enforcement professionals and reviewers of *Spanish for Law Enforcement*, Fifth Edition:

Joan W. Delzangle, Chaffey College
Dr. María R. Irizarry, Attorney, Boston Public Schools, Boston, MA
Hugo Muñoz-Ballesteros, Tarleton State University
Ana Rodríguez, North Miami Beach Police Department, North Miami Beach, FL
Alba Lucía Ulloa, Pitt Community College
Walter J. Weeks, University of Massachusetts Dartmouth

Finally, we extend our sincere appreciation to the Modern Languages Staff of D. C. Heath and Company, College Division: Denise St. Jean, Senior Acquisitions Editor; Sheila McIntosh, Developmental Editor; Julie Lane, Production Editor; Richard Tonachel, Production Coordinator; and Alwyn Velásquez, Senior Designer.

Ana C. Jarvis
Luis Lebredo
Walter Oliver

Contents

Appendixes

Spanish-English Vocabulary

English-Spanish Vocabulary

Preliminar

📼 *Conversaciones breves (Brief conversations)*

A. —Décima Estación de Policía, buenos días. ¿En qué puedo servirle?
—Buenos días. El agente Donoso, por favor.
—Un momento, por favor.

B. —Buenas tardes, señora.
—Buenas tardes, señorita. Pase y tome asiento. ¿Cómo está usted hoy?
—Bien, gracias.
—¿Qué se le ofrece?

c. —Buenas noches, señor, y muchas gracias por la información.
—De nada, señora. Para servirle. Adiós.

D.   —Hola, Mario. ¿Qué hay de nuevo?
—Nada, señor.
—Bueno, hasta luego.
—Hasta luego.

E. —¿Nombre y apellido?
—Roberto Santacruz.
—¿Dirección?
—Avenida Magnolia, número treinta.[1]
—¿Número de teléfono?
—Cuatro-tres-dos-cero-cinco-seis-ocho.

---

[1]In Spanish addresses, the name of the street precedes the number of the house.

Vocabulario (*Vocabulary*)

COGNADOS (*Cognates*)

el (la) agente officer
la avenida avenue
la información information
el momento moment

SALUDOS Y DESPEDIDAS (*Greetings and farewells*)

Adiós. Good-bye.
Buenos días. Good morning., Good day.
Buenas tardes. Good afternoon.
Buenas noches. Good evening., Good night.
¿Cómo está usted? How are you?
Bien. Fine., Well.
Hasta luego. So long., See you later.
Hola. Hello., Hi.
¿Qué hay de nuevo? What's new?

EXPRESIONES DE CORTESÍA (*Expressions of courtesy*)

De nada., No hay de qué. You're welcome., Don't mention it.
¿En qué puedo (podemos) servirle?, ¿Qué se le ofrece? What can I (we) do for you?
Gracias. Thank you.
Muchas gracias. Thank you very much.
para servirle at your service
por favor please

TÍTULOS (*Titles*)

señor (Sr.) Mr., sir, gentleman
señora (Sra.) Mrs., lady, Ma'am, Madam
señorita (Srta.) Miss, young lady

OTRAS PALABRAS Y EXPRESIONES (*Other words and expressions*)

el apellido last name, surname
bueno okay
con with
las conversaciones breves brief conversations
décimo(a) tenth
la dirección, el domicilio address
la estación de policía, la jefatura de policía, la comisaría police station
hoy today
nada nothing
el nombre name
el número de teléfono phone number
Pase. Come in.
por for
Tome asiento. Take a seat.
y and

Notas culturales (Cultural notes)

- Cognates (*Cognados*) are words that are similar in spelling and meaning in two languages. Some Spanish cognates are identical to English words. In other instances, the words differ only in minor or predictable ways. There are many Spanish cognates related to law enforcement, as illustrated in the following list. Learning to recognize and use cognates will help you to acquire vocabulary more rapidly and to read and speak Spanish more fluently.

accidente	accident	**menor**	minor
ambulancia	ambulance	**paramédico**	paramedic
contrabando	contraband	**problema**	problem
domicilio	domicile	**sargento**	sergeant
homicidio	homicide	**sección**	section
hospital	hospital	**teléfono**	telephone

- The title of **señorita** is given only to a woman who has never been married. A divorcée or widow is addressed or referred to as **señora**.

¿Recuerdan ustedes? (*Do you remember?*)

Write the appropriate responses to the following statements.

1. Buenos días.

   _____

2. Buenas tardes. ¿Cómo está usted?

   _____

3. Muchas gracias.

   _____

4. Buenas noches.

   _____

5. Pase y tome asiento, por favor.

   _____

6. ¿Nombre y apellido?

   _____

7. ¿Dirección?

   _____

8. ¿Número de teléfono?

   _____

9. Adiós.

_____

10. ¿Qué hay de nuevo?

_____

Vamos a practicar (*Let's practice*)

A. **You are a 911 dispatcher routing several phone calls. Write in Spanish the name of the place and the telephone number you would call in each of the following situations. Since many of the words are cognates, guess at their meaning.**

Garaje municipal 257–8493	Policía 112
Ambulancia 235–3001	Paramédicos 110
Clínica veterinaria 265–9267	

1. A distraught woman reports that her dog was run over by a car.

_____

2. A bystander was shot at the scene of a drive-by shooting.

_____

3. A husband says his wife is having a heart attack.

_____

4. A caller reports a car with a flat tire on the highway.

_____

5. A citizen calls in that a burglary is in progress at his/her neighbor's house.

_____

B. **You are responsible for logging all calls received at the police station today. In order to verify that you have written the following names correctly in the log book, spell each one aloud in Spanish.**

1. Sandoval   4. Ugarte

2. Fuentes   5. Barrios

3. Varela   6. Zubizarreta

C. **Write the definite article before each word and then write the plural form.**

1. _____ estación   _____

2. _____ señorita   _____

3. _____ agente   _____

4. _____ señor   _____

5. _____ momento   _____

6. _____ información   _____

7. _____ calle   _____

8. _____ número   _____

En estas situaciones (*In these situations*)

What would you say in the following situations? What might the other person say?

1. You greet a colleague in the morning and ask how he/she is.

2. Someone knocks on the door of your office.

3. You thank someone for giving you information.

4. You receive a phone call and ask what you can do for the caller.

5. You say good night to a colleague.

1

📼 *En una estación de policía*

El Sr. Pérez llama por teléfono para notificar un accidente.

SR. PÉREZ	—Yo no hablo inglés, pero deseo avisar de un accidente.
TELEFONISTA	—¿Dónde? Yo hablo un poco de español.
SR. PÉREZ	—Aquí, frente a mi casa, en la calle Central, entre Florida y Terracina.
TELEFONISTA	—Despacio, por favor.
SR. PÉREZ	—Calle Central, entre Florida y Terracina (*Deletrea.*) Te-e-erre-a-ce-i-ene-a.
TELEFONISTA	—Muy bien, gracias. ¿Hay heridos?
SR. PÉREZ	—Sí, hay dos heridos graves: una mujer y una niña.
TELEFONISTA	—Bien. Ahora necesito sus datos personales. ¿Quién habla? Necesito su nombre y apellido, por favor.
SR. PÉREZ	—José Antonio Pérez.
TELEFONISTA	—¿Domicilio?
SR. PÉREZ	—Calle Central, quinientos cuarenta y seis, apartamento siete.
TELEFONISTA	—¿Número de teléfono?
SR. PÉREZ	—Siete, seis, dos, cinco, cuatro, tres, cero.
TELEFONISTA	—Enseguida mando para allá a los paramédicos y un carro patrullero. Muchas gracias por su información.
SR. PÉREZ	—De nada.

En persona, la Sra. Vera denuncia un robo.

SRA. VERA	—Yo no hablo inglés, pero necesito ayuda. Deseo hablar con un policía.
TELEFONISTA	—¿Habla español? Un momento.
AGENTE LÓPEZ	—Buenos días, señora. ¿Qué desea Ud.?[1]
SRA. VERA	—Deseo denunciar un robo.
AGENTE LÓPEZ	—Un momento. Ud. necesita hablar con el sargento Viñas, de la Sección de Robos, pero primero necesita llenar un informe de robo.

La Sra. Vera llena el reporte de robo.

---

[1] *Usted, ustedes* are abbreviated as *Ud., Uds.*

🔊 Vocabulario

---

el accidente accident
el apartamento apartment
central central
el (la) paramédico(a) paramedic
la policía police (force)

el (la) policía police officer
el reporte report
el (la) sargento sergeant
la sección, la división section, division
el teléfono telephone

NOMBRES (*Nouns*)

la ayuda help
la calle street
el carro patrullero patrol car
la casa house, home
el dato personal personal data, information
el español Spanish (language)
el informe report
el inglés English (language)
la mujer woman
la niña child, girl
el niño child, boy
el robo robbery
el (la) telefonista, el (la) operador(a) telephone operator, dispatcher

VERBOS (*Verbs*)

avisar de, notificar to inform, to give notice, to report
deletrear to spell
denunciar to report (a crime)
desear to want, to wish
hablar to speak, to talk
llamar to call
llenar to fill out
mandar to send
necesitar to need

ADJETIVOS (*Adjectives*)

grave serious
herido(a) hurt, injured
mi my
su your

OTRAS PALABRAS Y EXPRESIONES (*Other words and expressions*)

ahora now
aquí here
de of
despacio slowly
¿dónde? where?
en in, on, at
en persona personally, in person
enseguida right away
entre between
frente a in front of
hay there is, there are
muy very
para for
para allá there, over there
pero but
por teléfono on the phone, by phone
primero first
¿qué? what?
¿quién? who?
sí yes
un poco de a little

12

Vocabulario adicional (Additional vocabulary)

ACTIVIDADES DELICTIVAS (*Criminal activities*)

asaltar   to assault, to mug, to hijack
el asalto   assault, mugging, hold-up, hijacking
asesinar   to murder
el asesinato   murder
el chantaje   blackmail
chantajear   to blackmail
contrabandear   to smuggle
el contrabando   contraband, smuggling
la estafa   swindle, fraud
estafar   to swindle
la falsificación   falsification, counterfeit, forgery
falsificar   to falsify, to counterfeit, to forge
el fuego intencional, el incendio intencional   arson
el homicidio   homicide, manslaughter
pegar fuego, dar fuego   to set on fire
secuestrar   to kidnap
el secuestro   kidnapping
la violación   rape
violar   to rape

Notas culturales

- Most Hispanic people usually say their phone numbers in Spanish using a sequence other than the one used in English. For example, 549-2732 would be said as *cinco–cuarenta y nueve–veintisiete–treinta y dos* (5–49–27–32). The phone number 890-1106 would be said as *ocho–noventa–once–cero–seis* (8–90–11–0–6). Puerto Ricans are an exception to this rule, as they generally say their phone numbers one digit at a time. Notice that Spanish speakers say *cero* and not "o" as is frequent in English.
- Different words are used to answer the telephone in different Spanish-speaking countries: in Mexico, *bueno* or *mande;* in Puerto Rico, *hola, diga,* or *aló;* in Cuba, *hola, oigo,* or *diga;* in Spain, *diga* or *¿sí?*

¿Recuerdan ustedes?

Answer the following questions, basing your answers on the dialogues.

1. ¿Habla inglés el Sr. Pérez?

   _____

2. Y la telefonista, ¿habla español?

   _____

3. ¿Qué desea el Sr. Pérez?

   _____

4. ¿Hay heridos?

_____

5. ¿Cuál es (*What is*) el número de teléfono del Sr. Pérez?

_____

6. ¿Qué necesita la Sra. Vera?

_____

7. ¿Con quiénes habla la Sra. Vera?

_____

8. ¿Qué desea la Sra. Vera?

_____

9. ¿Qué necesita llenar?

_____

Para conversar (*To talk*)

Interview a classmate, using the following questions. When you have finished, switch roles.

1. ¿Nombre y apellido, por favor?

_____

2. ¿Domicilio?

_____

3. ¿Número de teléfono?

_____

4. ¿Necesita Ud. un carro patrullero?

_____

5. ¿Habla Ud. español bien?

_____

6. ¿Con quién desea hablar?

_____

7. ¿Necesita ayuda?

_____

Vamos a practicar

A. Write affirmative sentences using the subjects and verbs given. Then rewrite them in the negative form.

Modelo: yo / desear

Yo deseo hablar con un policía.

Yo no deseo hablar con un policía.

1. Ud. / necesitar

   _____

   _____

2. yo / llenar

   _____

   _____

3. la telefonista / mandar

   _____

   _____

4. la señora / desear

   _____

   _____

5. nosotras / denunciar

   _____

   _____

6. el Sr. Pérez / hablar

   _____

   _____

7. tú / notificar

   _____

   _____

8. Uds. / llamar

   _____

   _____

B. Write appropriate questions that would elicit the following answers.

1. _____

   Sí, la Sra. Vera denuncia un robo.

2. _____

   No, la Sra. Vera no necesita llenar un informe de robo ahora.

3. _____

   Sí, ellos mandan un carro patrullero enseguida.

4. _____

   No, yo deseo notificar un accidente.

C. Give the Spanish equivalent of the following expressions. Remember to use the preposition *de* in each answer.

Modelo: police station

   estación de policía

1. telephone number

   _____

2. robbery division

   _____

3. accident report

   _____

4. police officer

   _____

D. Write the following numbers in Spanish.

1. 596 _____

2. 358 _____

3. 715 _____

4. 969 _____

5. 1.670 _____

E. ¿Qué hora es? (*What time is it?*)

1. _____ 2. _____ 3. _____

_____ _____ _____

Conversaciones breves

Complete the following dialogues, using your imagination and the vocabulary from this lesson.

Al teléfono:

TELEFONISTA —Estación de policía, buenos días.

SR. SOTO —_____

TELEFONISTA —¿Quién habla?

SR. SOTO —_____

TELEFONISTA —¿Domicilio, por favor?

SR. SOTO —_____

TELEFONISTA —¿Número de teléfono, por favor?

SR. SOTO —_____

TELEFONISTA —En seguida mando un carro patrullero, Sr. Soto.

SR. SOTO —_____

TELEFONISTA —_____

Un accidente:

SRA. MESA —Necesito ayuda.

TELEFONISTA —_____

SRA. MESA —Un accidente de tráfico (*traffic*) en la calle Magnolia.

TELEFONISTA —_____

SRA. MESA —¿El agente Muñoz... ?

TELEFONISTA —_____

En estas situaciones

What would you say in the following situations? What might the other person say?

1. You are a sergeant in the Traffic Division. Someone calls to report an accident in front of his/her house. Get the person's name, address, and telephone number. Thank the person for the information.

2. While patrolling a neighborhood you come across an elderly Hispanic person who has fallen down and needs help. Tell the person you don't speak Spanish very well; ask if he/she speaks English. Ask the person to talk slowly.

3. You are the switchboard operator at the police station. Someone calls to report a robbery. Refer the caller to officer Rojas of the Robbery Division.

Casos (*Cases*)

Act out the following scenarios with a partner.

1. You are a traffic officer helping a witness complete the standard accident report form.

2. Imagine yourself to be an excited witness reporting an accident to an officer.

3. You are a police officer talking to someone who has come to the station to report a robbery.

Un paso más (*One step further*)

A. **Review the *Vocabulario adicional* in this lesson and match the terms in column A with their English equivalents in column B.**

A	*B*
1. _____ el homicidio	a. *assault*
2. _____ el asesinato	b. *kidnapping*
3. _____ el fuego intencional	c. *forgery*
4. _____ la falsificación	d. *swindle*
5. _____ el asalto	e. *blackmail*
6. _____ el contrabando	f. *rape*
7. _____ el secuestro	g. *homicide*
8. _____ el chantaje	h. *smuggling*
9. _____ la estafa	i. *murder*
10. _____ la violación	j. *arson*

B. List each verb under the appropriate categories.

asaltar   falsificar
asesinar   pegar fuego
contrabandear   secuestrar
chantajear   violar
estafar

1. Crimes that involve money

   _____

   _____

2. Crimes that involve physical assault

   _____

   _____

3. Crimes that involve fire

   _____

   _____

2

🔲 *Con un agente hispano, en una calle de la ciudad*

Una señora solicita información.

SEÑORA	—Ud. habla español, ¿verdad?
AGENTE	—Sí, señora. ¿En qué puedo servirle?
SEÑORA	—Por favor, ¿dónde queda el Banco de América?
AGENTE	—En la calle Magnolia, entre las avenidas Roma y París.
SEÑORA	—¿Cómo llego allá?
AGENTE	—Debe seguir derecho hasta llegar a la calle Magnolia. Allí dobla a la izquierda.
SEÑORA	—¿Cuántas cuadras debo caminar por Magnolia?
AGENTE	—Unas cinco o seis cuadras.
SEÑORA	—Muchas gracias por su información.
AGENTE	—Para servirle, señora.

El agente habla con un muchacho en bicicleta.

AGENTE	—Un momento, por favor. ¿Por qué no llevas puesto el casco de seguridad?
MUCHACHO	—El casco es muy incómodo, señor.
AGENTE	—En este estado la ley exige el uso del casco y, además, los cascos salvan muchas vidas. ¿Dónde vives?
MUCHACHO	—A una cuadra de aquí, en la calle Madison.
AGENTE	—Bien, debes regresar a tu casa a pie y buscar el casco.
MUCHACHO	—¿Y la bicicleta?
AGENTE	—Debes llevar la bicicleta de la mano.

El agente habla con una niña.

AGENTE	—Niña, ¿por qué andas sola?
NIÑA	—Yo ya soy grande...
AGENTE	—No, todavía eres muy pequeña para andar sola por la calle.
NIÑA	—No es muy tarde...
AGENTE	—Sí, es tarde. ¿Dónde vives?
NIÑA	—Vivo en la calle California, número doscientos sesenta y siete, apartamento dieciocho.
AGENTE	—Bien, vamos. Yo necesito hablar con tu mamá.

Más tarde:

MADRE	—¡Ay, Dios mío! ¿Qué sucede? ¿Qué pasa con la niña?
AGENTE	—Nada, señora, pero la niña es muy pequeña para andar sola por la calle.
MADRE	—Desde luego, pero no me hace caso.

▣ Vocabulario

COGNADOS

el banco   bank
la bicicleta   bicycle
hispano(a)   Hispanic
el uso   use

NOMBRES

el casco de seguridad   safety (bike) helmet
la ciudad   city
la cuadra   block
el estado   state
la ley   law
la mamá, la madre   mom, mother
el (la) muchacho(a)   boy, girl
la vida   life

VERBOS

andar, caminar   to walk
buscar   to look for
deber   must, should
doblar, voltear (*Méx.*)   to turn
exigir[1]   to demand
llegar(a)   to arrive (at), to reach
llevar   to take; to carry; to wear
quedar   to be located
regresar   to return
salvar   to save
ser[2]   to be
solicitar   to ask for
suceder, pasar   to happen
vivir   to live

ADJETIVOS

este(a)   this
grande   big, large
incómodo(a)   uncomfortable
muchos(as)   many
pequeño(a)   small, little
solo(a)   alone
tu   your
unos(as)   about, around

OTRAS PALABRAS Y EXPRESIONES

a   to, at, on
a la izquierda, a la derecha   to the left, to the right
a pie   on foot
a una cuadra de aquí   a block from here
a veces   sometimes
además   besides
allá, allí   there
¡Ay, Dios mío!   Oh, goodness gracious!
¿cómo?   how?
¿cuántos(as)?   how many?
de la mano   by hand
desde luego   of course
en bicicleta   on a bike
hasta   until
llevar puesto(a)   to wear
más tarde   later
No me hace caso.   He/She doesn't pay attention to me.
por   on (by way of), through
¿por qué?   why?
seguir derecho   to go straight ahead
tarde   late
todavía   still, yet
Vamos.   Let's go.
¿verdad?   right?, true?
ya   already

---

[1]First person singular: *yo exijo*
[2]*Ser* is irregular in the present indicative: *soy, eres, es, somos, son.*

Vocabulario adicional

EN LA CIUDAD

el cine, el teatro (movie) theater
la estación de bomberos fire department
la estatua, el monumento statue, monument
la farmacia, la botica drugstore
la gasolinera, la estación de servicio gas station
el hospital hospital
el hotel hotel
la iglesia church
el mercado, el supermercado market, supermarket
el mercado al aire libre, el tianguis (*Méx.*) open-air market
la oficina de correos, la estación de correos post office
la parada de autobuses, la parada de guaguas (*Cuba*), **la parada de ómnibus** bus stop
el parque park
el restaurante restaurant

Nota cultural

- Many Hispanic immigrants in the United States come from countries in which the police force is a repressive institution that often fails to respect the rights of citizens. As a result, many Hispanics become frightened when they see a police officer arrive at their home. They also often prefer not to ask questions of police officers.

¿Recuerdan ustedes?

Answer the following questions, basing your answers on the dialogues.

1. ¿En qué calle queda el Banco de América?

   _____

2. ¿Entre qué avenidas queda el banco?

   _____

3. ¿Cuántas cuadras debe seguir derecho la señora?

   _____

4. ¿Por qué no lleva puesto el muchacho el casco de seguridad?

   _____

5. ¿Qué exige la ley? ¿Por qué?

   _____

6. ¿Dónde vive el muchacho?

   _____

7. Según (*According to*) el agente, ¿es grande o (*or*) pequeña la niña que anda sola?

   _____

8. ¿Dónde vive ella?

   _____

Para conversar

Interview a classmate, using the following questions. When you have finished, switch roles.

1. ¿Dónde queda la estación de policía en esta ciudad?

   _____

2. ¿Vive Ud. en una casa o (*or*) en un apartamento? ¿Es grande o pequeño(a)? ¿Dónde queda?

   _____

3. ¿A veces regresa a su casa a pie?

   _____

4. ¿Dónde vive su mamá?

   _____

5. ¿Regresa Ud. a su casa tarde?

   _____

Vamos a practicar

A. Write sentences using the subjects and verbs provided. Add words from the dialogues, as needed.

1. Ud. / deber

   _____

2. nosotras / vivir

   _____

3. el agente Smith / exigir

   _____

4. yo / vivir

   _____

5. tú / deber

   _____

B. Place the adjectives in parentheses before or after the nouns as appropriate. Make sure the adjectives agree in gender and number with the nouns they modify.

1. (incómodo) Ella lleva un _____ casco _____ .

2. (muchos) El casco salva _____ vidas _____ .

3. (solo) Hay un _____ niño _____ en la calle.

4. (dieciocho) Vivo en el _____ apartamento _____ .

C. Complete the following minidialogues with the appropriate form of the verb *ser*.

1. —¡Yo ya _____ grande!

   —No, tú _____ muy pequeño para andar solo por la calle.

   —¡No _____ tarde!

2. —¿ _____ Uds. hispanas?

   —Sí, _____ de México. ¿ _____ Ud. agente de policía?

   —Sí, señora.

Conversaciones breves

Complete the following dialogues, using your imagination and the vocabulary from this lesson.

El agente Varela habla con un niño.

NIÑO —_____

AGENTE VARELA —¿El Restaurante Azteca? Queda en la calle Magnolia.

NIÑO —_____

AGENTE VARELA —Debes caminar cinco cuadras y doblar a la izquierda en la calle Magnolia. ¿Dónde vives?

NIÑO —_____

El agente Varela llega a la casa de la Sra. Vega.

SRA. VEGA —Buenas tardes, señor.

AGENTE VARELA —_____

SRA. VEGA —Pase, por favor.

AGENTE VARELA —_____

SRA. VEGA   —¿Qué pasa con mi niño?

AGENTE VARELA   — _____

En estas situaciones

What would you say in the following situations? What might the other person say?

1. You are on traffic duty. Someone asks if you speak Spanish and wants to know where the bank is. Tell the person to go straight ahead to Seventh Street. There he/she should turn left and walk about three blocks.

2. Two teenagers are riding their bikes without helmets. Ask them why. Explain the law to them and point out that helmets save lives. Tell them they must wear their helmets.

3. You find a little girl who is apparently lost. Find out where she lives. Tell her she shouldn't walk in the street alone. Say that you need to speak with her mom.

Casos

Act out the following scenarios with a partner.

1. You are a lost tourist who asks a police officer how to get to a famous landmark.

2. You are a police officer, speaking to a lost child.

3. You have been asked to explain to a class of first-graders why bike helmets must be worn.

Un paso más

Review the *Vocabulario adicional* in this lesson and write sentences telling where some of the places listed on p. 23 are located in your city.

Modelo: **El hospital queda en** la calle Arizona.

1. _____

   _____

2. _____

   _____

3. _____

   _____

4. _____

   _____

5. _____

   _____

3

▦ *Con el agente Smith*

El agente Smith habla con dos miembros de una pandilla.

AGENTE SMITH	—(*A uno de ellos*) ¿Qué hacen Uds. en la calle a esta hora?
JOSÉ	—Nada. ¿Por qué?
AGENTE SMITH	—Porque hay un toque de queda para las personas menores de edad y Uds. deben estar en su casa antes de la medianoche.
MARIO	—Nosotros siempre estamos en esta esquina con nuestros amigos.
AGENTE SMITH	—Vamos a la comisaría. Voy a llamar a sus padres.

Los muchachos protestan, pero suben al carro patrullero sin problema.

El agente Smith habla con un hombre que está en el patio de una casa desocupada.

AGENTE SMITH	—Buenos días, señor. ¿Por qué está Ud. en el patio de una casa desocupada?
HOMBRE	—Soy el jardinero.
AGENTE SMITH	—Su identificación, por favor.
HOMBRE	—Mi tarjeta verde, ¿está bien?
AGENTE SMITH	—Necesito una identificación con su fotografía.
HOMBRE	—Bien, aquí está mi licencia de conducir.
AGENTE SMITH	—Muy bien, muchas gracias por su cooperación.
HOMBRE	—A sus órdenes, agente.

El agente Smith arresta a un ladrón.

AGENTE SMITH	—¡Policía! ¡Alto! ¡Alto o disparo! ¡Quieto!

📼 Vocabulario

COGNADOS

la cooperación   cooperation
la fotografía   photograph
la identificación   identification, I.D.
la persona   person
el problema   problem

NOMBRES

el (la) amigo(a)   friend
la esquina   (street) corner
el hombre   man
la hora   time, hour
el (la) jardinero(a)   gardener
el ladrón, la ladrona   thief
**la licencia de conducir, la licencia para
  manejar**   driver's license
la medianoche   midnight
el (la) menor de edad   minor
el (la) miembro[1]   member
los padres   parents
la pandilla   gang
el patio   yard
la tarjeta   card
el toque de queda   curfew

VERBOS

arrestar, prender   to arrest
dar[2]   to give
disparar   to shoot
estar[3]   to be
hacer[4]   to do, to make
ir[5]   to go
protestar   to complain, to protest
subir   to get in (a car, etc.)

ADJETIVOS

desocupado(a)   vacant, empty
su   his, her
verde   green

OTRAS PALABRAS Y EXPRESIONES

a esta hora   at this time, at this hour
a sus órdenes   at your service, any time
¡Alto!   Halt!, Stop!
antes de   before
¿Está bien?   Is that okay?
o   or
porque   because
que   that
¡Quieto(a)!   Freeze!
siempre   always
sin   without

---

[1]The feminine form *miembra* is rarely used.
[2]Irregular first-person present indicative: *yo doy.*
[3]Irregular first-person present indicative: *yo estoy.*
[4]Irregular first-person present indicative: *yo hago.*
[5]*Ir* is irregular in the present indicative: *voy, vas, va, vamos, van.*

Vocabulario adicional

LA FAMILIA HISPÁNICA

la abuela   grandmother
el abuelo   grandfather
la esposa, la mujer   wife
el esposo, el marido   husband
la hermana   sister
el hermano   brother
la hija   daughter
el hijo   son
los hijos[1]   children
la madre   mother
la nieta   granddaughter
el nieto   grandson
el padre   father
los parientes   relatives
el (la) primo(a)   cousin
la sobrina   niece
el sobrino   nephew
la tía   aunt
el tío   uncle

LOS PARIENTES POLÍTICOS (*The in-laws*)

la cuñada   sister-in-law
el cuñado   brother-in-law
la nuera   daughter-in-law
la suegra   mother-in-law
el suegro   father-in-law
el yerno   son-in-law

OTROS MIEMBROS DE LA FAMILIA (*Other members of the family*)

la ahijada   goddaughter
el ahijado   godson
la hijastra   stepdaughter
el hijastro   stepson
la madrastra   stepmother
la madrina[2]   godmother
el padrastro   stepfather
el padrino[2]   godfather

---

[1]The plural form *hijos* may mean "sons" or it may mean "children" if it refers to son(s) and daughter(s).
[2]*La comadre* and *el compadre* are the names by which the parents of a child and the godparents address each other.

Notas culturales

- In many Hispanic countries, adults must always carry an official identification card, and the police can ask anyone to show his/her identification document. Because of this, Hispanic immigrants generally cooperate with the police when asked to identify themselves.
- It is important to remember that Hispanics in the United States and Canada do not constitute a homogeneous ethnic group. They have significant cultural, racial, and ethnic differences resulting from various combinations of Spanish, indigenous, African, European, and mestizo traditions. They have different immigration stories, even within a single national group. The term "Mexican American," for example, may identify both recent immigrants and persons whose families have lived in what is now the United States since the sixteenth century. Nevertheless, certain underlying cultural traditions and values prevail; familiarity with them may provide law enforcement professionals with insights into the behaviors and attitudes of Hispanics with whom they interact.

¿Recuerdan ustedes?

Answer the following questions, basing your answers on the dialogues.

1. ¿Con quiénes habla el agente Smith?

   _____

2. ¿Por qué deben estar los muchachos en su casa antes de la medianoche?

   _____

3. ¿Adónde van el agente Smith y los muchachos? ¿Por qué?

   _____

4. ¿Dan los muchachos problemas antes de subir al carro patrullero?

   _____

5. ¿Es inmigrante el jardinero?

   _____

6. ¿Qué identificación desea el agente Smith?

   _____

7. ¿Qué tiene (*has*) el jardinero?

   _____

8. ¿A quién arresta el agente Smith?

   _____

Para conversar

Interview a classmate, using the following questions. When you have finished, switch roles.

1. ¿Está Ud. solo(a) ahora?

   _____

2. ¿Es Ud. menor de edad?

   _____

3. ¿Está Ud. siempre con sus amigos(as) por la noche (*at night*)?

   _____

4. ¿Da Ud. muchos problemas?

   _____

5. ¿Es Ud. policía?

   _____

Vamos a practicar

A. Complete the following sentences, using the Spanish equivalent of the words in parentheses.

1. Ella es _____ (*Ana's mom*).

2. ¿Dónde están _____ (*Javier's reports*)?

3. ¿Ésta es _____ (*Teresa's photograph*)?

4. Yo tengo (*have*) _____ (*my friend's driver's license*).

5. ¿Dónde queda _____ (*your parents' house*), señorita?

B. Complete each of the following sentences with the appropriate form of the verb *ir* and a possessive adjective based on the subject provided.

   Modelo: Yo _____ a _____ patio.

   Yo **voy** a **mi** patio.

1. Tú _____ a _____ casa.

2. ¿Ud. _____ a hablar con _____ amigo?

3. Ella _____ a deletrear _____ apellido.

4. Nosotros _____ a llamar a _____ padres.

5. Nosotros _____ a _____ casa.

C. Fill in the blanks with the correct forms of *ser* or *estar*, as needed.

1. Ellas _____ agentes de policía.

2. ¿Dónde _____ el carro?

3. ¿_____ Ud. herido(a)?

4. Él y ella _____ en el patio.

5. Yo no _____ la mamá de Roberto.

6. El sargento Viñas _____ agente de policía.

7. Él _____ en la estación de policía.

8. Tú _____ menor de edad.

9. ¿Dónde _____ tus padres?

10. Mi papá _____ en el patio. Mi mamá _____ en casa.

11. A esta hora debes _____ en casa.

12. ¿_____ Ud. el amigo de Roberto?

Conversaciones breves

Complete the following dialogues, using your imagination and the vocabulary from this lesson.

El agente Robles habla con el papá de María Soto.

AGENTE ROBLES — _____

SR. SOTO —Sí, señor. Soy el papá de María Soto. ¿Qué pasa?

AGENTE ROBLES — _____

SR. SOTO —¿En la esquina? ¿Con quiénes?

AGENTE ROBLES — _____

El agente Robles habla con la señorita Roca.

AGENTE ROBLES — _____

SRTA. ROCA —Mariana Roca, señor.

AGENTE ROBLES — _____

SRTA. ROCA —Aquí está mi tarjeta verde.

AGENTE ROBLES — _____

En estas situaciones

What would you say in the following situations? What might the other person say?

1. You see a fifteen-year-old girl walking on the street late at night. Ask her why she's not home and where her parents are. Tell her she is a minor and she must be home before midnight.

2. Tell someone you need to see an I.D. with a photograph. Thank the person for cooperating.

3. You want a suspect to stop. Tell him to halt or you'll shoot. Another man appears. Tell him to freeze.

Casos

Act out the following scenarios with a partner.

1. Stop a suspect who is attempting to flee the scene of a crime.

2. While working the graveyard shift, you see a minor walking alone. Find out why he/she is on the street alone at this time of night.

Un paso más

Review the *Vocabulario adicional* in this lesson and complete the following definitions.

1. La esposa de mi hermano es mi _____.

2. El esposo de mi hermana es mi _____.

3. La mamá de mi esposo es mi _____.

4. El papá de mi esposo es mi _____.

5. El hermano de mi mamá es mi _____.

6. La hija de mi tía es mi _____.

7. El hijo de mi hermana es mi _____.

8. La mamá de mi papá es mi _____.

9. La esposa de mi hijo es mi _____.

10. El hijo de mi hija es mi _____.

11. La hija de mi hermano es mi _____.

12. Yo soy la nieta de mi _____.

13. El hijo de mi tío es mi _____.

14. El esposo de mi hija es mi _____.

15. Es la esposa de mi papá, pero no es mi mamá. Es mi _____.

16. Es el esposo de mi mamá, pero no es mi papá. Es mi _____.

17. Mis tíos, primos, abuelos, etcétera, son mis _____.

18. Mi mamá y mi papá son mis _____.

19. No es mi hijo; es el hijo de mi esposa. Es mi _____.

20. Ella es mi madrina y él es mi _____.

4

🔲 *Denuncias por teléfono*

La telefonista de la Comisaría Cuarta recibe una llamada de emergencia.

TELEFONISTA	—Departamento de Policía, buenas noches.
SEÑORA	—¡Por favor! ¡Necesito ayuda urgente!
TELEFONISTA	—¿Qué sucede, señora?
SEÑORA	—Hay un hombre extraño en el patio de mi casa y estoy sola con mis hijos.
TELEFONISTA	—Bien. ¿Cuál es su dirección?
SEÑORA	—Avenida Tercera, número setecientos nueve, entre las calles Once y Trece. A dos cuadras del hospital.
TELEFONISTA	—Enseguida mando un carro patrullero. Si el hombre trata de entrar, debe prender la luz.
SEÑORA	—¡Tiene que venir pronto! Mi esposo tiene un revólver en la casa...
TELEFONISTA	—¿Está Ud. entrenada en el uso de armas de fuego?
SEÑORA	—No, señora.
TELEFONISTA	—Entonces, usar el revólver es más peligroso para Ud. que para él. ¿Cómo es el hombre? ¿Es alto o bajo?
SEÑORA	—Es alto y creo que es blanco.
TELEFONISTA	—¿Cómo está vestido?
SEÑORA	—Con ropa oscura. El pantalón es azul o negro y la camisa es azul... no tan oscura como el pantalón.
TELEFONISTA	—¿Lleva sombrero?
SEÑORA	—Una gorra.

La telefonista recibe otra llamada.

SEÑOR	—Llamo para avisar que hay un hombre y una mujer en la casa de mis vecinos y ellos están de vacaciones y no vienen hasta la semana próxima.
TELEFONISTA	—El hombre y la mujer, ¿están dentro o fuera de la casa?
SEÑOR	—Dentro. La casa está oscura, pero ellos tienen una linterna.
TELEFONISTA	—¿Cómo son ellos?
SEÑOR	—El hombre es de estatura mediana y la muchacha es un poco más bajita que él.
TELEFONISTA	—¿Son jóvenes?
SEÑOR	—Sí, pero ella parece mucho menor que él. Ella debe tener menos de veinte años.
TELEFONISTA	—Muy bien. Ahora necesito la dirección de la casa de sus vecinos.

🔊 Vocabulario

COGNADOS

el departamento department	**la pistola** pistol
la emergencia emergency	**el revólver** revolver
el hospital hospital	**urgente** urgent
mucho much	

NOMBRES

el arma de fuego firearm
la camisa shirt
la denuncia report (of a crime)
el esposo, el marido husband
la gorra cap
los hijos children
la linterna flashlight
la luz light
la llamada call
el pantalón, los pantalones trousers, pants
la ropa clothes, clothing
la semana week
el sombrero hat
el (la) vecino(a) neighbor

VERBOS

creer to believe, to think
entrar (en) to go in
parecer[1] to seem
prender to turn on (a light)
recibir to receive
tener[2] to have
tratar (de) to try (to)
usar to use
venir[3] to come

ADJETIVOS

alto(a) tall
azul blue
bajo(a), bajito(a) (*Cuba*), **chaparro(a)** (*Méx.*) short
blanco(a) white
cuarto(a) fourth
entrenado(a) trained
extraño(a) strange
joven[4] young
menor younger
negro(a) black
oscuro(a) dark
otro(a) other, another
peligroso(a) dangerous
próximo(a) next
vestido(a) dressed

OTRAS PALABRAS Y EXPRESIONES

¿Cómo es? What does he/she/you look like?
¿cuál? which?, what?
de estatura mediana of medium height
de vacaciones[5] on vacation
dentro inside
entonces then
fuera outside
más... que (de)[6] more ... than
menos que (de)[6] less than, fewer than
pronto soon
si if
tan... como as ... as
tener... años[7] to be ... years old
tener que + *infinitivo* to have to (do something)

---

[1]Irregular first-person present indicative: *yo parezco.*
[2]*Tener* is irregular in the present indicative: *tengo, tienes, tiene, tenemos, tienen.*
[3]*Venir* is irregular in the present indicative: *vengo, vienes, viene, venimos, vienen.*
[4]The plural of *joven* is *jóvenes.*
[5]*Vacación* (*f.*) is rarely used in the singular.
[6]*De* is used with numbers: *más de ochenta pesos.*
[7]To ask how old a person is, use: *¿Cuántos años tiene(s)?*

Vocabulario adicional

LA ROPA

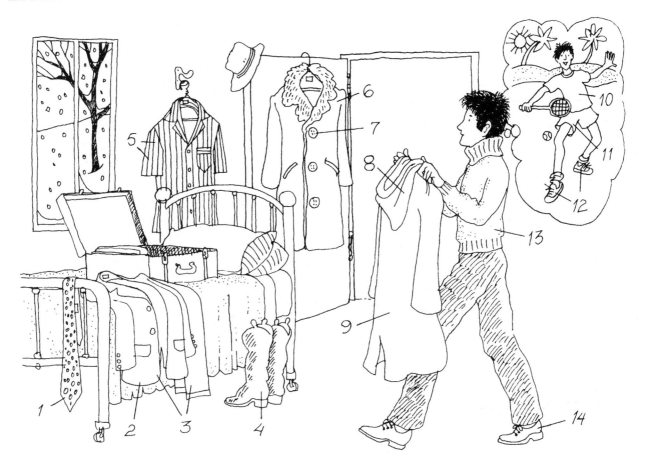

1. la corbata
2. el saco (*jacket*)
3. el traje
4. las botas
5. a rayas (*pinstriped*)
6. el abrigo
7. el botón

8. la capucha
9. el impermeable (*raincoat*)
10. la camiseta (*T-shirt*)
11. los shorts
12. el zapato de tenis
13. el suéter
14. el zapato

MÁS ROPA

1. la blusa

2. floreado(a) (*flowered*)

3. de mangas cortas (*short-sleeved*)

4. a cuadros (*plaid*)

5. el cuello

6. de mangas largas (*long-sleeved*)

7. el abrigo de piel

8. sin mangas (*sleeveless*)

9. de lunares (*polka dot*)

10. el cinturón, el cinto

11. la falda

12. la sandalia

13. estampado(a) (*print*)

14. el vestido

15. los guantes

16. la bolsa, la cartera

17. la chaqueta

18. el bolsillo

Nota cultural

Generally, Hispanic families interact socially with their neighbors more than do North American families. They tend to make and receive unannounced visits and to do small favors for each other with some frequency. In addition, in many neighborhoods in Hispanic countries, the local grocery store often becomes a sort of mini social center at which people chat and exchange community information.

¿Recuerdan ustedes?

Answer the following questions, basing your answers on the dialogues.

1. ¿Por qué llama la señora a la comisaría?

   _____

2. ¿Cuál es la dirección de la señora?

   _____

3. ¿Debe usar el revólver de su esposo la señora? ¿Por qué?

   _____

4. ¿Cómo es el hombre que está en el patio?

   _____

5. ¿Qué ropa lleva puesta el hombre?

   _____

6. ¿Qué tiene que mandar enseguida la telefonista?

   _____

7. ¿Por qué llama el señor a la comisaría?

   _____

8. ¿Dónde están los vecinos del señor?

   _____

9. ¿Dónde están el hombre y la mujer? ¿Dentro o fuera de la casa?

   _____

10. ¿Qué tienen ellos? ¿Por qué?

    _____

11. ¿El hombre es alto o bajo?

   _____

12. ¿Quién parece menor: el hombre o la muchacha?

   _____

Para conversar

Interview a classmate, using the following questions. When you have finished, switch roles.

1. ¿Cómo es Ud.? ¿Alto(a)? ¿Bajo(a)? ¿De estatura mediana?

   _____

2. ¿Tiene un revólver en la casa?

   _____

3. Si una persona desea usar un revólver, ¿debe estar entrenada? ¿Por qué?

   _____

4. ¿Manda Ud. un carro patrullero enseguida si hay una emergencia?

   _____

5. ¿Qué tiene que hacer hoy?

   _____

6. ¿Cuántos años tiene Ud.?

   _____

Vamos a practicar

A. Write sentences using the subjects and verbs given.

1. yo / tener / un pantalón azul oscuro

   _____

2. ella / tener / una pistola

   _____

3. nosotros / no tener / armas de fuego en la casa

   _____

4. yo / venir / vestido(a) con ropa oscura

   _____

5. Ud. / venir / con mi esposo(a)

   _____

6. nosotras / venir / la semana próxima

   _____

B. Express comparisons by giving the Spanish equivalent of the words in parentheses.

1. Los pantalones son _____ (*darker than*) la camisa.

2. El revólver es _____ (*more dangerous*) para Ud. que para el ladrón.

3. Este accidente no es _____ (*as serious as*) el otro.

4. Ud. tiene que mandar _____ (*as many patrol cars as*) yo.

5. Esta gorra no es _____ (*as big as*) mi sombrero.

6. Mi casa es _____ (*the smallest on*) la calle.

7. Ella es _____ (*younger than*) Uds.

8. ¿Es este hospital _____ (*the best in*) la ciudad?

Conversaciones breves

Complete the following dialogue, using your imagination and the vocabulary from this lesson.

La telefonista y la Sra. Díaz:

TELEFONISTA — _____

SRA. DÍAZ —Necesito ayuda. Hay un hombre extraño en el patio de mi casa.

TELEFONISTA — _____

SRA. DÍAZ —Estoy con mi hijo de seis años, pero mi esposo no está.

TELEFONISTA — _____

SRA. DÍAZ —De estatura mediana.

TELEFONISTA — _____

SRA. DÍAZ —Creo que lleva puesto un pantalón verde o azul. No tiene camisa.

TELEFONISTA — _____

SRA. DÍAZ —Calle Quinta, número seiscientos treinta y dos.

TELEFONISTA — _____

En estas situaciones

What would you say in the following situations? What might the other person say?

1. You are a police dispatcher, and a child calls to report a strange man in the yard. Ask if the child is alone, find out the address, including the cross streets, and get a description of the intruder.

2. You receive an emergency call from someone who says a strange man with a gun is trying to enter his/her apartment. He/She says you have to send a patrol car right away.

3. Someone calls to report a robbery at a bank. The caller says a woman and a man with guns are in the bank. You ask for a description, and the caller says the man is white and the woman is Hispanic; both are dressed in dark clothes and wearing caps. You get the address of the bank and thank the caller.

Casos

Act out the following scenarios with a partner.

1. You are a police dispatcher taking a call about an intruder in someone's yard.

2. While working the night shift as a police dispatcher, you receive a call from a person reporting that someone with a gun is trying to enter his/her house.

Un paso más

A. Review the *Vocabulario adicional* in this lesson and name the following articles of clothing and other clothing-related terms.

1. _____
2. _____
3. _____
4. _____
5. _____
6. _____
7. _____
8. _____
9. _____

10. _____
11. _____
12. _____
13. _____
14. _____
15. _____
16. _____
17. _____

B. Identify the articles of clothing and other clothing-related terms in the spaces provided.

1. _____

2. _____

3. _____

4. _____

5. _____

6. _____

7. _____

8. _____

9. _____

10. _____

11. _____

12. _____

13. _____

14. _____

15. _____

16. _____

17. _____

18. _____

C. Read the information in the following brochure about reporting suspicious activities. Try to guess the meaning of all cognates. Then, do the two exercise items that follow on the next page.

Denunciando actividades sospechosas°

¡La policía necesita la ayuda de todos los miembros de la comunidad! Cuando° Ud. ayuda a la policía, también se ayuda a sí mismo.° Si Ud. toma responsabilidad, puede evitar° ser víctima de un crimen. ¡La atención de la comunidad es la mejor prevención!

Recuerde°:

1. Si Ud. ve° alguna° actividad criminal, llame a la policía enseguida. Describa con exactitud lo que vio.°
2. No deje de° llamar a la policía si Ud. sospecha° algo.° No importa si es una falsa alarma.
3. En cuanto pueda,° anote° lo que recuerda.
4. Guarde° una copia de las siguientes° formas. Es posible que Ud. las necesite° en el futuro.

suspicious

When
sí... *yourself*
avoid

Remember
see / any
lo... *what you saw*
No... *Don't fail to / suspect / anything*

En... *As soon as you can / write down*
Keep / following
Ud... *you may need them*

Descripción de la persona	Descripción del vehículo	
Sexo _____	2 puertas° _____ 4 puertas _____	*doors*
Raza _____	Convertible/camión° _____	*truck*
Edad _____	Carro deportivo° _____	**Carro...** *sports car*
Estatura _____	Motocicleta _____	
Peso° _____	Otro _____	*weight*
Pelo° _____	Marca° _____	*hair / make*
Ojos° _____	Modelo _____ Año ____	*eyes*
Armas _____	Color _____	
Ropa _____	N° de placa° _____	*license plate*
Complexión° (delgado,° grueso,°	Estado _____	*build / thin / fat*
mediano°) _____	N° de personas en el vehículo _____	*average*
Características (lentes,° bigote,°	Hombre(s) _____ Mujer(es) _____	*glasses / moustache*
cicatrices,° etc.) _____	¿Dónde fue visto últimamente?	*scars*
_____	_____	
¿Dónde fue visto últimamente°?	_____	**fue...** *was he/she last seen?*
_____	_____	
_____	Dirección en que se fue° _____	**se...** *he/she went*
Dirección en que se fue _____	_____	
_____	_____	

1. Which of the following points does the brochure recommend?
   Si Ud. ve alguna actividad criminal...

   _____ a. debe esperar (*wait*) hasta mañana para llamar a la policía.

   _____ b. Ud. necesita guardar una copia de la descripción de la persona
   y de la descripción del vehículo.

   _____ c. primero debe hablar con los vecinos.

   _____ d. debe anotar una descripción exacta de lo que vio.

2. An elderly woman has just reported a robbery next door. She is unable to fill out the two description forms included in the brochure, but describes the following scene to you. Fill out the forms according to the information contained in the scene.

5

🔲 *La operadora contesta el teléfono*

Esta noche la telefonista de la Comisaría Cuarta en Los Ángeles contesta varias llamadas telefónicas.

A las siete y media:

OPERADORA	—Comisaría Cuarta, buenas noches.
SRA. VALLES ROJAS	—Buenas noches. Soy Isabel Valles Rojas. Mi marido y yo vamos a ir de vacaciones y quiero avisar a la policía...
OPERADORA	—Muy bien. ¿Cuál es su dirección completa y su número de teléfono, señora?
SRA. VALLES ROJAS	—Fairfax, número quinientos noventa y seis, Los Ángeles. Mi teléfono es 232–0649.
OPERADORA	—¿Cuánto tiempo piensan estar de vacaciones?
SRA. VALLES ROJAS	—Dos semanas. Vamos a estar de vuelta el primero de enero.
OPERADORA	—¿Van a dejar una luz encendida?
SRA. VALLES ROJAS	—Sí, vamos a dejar prendida la luz de la cocina.
OPERADORA	—¿Alguien tiene la llave de su casa?
SRA. VALLES ROJAS	—Sí, mi vecina. Ella vive enfrente de nuestra casa: Fairfax, número quinientos noventa y uno.
OPERADORA	—Muy bien. ¿Ella va a recoger su correspondencia?
SRA. VALLES ROJAS	—No, no es necesario. Nosotros vamos a suspender la entrega de la correspondencia y del periódico.
OPERADORA	—¿Alguien va a cortar el césped?
SRA. VALLES ROJAS	—Sí, y tenemos un sistema de riego automático.
OPERADORA	—Muy bien, señora. Gracias por llamar. Voy a comunicar esta información a la patrulla de su barrio.
SRA. VALLES ROJAS	—Gracias.

A las ocho menos cuarto:

NIÑO	—¡Socorro! Hay un incendio en mi casa y mi mamá y mi papá no están...
OPERADORA	—¿Tú estás dentro de la casa ahora?
NIÑO	—Sí. Tengo miedo... Hay mucho humo...
OPERADORA	—Tienes que salir de la casa enseguida. Debes ir a la casa de un vecino. ¡Rápido! Voy a llamar a los bomberos.

📼 Vocabulario

COGNADOS

automático(a)   automatic
completo(a)   complete
necesario(a)   necessary
el sistema   system

NOMBRES

el barrio, la colonia (*Méx.*)   neighborhood, district
el (la) bombero(a)   firefighter
el césped, el zacate (*Méx.*)   lawn
la cocina   kitchen
la correspondencia, el correo   mail
la entrega   delivery
el humo   smoke
el incendio, el fuego   fire
la llamada telefónica   phone call
la llave   key
la noche   night
el papá, el padre   dad, father
la patrulla   patrol
el periódico, el diario   newspaper
el riego   watering

VERBOS

comunicar   to communicate
contestar   to answer
cortar   to mow, to cut
dejar   to leave (behind)
encender (e:ie)   to turn on (a light)
pensar (e:ie) + *infinitivo*   to plan (to do something)
querer (e:ie)   to want, to wish
recoger[1]   to pick up
salir[2]   to get out, to leave, to go out
suspender   to stop

ADJETIVOS

encendido(a), prendido(a)   on (a light, a TV set)
nuestro(a)   our
varios(as)   several

OTRAS PALABRAS Y EXPRESIONES

alguien   someone
¿cuánto tiempo?   how long?
enfrente de   across the street from
esta noche   tonight
estar de vuelta, estar de regreso   to be back
ir a + *infinitivo*   to be going (to do something)
el primero de enero (abril, etc.)   the first of January (April, etc.)
rápido   quick, quickly, fast
¡Socorro!, ¡Auxilio!   Help!
tener miedo   to be afraid

---

[1]First-person present indicative: *yo recojo.*
[2]First-person present indicative: *yo salgo.*

Vocabulario adicional

LA CASA

el baño, el escusado[1] (*Méx.*) bathroom	**el portal** porch
el comedor dining room	**la puerta** door
el cuarto, la habitación room	**la sala** living room
el dormitorio, la recámara (*Méx.*) bedroom	**la sala de estar** family room
la entrada entrance	**el sótano** basement
el garaje garage	**el techo (de tejas)** (tile) roof
el jardín garden	**la terraza** terrace
la pared wall	**la ventana** window
el pasillo hall	

Notas culturales

- In Hispanic countries, people generally have two surnames: the father's surname and the mother's maiden name. For example, the children of María *Rivas* and Juan *Pérez* would use the surnames *Pérez Rivas*. In this country, this custom may cause some confusion when completing forms, making appointments, or filing records. The proper order for alphabetizing Hispanic names is to list people according to the father's surname.

  Peña Aguilar, Rosa
  Peña Aguilar, Sara Luisa
  Peña Gómez, Raúl
  Quesada Álvarez, Javier
  Quesada Benítez, Ana María

- In Spanish-speaking countries a woman doesn't change her last name when she marries, but she may add her husband's last name after her own, preceded by *de:* i.e., if Teresa Gómez marries Juan Pérez she may sign Teresa Gómez de Pérez. Many Hispanic women in the U.S., however, do use their husband's last name.

¿Recuerdan ustedes?

Answer the following questions, basing your answers on the dialogues.

1. ¿Con quién tiene que hablar primero la operadora esta noche?

   _____

2. ¿Por qué llama la Sra. Valles Rojas?

   _____

3. ¿Cuánto tiempo piensan estar de vacaciones los Valles Rojas?

   _____

4. ¿Cuándo van a estar de vuelta?

   _____

---

[1]Also *excusado*.

5. ¿Dónde piensan dejar una luz encendida?

   _____

6. ¿Quién tiene la llave de su casa?

   _____

7. ¿Dónde vive la vecina?

   _____

8. ¿Qué pasa en la casa del niño?

   _____

9. ¿Por qué tiene miedo el niño?

   _____

10. En caso de incendio, ¿a quiénes hay que llamar?

    _____

Para conversar

Interview a classmate, using the following questions. When you have finished, switch roles.

1. ¿Contesta Ud. las llamadas telefónicas en la comisaría?

   _____

2. ¿Siempre avisa Ud. a la policía cuando va a ir de vacaciones?

   _____

3. ¿Cuál es su dirección completa y su número de teléfono?

   _____

4. ¿A qué hora va a estar de vuelta en su casa mañana?

   _____

5. ¿Va a dejar Ud. una luz prendida en casa esta noche?

   _____

6. ¿Quién recoge su correo cuando Ud. está de vacaciones?

   _____

7. ¿Tiene Ud. miedo a veces?

   _____

8. ¿Tiene Ud. césped en su casa?

   _____

Vamos a practicar

A. Complete the following exchanges, using the verbs given.

1. pensar —¿Uds. _____ ir de vacaciones en enero?

    —Sí, y _____ estar de regreso en febrero.

    —¿Adónde _____ ir Ud.?

    —Yo _____ ir a Acapulco.

2. querer —¿Tú _____ suspender la entrega de la correspondencia?

    —Sí, y también _____ suspender la entrega del periódico.

3. encender —¿Teresa va a encender la luz?

    —No, ella no _____ la luz durante (*during*) el día.

**B. Complete the following sentences with the appropriate form of
ir a + infinitivo.**

1. Nosotros _____ de vacaciones.

2. Yo _____ de vuelta el 4 de julio.

3. La Sra. Vera _____ encendida una luz.

4. Mis vecinos _____ la correspondencia.

5. Yo _____ la información.

6. El niño _____ a los bomberos.

7. Nosotros _____ el césped.

8. Tú _____ de la casa enseguida, ¿no?

Conversaciones breves

Complete the following dialogues, using your imagination and the vocabulary from this lesson.

El Sr. Nieto llama a los bomberos.

BOMBERO   —_____

SR. NIETO   —¡Hay un incendio en la casa de mi vecino!

BOMBERO   —_____

SR. NIETO   —Magnolia, número cuatrocientos ochenta y dos.

BOMBERO   —_____

SR. NIETO —Sí, hay tres niños dentro de la casa. ¡Y los padres no están!

BOMBERO — _____

La operadora habla con la Srta. Gómez.

OPERADORA —Comisaría Cuarta, buenas noches.

SRTA. GÓMEZ — _____

OPERADORA —Bien. ¿Cuál es su dirección completa?

SRTA. GÓMEZ — _____

OPERADORA —¿Cuánto tiempo va a estar de vacaciones, señorita?

SRTA. GÓMEZ — _____

OPERADORA —¿Va a dejar una luz encendida?

SRTA. GÓMEZ — _____

OPERADORA —¿Alguien tiene la llave de su casa?

SRTA. GÓMEZ — _____

En estas situaciones

What would you say in the following situations? What might the other person say?

1. You are going on vacation. Call the police and tell them how long you'll be gone and when you'll be back. Also inform them that your neighbor is going to pick up your mail and the paper.

2. You are a dispatcher at a police station. A child calls to tell you that there's a fire in his/her house and that he/she is all alone.

Casos

Act out the following scenarios with a partner.

1. You are a police dispatcher and you receive a call from someone informing you that he/she is going on vacation in a week.

2. You are a police dispatcher and you receive a call from a child reporting a fire in his/her home. Tell the child what to do.

Un paso más

Review the *Vocabulario adicional* in this lesson and then draw a floor plan of your dream house in which you label each part and room of the house.

Repaso

LECCIONES 1–5

PRÁCTICA DE VOCABULARIO

A. Circle the word or phrase that does not belong in each group.

1. apellido, nombre, pandilla

2. domicilio, mujer, dirección

3. exigir, notificar, avisar

4. querer, desear, recibir

5. venir, llegar, salvar

6. pasa, da, sucede

7. grande, pequeño, mucho

8. parecer, arrestar, prender

9. ¡alto!, ¡siempre!, ¡quieto!

10. revólver, arma de fuego, camisa

11. esposo, vecino, marido

12. próximo, joven, menor de edad

13. dentro, fuera, entonces

14. alta, baja, extraña

15. negro, entrenado, azul

16. estado, estación de policía, comisaría

17. fuego, incendio, césped

18. encendida, vestida, prendida

B.   Circle the word or phrase that best completes each sentence.

1. Vivo en la (dirección, calle, casa) Magnolia, número cien.

2. ¿Cuál es su (número, robo, denuncia) de teléfono?

3. Debo (deletrear, llenar, buscar) a tus padres.

4. Hay dos heridos (bajos, altos, graves).

5. Vive enfrente de mi casa; es mi (vecina, domicilio, informe).

6. Tienen que mandar un carro patrullero (un poco, enseguida, además).

7. Tengo que usar (un casco de seguridad, una vida, una cuadra).

8. Van a (solicitar, llevar, doblar) a la izquierda.

9. Voy a dejar una luz (peligrosa, incómoda, prendida).

10. ¿Es azul o (verde, de estatura mediana, bajo)?

11. Lleva puesta (una semana, una fotografía, una camisa) blanca.

12. Está muy oscuro. Necesito (un pantalón, una linterna, un periódico).

13. Hay un incendio. Voy a llamar a (los jardineros, los maridos, los bomberos).

14. ¿Quién quiere (contestar, recoger, creer) el teléfono?

15. ¡Tengo miedo! Tienes que (venir rápido, hablar con alguien, protestar).

C. Match the questions in column A with the appropriate word or phrase
    in column B.

A	*B*
1. _____ ¿Hay heridos?	a. Arrestan a dos miembros de la pandilla.
2. _____ ¿Cuál es su apellido?	b. De la mano.
3. _____ ¿Qué necesita ahora?	c. No, en la esquina.
4. _____ ¿Qué desea denunciar?	d. Unas cuatro.
5. _____ ¿Qué hacen los agentes?	e. Sí, para las personas menores de edad.
6. _____ ¿Cuántas cuadras debo caminar?	f. Sus datos personales.
7. _____ ¿Qué exige la ley?	g. Alto.
8. _____ ¿Cómo llevo la bicicleta?	h. Sí, pero no graves.
9. _____ ¿Hay un toque de queda?	i. En agosto.
10. _____ ¿Están en tu casa?	j. Un robo.
11. _____ ¿Cómo es el hombre?	k. El uso del casco.
12. _____ ¿Cuándo vas a estar de regreso?	l. Torres.

D. Crucigrama

HORIZONTAL

2. opuesto (*opposite*) de *grande*

6. incendio

7. En Washington hablan inglés y en México hablan _____ .

10. sección

11. Tenemos un sistema de riego _____ para el césped.

12. operadora

14. Las personas heridas y los _____ van en la ambulancia.

15. *smoke*, en español

16. California y Arizona son _____ .

18. masculino: hombre; femenino: _____

19. pasar

21. arma de fuego

22. ¡Son las once de la noche! ¡Es muy _____ !

24. notificar

26. verbo: cooperar; nombre: _____

29. ¿Tiene Ud. su _____ verde?

31. prendido

33. *to shoot*, en español

34. opuesto de *alto*

35. opuesto de *fuera*

VERTICAL

1. correo

3. deseo

4. dirección

5. opuesto de *mucho*

8. anda

9. Debe _____ a la izquierda.

13. opuesto de *derecha*

14. *patrol car:* carro _____

17. las doce de la noche

20. La casa no está ocupada; está _____ .

23. hombre que roba

25. opuesto de *con*

27. *shirt*, en español

28. ¡Auxilio!

30. zacate

32. ¡Es muy _____ ! ¡Tiene catorce años!

🔊 PRÁCTICA ORAL

Listen to the following exercise on the audio program. The speaker will ask you some questions. Answer each question, using the cue provided. The speaker will verify your response. Repeat the correct answer.

1. ¿En qué calle vive Ud.? (en la calle París)

2. ¿Vive Ud. en una casa o en un apartamento? (en una casa)

3. ¿Tiene Ud. jardinero? (no)

4. ¿Está Ud. con sus amigos ahora? (no)

5. ¿Ud. habla español o inglés con sus amigos? (inglés)

6. ¿Habla Ud. español rápido o despacio? (despacio)

7. ¿Con quién desea salir Ud. ahora? (con mi amiga)

8. ¿Es Ud. menor que su amiga? (no)

9. ¿Tiene Ud. mis datos personales? (sí)

10. ¿Dónde queda la comisaría? (en la calle Roma)

11. Para llegar a la comisaría, ¿tengo que seguir derecho o doblar? (doblar)

12. ¿Hay muchas pandillas en su ciudad? (sí)

13. ¿A qué hora debe estar en su casa una persona menor de edad? (antes de la medianoche)

14. ¿Qué arma de fuego tiene Ud. en su casa? (una pistola)

15. ¿Qué debe tener siempre una identificación? (una fotografía)

16. ¿Tiene Ud. fotografías de sus padres? (sí, muchas)

17. ¿Su mamá es alta, baja o de estatura mediana? (de estatura mediana)

18. ¿Su mamá es más baja o más alta que su papá? (un poco más baja)

19. ¿Está Ud. de vacaciones? (no)

20. ¿Piensa Ud. ir de vacaciones esta semana o la semana próxima? (la semana próxima)

21. ¿Cuánto tiempo piensa estar de vacaciones? (una semana)

22. ¿Cuántas luces va a dejar Ud. encendidas en su casa? (dos)

23. ¿Quién va a recoger su correspondencia? (mi vecino)

24. ¿Lleva Ud. sombrero o gorra? (gorra)

25. ¿A qué hora va a estar de regreso esta noche? (a las nueve)

6

🔊 *El agente Chávez lee la advertencia Miranda*

El agente detiene a dos jóvenes que están escribiendo en la pared de un edificio.

AGENTE CHÁVEZ — ¡Policía! ¡Alto! ¡No se muevan! ¡Están detenidos!

JOVEN 1 — ¿Por qué? No estamos haciendo nada malo.

AGENTE CHÁVEZ — Están cometiendo un delito de vandalismo. No se puede escribir en la pared de un edificio. (*El agente saca una tarjeta de su bolsillo y lee la advertencia Miranda.*)

LA ADVERTENCIA MIRANDA

1. Ud. tiene el derecho de permanecer callado.

2. Cualquier cosa que diga puede usarse y se usará en contra de Ud. en el juzgado.

3. Ud tiene el derecho de hablar con un abogado, y de tenerlo presente durante el interrogatorio.

4. Si Ud. no puede pagar un abogado, se le nombrará uno para que lo represente antes de que lo interroguen, si Ud. lo desea.

AGENTE CHÁVEZ — ¿Entienden Uds. cada uno de estos derechos?

JÓVENES 1 Y 2 — Sí.

JOVEN 2 — ¿Nos va a llevar presos? Conmigo pierde su tiempo. Yo tengo menos de quince años; dentro de unas horas estoy en mi casa otra vez.

AGENTE CHÁVEZ — Ahora van a la estación de policía conmigo. Yo no decido lo demás.

Horas después, el agente detiene al chofer de un automóvil que comete una infracción de tránsito. Cuando habla con él, nota que el hombre está endrogado.

AGENTE CHÁVEZ — Buenos días. Su licencia de manejar y el registro del carro, por favor.

CHOFER — ¿Me va a dar una multa? ¿Por qué? No estoy borracho. Además, yo manejo mejor que nunca cuando tomo un par de tragos.

El agente nota marcas de aguja en el brazo y la mano del hombre. Las marcas son nuevas.

AGENTE CHÁVEZ	—A ver el brazo. ¿Tiene diabetes?
CHOFER	—No.
AGENTE CHÁVEZ	—¿Da Ud. sangre a menudo?
CHOFER	—Sí, doy sangre a veces.
AGENTE CHÁVEZ	—¿Dónde está el banco de sangre?
CHOFER	—En... No recuerdo ahora.
AGENTE CHÁVEZ	—Mire aquí, por favor. Debe tratar de no parpadear.
CHOFER	—No puedo dejar de parpadear. Tengo mucho sueño...
AGENTE CHÁVEZ	—Lo siento, pero tiene que venir conmigo. Ud. no está en condiciones de manejar.
CHOFER	—¿Estoy detenido? ¿Cuál es mi delito?
AGENTE CHÁVEZ	—Conducir bajo los efectos de alguna droga. (*El agente lee la advertencia Miranda.*)

Vocabulario

COGNADOS

el automóvil automobile	**el interrogatorio** interrogation, questioning
la condición condition	**la marca** mark
la diabetes diabetes	**presente** present
la droga drug	**el vandalismo** vandalism

NOMBRES

el (la) abogado(a) lawyer
la aguja needle
el banco de sangre blood bank
el bolsillo pocket
el brazo arm
el carro, el coche, la máquina (*Cuba*) car
la cosa thing
el (la) chofer driver
el delito crime, misdemeanor, felony
el derecho right
el edificio building
la infracción de tránsito traffic violation
el (la) joven young man, young woman
el juzgado, la corte court (of law)
la mano hand
la multa ticket, fine
la pared wall
el registro registration
el tiempo time
el trago drink

VERBOS

cometer to commit, to perpetrate
decidir to decide
detener[1] to detain, to stop
entender (e:ie) to understand
escribir to write
interrogar to question, to interrogate
leer to read
manejar, conducir[2] to drive
notar to notice
pagar to pay (for)
parpadear to blink
perder (e:ie) to waste, to lose
permanecer[3] to stay, to remain
poder (o:ue) can, to be able
recordar (o:ue) to remember
sacar to take out
tomar to drink, to take

---

[1]*Detener* is irregular in the present indicative: *detengo, detienes, detiene, detenemos, detienen.*
[2]Irregular first-person present indicative: *yo conduzco.*
[3]Irregular first-person present indicative: *yo permanezco.*

ADJETIVOS

algún, alguno(a)   some
borracho(a)   drunk
cada   each, every
callado(a)   silent, quiet
cualquier   any
detenido(a), arrestado(a), preso(a)   arrested
endrogado(a)   on drugs, drugged
estos(as)   these
malo(a)   bad
nuevo(a)   new, fresh

OTRAS PALABRAS Y EXPRESIONES

a menudo   often
a ver   let's see
la advertencia Miranda   Miranda warning
antes de que lo interroguen   before they
  question you
bajo los efectos (de)   under the influence (of)
con él   with him
conmigo   with me
cualquier cosa que diga   anything you say
cuando   when
dejar de + *infinitivo*   to stop (doing something)
dentro de   in, within
después   later
durante   during
en contra de   against
estar en condiciones de + *infinitivo*   to be in a
  condition to (do something)
lo   you, him
lo demás   the rest

Lo siento.   I'm sorry.
mejor que nunca   better than ever
Mire.   Look.
¡No se muevan![1]   Don't move!, Freeze!
No se puede escribir...   You (One) cannot
  write . . .
¿Nos va a llevar presos?   Are you going to arrest
  us?
nunca   never
otra vez   again, once again
para que lo represente   to represent you
puede usarse   can be used
se le nombrará uno   one will be appointed for
  you
se usará   will be used
si Ud. lo desea   if you wish
tener el derecho de (tenerlo presente)   to have
  the right to (have him present)
tener (mucho) sueño   to be (very) sleepy
un par de   a couple of

Vocabulario adicional

el (la) compañero(a)   pal, peer
la declaración falsa   false statement
el (la) delincuente juvenil   juvenile delinquent
el (la) droguero(a)   drug user, drug pusher
el grafiti   graffiti
el juramento   oath
bajo juramento   under oath
jurar   to take an oath, to swear
la mentira   lie
la pregunta   question
la respuesta, la contestación   answer
la verdad   truth

---

[1]When speaking to only one person: *¡No se mueva!*

Nombre _____ Sección _____ Fecha _____

Notas culturales

- Alcoholism and cirrhosis are important health issues that affect the Hispanic population in North America. The incidence rate is particularly high among Mexican Americans and Puerto Ricans. In addition, Hispanics have a disproportionate number of deaths due to narcotic addictions. In a recent Hispanic Health and Nutrition Survey done in the United States, 21.5% of Puerto Ricans reported having used cocaine, while the figure was 11.1% for Mexican Americans, and 9.2% for Cuban Americans.
- In Spanish, the word *droga* does not mean "medicine" as in English. Hispanics use this term to refer to narcotics and other illegal drugs. Similarly, a *droguero(a)* is a person who uses or sells illicit drugs.

¿Recuerdan ustedes?

Answer the following questions, basing your answers on the dialogues.

1. ¿A quiénes detiene el agente Chávez?

2. ¿Qué están haciendo?

3. ¿Cuál es el delito que están cometiendo?

4. ¿Qué lee el agente Chávez?

5. Según (*According to*) el joven 2, ¿por qué pierde el agente Chávez su tiempo con él?

6. ¿Adónde van los tres?

7. ¿Qué comete el chofer de un automóvil?

8. Cuando el agente Chávez habla con el chofer, ¿qué nota? ¿Qué tiene en el brazo y en la mano?

9. ¿Por qué cree Ud. que el chofer no recuerda dónde está el Banco de Sangre?

_____

10. ¿Por qué tiene que venir el chofer con el agente Chávez? ¿Cuál es su delito?

_____

Para conversar

Interview a classmate, using the following questions. When you have finished, switch roles.

1. ¿Se puede escribir en las paredes de los edificios? ¿Por qué o por qué no?

_____

2. ¿Da Ud. sangre a veces?

_____

3. ¿Siempre toma un par de tragos antes de manejar?

_____

4. ¿Está Ud. en condiciones de manejar ahora? ¿Por qué?

_____

5. ¿Puede venir a la estación de policía conmigo?

_____

6. ¿Qué está haciendo ahora?

_____

Vamos a practicar

A. Rewrite the following sentences using the new subjects and making all necessary changes.

1. No podemos arrestar al chofer. (yo)

_____

2. Volvemos (*We return*) al juzgado con ella. (ellos)

_____

3. No recordamos nada. (Ud.)

_____

4. Nosotros dormimos (*sleep*) en la estación de policía. (ellos)

   _____

5. Podemos leer la advertencia ahora. (Ud.)

   _____

B. **Change the following sentences to the present progressive to convey the idea that the action is just taking place.**

1. El agente saca una tarjeta del bolsillo.

   _____

2. Ud. pierde su tiempo.

   _____

3. Ella maneja mejor que nunca.

   _____

4. La agente lee la advertencia Miranda.

   _____

C. **Answer the following questions in the negative, using one of the following words in your answer.**

   nada   nunca
   nadie   tampoco
   ni... ni

1. ¿Da sangre a veces?

   _____

2. ¿Tiene que hacer algo (*something*) hoy?

   _____

3. ¿Siempre toma un trago cuando maneja?

   _____

4. ¿Hay alguien en su carro ahora?

   _____

5. Yo no escribo en las paredes de los edificios. ¿Y Ud.?

   _____

Conversaciones breves

Complete the following dialogue, using your imagination and the vocabulary from this lesson.

El agente Mora detiene a un chofer.

AGENTE MORA —_____

CHOFER —Tengo marcas de aguja en el brazo porque doy sangre muy a menudo.

AGENTE MORA —_____

CHOFER —No recuerdo en este momento. Además, las marcas de aguja no son nuevas...

AGENTE MORA —_____

CHOFER —Trato de no papardear, pero tengo mucho sueño...

AGENTE MORA —_____

CHOFER —No, no uso drogas nunca.

AGENTE MORA —_____

CHOFER —¿Yo? ¿Detenido? Pero, ¿cómo puede ser?

AGENTE MORA —_____

En estas situaciones

What would you say in the following situations? What might the other person say?

1. You catch three teenagers vandalizing cars. Identify yourself as a police officer and tell them to halt. They say they're not afraid because they are minors. Inform them that they are under arrest and that they are going to the police station with you.

2. You see someone trying to break into a bank. Tell the person to halt and not to move, or you'll shoot and arrest him/her. The suspect says he/she isn't doing anything. Read the Miranda warning.

3. You stop a driver and ask to see a driver's license and car registration. Say that you think that he/she is drunk and is under arrest for driving under the influence of alcohol. The driver doesn't want to go to the police station with you.

Casos

Act out the following scenarios with a partner.

1. You are a police officer talking to someone who shows signs of being under the influence of alcohol and/or drugs.

2. You arrest some minors for committing vandalism.

Un paso más

Review the *Vocabulario adicional* in this lesson and complete the following sentences.

1. ¡Son mentiras! Él nunca dice _____ .

2. Tengo las preguntas, pero no tengo _____ .

3. En la pared hay mucho _____ , pero mi _____ y yo no escribimos

   nada. ¡No somos _____ !

4. Ella jura que no está endrogada, pero ésa es una _____ .

5. Antes de contestar, debe recordar que Ud. está _____ .

7

🔊 *Problemas de la ciudad*

Por la mañana: El agente Flores habla con el dueño de una licorería después de un robo.

AGENTE FLORES	—¿Dice Ud. que los ladrones son muy jóvenes? ¿Puede describirlos?
DUEÑO	—Sí. El hombre es rubio, de ojos azules, y la mujer es pelirroja, de ojos verdes.
AGENTE FLORES	—¿Qué más recuerda?
DUEÑO	—El hombre mide unos seis pies, y ella mide unos cincos pies, dos pulgadas. Él es delgado. Ella es más bien gorda.
AGENTE FLORES	—¿Algunas marcas visibles?
DUEÑO	—Él tiene un tatuaje en el brazo izquierdo. Ella tiene pecas.
AGENTE FLORES	—Ud. no los conoce, ¿verdad? No son clientes...
DUEÑO	—No, pero sé que los puedo reconocer si los veo otra vez.
AGENTE FLORES	—¿Qué clase de carro manejan?
DUEÑO	—Un Chevrolet amarillo, de dos puertas. Es un carro viejo.
AGENTE FLORES	—¿Algo más?
DUEÑO	—Sí, creo que sí. Él fuma cigarrillos negros... de México... ¡y es zurdo!
AGENTE FLORES	—Si recuerda algo más, ¿puede llamarme a este número?
DUEÑO	—Cómo no, señor.

Por la tarde: El agente Flores ve a un hombre que está parado frente a una escuela. Sospecha que el hombre tiene drogas para vender, porque hay muchos estudiantes que toman drogas.

AGENTE FLORES	—¿Qué hace Ud. aquí? ¿Espera a alguien?
HOMBRE	—No... no hago nada...
AGENTE FLORES	—¿Tiene alguna identificación? ¿Su licencia de conducir, por ejemplo?
HOMBRE	—No, aquí no. La tengo en casa...
AGENTE FLORES	—¿Quiere acompañarme al carro, por favor? Quiero hablar con Ud.

Por la noche: El agente Flores sale de la comisaría para ir a su casa. En la zona de estacionamiento, ve a un hombre en el suelo. Corre hacia él.

AGENTE FLORES	—¿Qué tiene? ¿Está lastimado?
HOMBRE	—No... creo que... un ataque al corazón...
AGENTE FLORES	—¿Tiene alguna medicina para el corazón?
HOMBRE	—Sí... en la guantera del carro...
AGENTE FLORES	—(*Trae la medicina.*) Aquí está. Ahora voy a llamar a los paramédicos.

⏹ Vocabulario

COGNADOS

el (la) estudiante   student
la medicina   medicine
visible   visible

NOMBRES

el cigarrillo   cigarette
la clase   kind, type, class
el (la) cliente(a)   customer
el corazón   heart
el (la) dueño(a)   owner
la escuela   school
la guantera   glove compartment
la licorería   liquor store
la peca   freckle
el pie   foot
la puerta   door
la pulgada   inch
el suelo   floor
el tatuaje   tattoo
la zona de estacionamiento   parking lot

VERBOS

acompañar   to accompany, to go (come) with
conocer[1]   to know
correr   to run
decir (e:i)[2]   to say, to tell
describir   to describe
esperar   to wait (for)
fumar   to smoke
medir (e:i)   to measure
reconocer[3]   to recognize
saber[4]   to know
sospechar   to suspect
traer[5]   to bring
vender   to sell
ver[6]   to see

ADJETIVOS

amarillo(a)   yellow
delgado(a)   thin
gordo(a)   fat
izquierdo(a)   left
lastimado(a)   hurt, injured
parado(a)   standing
pelirrojo(a)   red-haired
rubio(a), güero(a)[7] (*Méx.*)   blonde
viejo(a)   old
zurdo(a)   left-handed

OTRAS PALABRAS Y EXPRESIONES

¿Algo más?   Anything else?
el ataque al corazón   heart attack
¡Cómo no!   Certainly!, Gladly!, Sure!
Creo que sí.   I think so.
de ojos (azules)   with (blue) eyes
después de   after
hacia   toward
más bien, medio   rather
por ejemplo   for example
por la mañana   in the morning
por la noche   in the evening
por la tarde   in the afternoon
¿Qué más?   What else?
¿Qué tiene?   What's wrong?

---

[1]Irregular first-person present indicative: *yo conozco.*
[2]Irregular first-person present indicative: *yo digo.*
[3]Irregular first-person present indicative: *yo reconozco.*
[4]Irregular first-person present indicative: *yo sé.*
[5]Irregular first-person present indicative: *yo traigo.*
[6]Irregular first-person present indicative: *yo veo.*
[7]Also applies to anyone with fair skin.

Vocabulario adicional

EL TAMAÑO (*Size*)

flaco(a)   thin, skinny
grueso(a)   fat

LA RAZA/EL COLOR DE LA PIEL (*Race/Color of the skin*)

asiático(a)   Asian
mestizo(a)   mixed (any of two or more races)
mulato(a)   mixed (black and white)

EL PELO (*Hair*)

calvo(a), pelón(ona)   bald
canoso(a)   grey-haired
castaño(a), café   brown
claro(a)   light
corto(a)   short
lacio(a)   straight
largo(a)   long
rizado(a), rizo(a), crespo(a)   curly
rojo(a), colorado(a)   red

OTRAS CARACTERÍSTICAS

ciego(a)   blind
cojo(a)   lame
inválido(a)   disabled, crippled
sordo(a)   deaf

Nota cultural

Recreational use of drugs is a relatively recent phenomenon in Hispanic countries, and it is generally limited to the large cities. Because the majority of Hispanic immigrants come from villages and small towns, there are few drug addicts among first-generation immigrants. Nonetheless, their numbers increase dramatically beginning with the second generation, owing possibly to culture shock and living conditions.

¿Recuerdan ustedes?

Answer the following questions, basing your answers on the dialogues.

1. ¿Con quién habla el agente Flores después del robo?

    _____

2. ¿Puede el dueño describir a los ladrones?

    _____

3. ¿Cómo es el hombre? ¿Y la mujer?

    _____

4. ¿Qué marcas visibles tiene el hombre? ¿Y la mujer?

_____

5. ¿Conoce el dueño de la licorería a los ladrones?

_____

6. ¿Cree el dueño que puede reconocer a los ladrones si los ve otra vez?

_____

7. ¿Qué clase de carro manejan los ladrones?

_____

8. ¿Qué ve el agente Flores por la tarde?

_____

9. ¿Qué sospecha el agente Flores?

_____

10. ¿Tiene el hombre alguna identificación?

_____

11. ¿Qué ve el agente Flores en la zona de estacionamiento?

_____

12. ¿Qué tiene el hombre?

_____

13. ¿Qué hace el agente Flores para ayudar al hombre?

_____

Para conversar

**Interview a classmate, using the following questions. When you have
finished, switch roles.**

1. ¿Cómo es Ud.? ¿Cuánto mide?

_____

2. ¿Puede describir a alguien de su familia?

_____

3. ¿Qué clase de coche maneja Ud.?

_____

4. ¿Su coche está en la zona de estacionamiento?

    _____

5. ¿Puede Ud. llamarme por teléfono mañana?

    _____

Vamos a practicar

A. **Rewrite the following sentences, using the new subjects and making all necessary changes.**

1. Nosotros medimos la puerta. (ellos)

    _____

2. Nosotros seguimos (*follow*) a los ladrones. (yo)

    _____

3. Nosotras pedimos (*ask for*) más información. (el policía)

    _____

4. Nosotros conseguimos (*get*) la medicina. (Ud.)

    _____

5. Nosotros decimos la verdad (*truth*). (tú)

    _____

B. **Imagine that you are Officer Flores. Form sentences to tell what you do in your investigation of the liquor store hold-up.**

    Modelo: ir / a la licorería

    　　　　Voy a la licorería.

1. ver / al dueño de la licorería

    _____

2. hacer / la descripción de los ladrones

    _____

3. decir / lo que (*what*) el dueño debe hacer mañana

    _____

4. salir / de la licorería

    _____

5. conducir / a la estación de policía

    _____

C. A police officer is questioning you about the hold-up that just took place at your store. Answer the questions, according to the model.

Modelo: ¿Conoce a **los ladrones**?

No, no **los** conozco.

1. ¿Sabe los nombres de los ladrones?

   _____

2. ¿Sabe si toman drogas?

   _____

3. ¿Puede describir a los ladrones?

   _____

4. ¿Reconoce a las personas en esta fotografía?

   _____

5. ¿Recuerda el color de su coche?

   _____

6. ¿Tiene mi tarjeta?

   _____

7. Ud. debe venir a la estación de policía mañana. ¿Sabe la dirección?

   _____

Conversaciones breves

Complete the following dialogue, using your imagination and the vocabulary from this lesson.

El Sr. Rivas describe a una ladrona.

AGENTE ALCALÁ — _____

SR. RIVAS —Sí, es alta, rubia, de ojos verdes, más bien delgada y muy bonita.

AGENTE ALCALÁ — _____

SR. RIVAS —No recuerdo mucho... Mide unos cinco pies y diez pulgadas.

AGENTE ALCALÁ — _____

SR. RIVAS —No, no tiene ninguna (*any*) marca visible.

AGENTE ALCALÁ — _____

SR. RIVAS	—Sí, yo creo que puedo reconocerla.
AGENTE ALCALÁ	— _____
SR. RIVAS	—Un Mazda amarillo de cuatro puertas.
AGENTE ALCALÁ	— _____
SR. RIVAS	—¡Ah, sí! ¡Ahora recuerdo! ¡Es zurda!
AGENTE ALCALÁ	— _____

En estas situaciones

What would you say in the following situations? What might the other person say?

1. You are investigating a burglary. Ask if the witness can recognize the burglar if he/she sees him/her again. Ask how tall the burglar is, and if he/she has any visible marks. Ask also what kind of car the burglar drives.

2. You see a suspect standing near a school. Ask what he/she is doing there. Ask if he/she is waiting for a student, and if he/she has any identification.

3. You see someone who seems to be sick. Ask what's wrong. You get the person's heart medicine from his/her pocket and then say that you're going to call the paramedics.

4. Your partner is hurt. Ask a passerby to please call the police, because there is a police officer who needs help.

Casos

Act out the following scenarios with a partner.

1. You are a police officer. Interview a witness of a burglary.

2. You are a police officer and you see a suspicious-looking person standing near a playground. Approach the person and question him/her.

3. You are a police officer and notice a person lying on the sidewalk. Find out what the person's problem is and try to help him/her.

Un paso más

A. Review the *Vocabulario adicional* in this lesson and describe several people, using as many words as possible from the list.

1. _____

_____

2. _____

_____

3. _____

_____

4. _____

_____

5. _____

_____

B. Read the information about shoplifting in the following brochure for shop owners. Try to guess the meaning of all cognates. Then, answer the questions that follow.

Recomendaciones para prevenir° el robo en las tiendas°

prevent / stores

1. Los empleados tienen que estar alertas. Ud. debe formular un método comprensivo que todos los empleados pueden seguir en caso de que vean a una persona robando.
2. Los empleados tienen que poder ver lo que° pasa en toda la tienda.° Los mostradores° no deben ser más altos que el nivel de la cintura.° Se recomienda poner° espejos° en los rincones de la tienda.
3. Arregle° los mostradores para que° no se pueda salir de la tienda sin pasar frente a un cajero.°
4. No se recomienda poner la mercancía más cara° cerca de° la puerta.
5. Arregle la mercancía para que los empleados puedan notar fácilmente° si algo falta.°

lo... *what*
toda... *the whole store / counters*
el... *waist-high / to put / mirrors*

Arrange / **para...** *so that*
cashier
expensive / **cerca...** *near*

easily / **algo...** *something is missing*

Recuerde...
¡Una advertencia contra° el robo en las tiendas siempre debe estar a la vista°!

against

estar... *be visible, be easily seen*

1. Which of the following suggestions does the brochure make to prevent shoplifting?

    _____ a. Se recomienda tener una puerta en el fondo (*in the back*) de la tienda.

    _____ b. Cada empleado(a) debe decidir por sí mismo(a) (*by him/herself*) qué hacer si ve a una persona robando.

    _____ c. Se necesita poner en un lugar (*a place*) muy visible una advertencia contra el robo en las tiendas.

    _____ d. Los mostradores deben ser muy bajos.

    _____ e. No se debe poner los productos más caros cerca de la puerta.

2. If you were advising the owner of a store in a high-crime area, which of the anti-shoplifting measures in the Spanish brochure would you present as the most effective?

    _____

    _____

    _____

8

🔊 *Casos de maltrato de miembros de la familia*

Julia, una niña, llama a la policía porque su padrastro le está pegando a su mamá. El agente Vera va a la casa de la familia Aguirre para investigar la denuncia.

AGENTE VERA	—Buenas tardes. ¿Es ésta la casa de la familia Aguirre?
JULIA	—Sí. Pase, por favor. Mi mamá y mi padrastro están encerrados en su recámara.
AGENTE VERA	—¿Cuál es el problema?
JULIA	—Mi padrastro no tiene trabajo ahora y, en lugar de buscar otro trabajo, todos los días va a la cantina y vuelve borracho.
AGENTE VERA	—¿Cómo consigue el dinero para la bebida?
JULIA	—Se lo pide a mi mamá, y si ella no se lo da, le pega, y se lo quita a la fuerza.
AGENTE VERA	—¿Le pega con la mano?
JULIA	—Con la mano y con el cinto. A veces le dice que la va a matar.
AGENTE VERA	—¿Tiene algún arma él?
JULIA	—Sí, tiene una navaja y una pistola.
AGENTE VERA	—(*Toca a la puerta de la recámara.*) Sr. Aguirre, soy agente de policía y necesito hablar con Ud. ¿Quiere salir un momento, por favor?
SR. AGUIRRE	—(*Desde adentro*) Ésta es mi casa. ¿Ud. tiene una orden del juez para entrar? Yo no tengo nada que hablar con Ud.
SRA. AGUIRRE	—(*Saliendo de la recámara*) Está enojado conmigo porque quiere dinero para bebidas.
SR. AGUIRRE	—(*Saliendo también*) Ése es un problema entre mi mujer y yo, y Ud. no tiene por qué entrometerse.
AGENTE VERA	—Sra. Aguirre, Ud. está bastante lesionada. Debe ver a un médico inmediatamente. ¿Está dispuesta a acusar a su marido de maltrato?
SR. AGUIRRE	—No. Ella hace lo que yo le digo. Y si Ud. quiere saber algo, me lo pregunta a mí.
SRA. AGUIRRE	—(*No le hace caso a su marido y le contesta al policía.*) Sí, señor agente.
SR. AGUIRRE	—(*A su esposa*) Tú no me debes hacer eso. Tú sabes que yo te trato bien cuando no estoy borracho. Te pido perdón.
SRA. AGUIRRE	—No. Esta vez no te perdono. Ya estoy cansada de tus maltratos.

El Dr. Andrade notifica a la policía sus sospechas de que el niño Carlos Jiménez está siendo maltratado. La agente Rodríguez, a cargo del caso, habla con sus padres.

AGENTE RODRÍGUEZ	—Buenos días. ¿Es Ud. el padre del niño Carlos Jiménez?
SR. JIMÉNEZ	—Sí, soy yo. ¿Qué se le ofrece?
AGENTE RODRÍGUEZ	—Soy la agente Rodríguez, de la policía local. Ésta es mi identificación.
SR. JIMÉNEZ	—Pase y siéntese. ¿En qué puedo servirle?
AGENTE RODRÍGUEZ	—Su hijo está ingresado en el hospital desde ayer. Ésta es la tercera vez que el niño ingresa en el hospital con lesiones más o menos graves y el médico sospecha que alguien lo está maltratando frecuentemente.
SR. JIMÉNEZ	—¿Qué? ¿Quién dice eso? Eso es mentira. Además, nadie tiene autoridad para decirnos cómo debemos disciplinar a nuestros hijos.
AGENTE RODRÍGUEZ	—Está equivocado, Sr. Jiménez. En este país no se aceptan ciertas formas de disciplinar a los niños.

Vocabulario

COGNADOS

la autoridad   authority
la familia   family
frecuentemente   frequently
inmediatamente   immediately
local   local

NOMBRES

el arma (*fem.*)   weapon
la bebida   drinking, drink
la cantina, la barra, el bar   bar
el cinto, el cinturón, la correa   belt
el dinero   money
la forma   way
el (la) juez(a)   judge
la lesión   injury
el maltrato   abuse
el (la) médico(a), el (la) doctor(a)   doctor
la mentira   lie
la navaja   switchblade, razor
la orden   warrant, order
el padrastro   stepfather
el país   country
el perdón   pardon, forgiveness
el por qué   reason
la recámara (*Méx.*), **el dormitorio**   bedroom
la sospecha   suspicion
el trabajo   work, job
la vez   time

VERBOS

aceptar   to accept
acusar   to accuse
conseguir (e:i)   to get, to obtain
disciplinar   to discipline
entrometerse, entremeterse   to meddle, to butt in
ingresar   to be admitted (to), to enter
investigar   to investigate
maltratar, abusar (de)   to abuse
matar (a)   to kill
pedir (e:i)   to ask (for)
pegar   to beat
perdonar   to forgive
preguntar   to ask (a question)
quitar   to take away
tratar   to treat
volver (o:ue)   to come back, to return

ADJETIVOS

cansado(a)   tired
cierto(a)   certain
dispuesto(a)   willing
encerrado(a)   locked up, closeted
enojado(a)   angry
ingresado(a)   admitted (to)
lesionado(a)   injured
tercero(a)   third

OTRAS PALABRAS Y EXPRESIONES

a cargo de   in charge of
a la fuerza   by force
adentro   inside
algo   something, anything
ayer   yesterday
bastante   quite, rather
desde   from
en lugar de   instead of
ése, ésa   that one
eso   that
esta vez   this time

estar equivocado(a)   to be wrong
éste, ésta   this one
hacerle caso a   to pay attention (to someone)
lo que   what
más o menos   more or less
nadie   nobody
Siéntese.   Sit down.
también   also, too
tocar a la puerta   to knock at the door
todos los días   every day
ya   at last, finally

Vocabulario adicional

ARMAS DE FUEGO

la ametralladora   machine gun
la escopeta   shotgun
el rifle   rifle

ARMAS BLANCAS (*Blades*)

el cuchillo   knife
el puñal, la daga   dagger

EXPLOSIVOS (*Explosives*)

la bomba (de tiempo)   (time) bomb
la dinamita   dynamite
la granada de mano   hand grenade

ALGUNOS CASTIGOS CORPORALES (*Some corporal punishments*)

la bofetada, la galleta (*Cuba*)   slap
la mordida   bite
la nalgada   spanking, slap on the buttocks
la paliza   beating
la patada   kick
la trompada, el puñetazo   punch

Notas culturales

- In Spanish-speaking cultures, the concept of *machismo*, in which males are seen as aggressive and authoritative, plays a part in traditional views of gender roles and family. While *machismo* and these traditional views may still linger in some Hispanic countries, among Hispanics in the United States, these views are not frequently a reality. Degrees of male authoritarianism vary widely, and in general, women are important contributors to decision making and share authority in the family. Many Hispanic women are also part of the work force, and more and more Hispanic men help with household chores and care of the children.
- In some Hispanic countries, parents are still accustomed to disciplining their children through corporal punishment. This type of discipline is either not prohibited by law or it is tolerated by the authorities. Generally speaking, mothers do the spanking, but if the misbehavior is serious, the father administers more serious punishment. He may hit the children with a belt or a leather strap. It is important, however, not to over-generalize this disciplinary practice and to keep in mind that, in general, Hispanic families tend to be close-knit units in which all family members spend time together and help and support each other. Usually, unless questions of study or work arise, children continue to live with their parents until they get married, even beyond the time when they are no longer minors.

¿Recuerdan ustedes?

Answer the following questions, basing your answers on the dialogues.

1. ¿Cuál es el problema en la casa de Julia?

   _____

2. ¿Por qué le pega el padrasto de Julia a su mamá? ¿Con qué le pega?

   _____

3. ¿Cómo está el Sr. Aguirre en este momento? ¿Y la señora? ¿A quién debe ver ella inmediatamente?

   _____

4. ¿Quiere hablar con el agente Vera el Sr. Aguirre?

   _____

5. ¿Qué cree el Sr. Aguirre de la situación?

   _____

6. ¿Qué decide hacer la Sra. Aguirre?

   _____

7. ¿Es un hombre peligroso el Sr. Aguirre?

   _____

8. ¿Por qué está en el hospital el niño Carlos Jiménez?

_____

9. ¿Es la primera vez que el niño está allí?

_____

10. ¿Qué sospecha el Dr. Andrade?

_____

11. ¿Qué es lo que no se acepta en este país, según (*according to*) la agente Rodríguez?

_____

Para conversar

Interview a classmate, using the following questions. When you have finished, switch roles.

1. ¿Investiga Ud. a menudo casos de maltrato de miembros de familia?

_____

2. Si Ud. viene a una casa para investigar una denuncia, ¿qué le dice primero a la familia?

_____

3. Si Ud. sospecha que una persona le está pegando a un miembro de la familia, ¿qué hace?

_____

4. ¿Está Ud. enojado(a) con alguien hoy? ¿Por qué?

_____

Vamos a practicar

A. Change the demonstrative adjectives so that they agree with the new nouns.

1. Este dinero, _____ mentira, _____ maltratos, _____ cantinas

2. Esas recámaras, _____ arma, _____ miembros de su familia, _____ caso

3. Aquel (*that, over there*) país, _____ formas, _____ jueces, _____ familia

B. Complete the following sentences with the appropriate Spanish demonstrative pronouns.

1. Voy a investigar este caso y _____ (*that one*).

2. Sospechamos que el papá les pega a sus niños con ese cinto y con _____ (*this one*).

3. El Sr. Ramírez va a esta cantina o a _____ (*that one over there*) todos los días.

4. ¿Qué es _____ (*that*)?

5. Esta lesión y _____ (*those*) son graves.

C. You are needed as an translator. Translate the following conversational exchanges into Spanish. Use direct and/or indirect object pronouns.

1. "What are you going to do, Anita?"

    "I'm going to tell him that I'm going to call the police."

    _____

    _____

2. "Do you give them money, Mr. Soto?"

    "No, I never give them anything!"

    _____

    _____

3. "Does your husband hit you, Mrs. Varela?"

    "Yes, he hits me when he's drunk."

    _____

    _____

D. Answer the following questions, using the cues provided. Substitute direct and indirect object pronouns for the italicized objects.

   Modelo: ¿Quién *le* quita *el dinero a esa mujer*? (su marido)

   Su marido **se lo** quita.

1. ¿Quién *le* dice *la verdad a Ud.*? (mi amigo)

    _____

2. ¿Quién no *les* perdona *los delitos a los ladrones*? (mi padre)

    _____

3. ¿Quién *les* consigue *bebidas a los menores de edad*? (nadie)

_____

4. ¿Quién *le* va a preguntar *eso al padrastro*? (el agente)

_____

Conversaciones breves

Complete the following dialogue, using your imagination and the vocabulary from this lesson.

Un caso de maltrato:

AGENTE ROCHA —_____

VECINA —El marido de mi vecina le está pegando.

AGENTE ROCHA —_____

VECINA —Sí, siempre le pega. Y cuando está borracho, le pega mucho.

AGENTE ROCHA —_____

VECINA —¿El dinero para bebidas? Su mujer me dice que si ella no se lo da, él se lo quita.

AGENTE ROCHA —_____

VECINA —No sé si tiene armas.

AGENTE ROCHA —_____

VECINA —No sé si va a estar dispuesta a acusar a su marido esta vez.

AGENTE ROCHA —_____

En estas situaciones

What would you say in the following situations? What might the other person say?

1. You arrive at a house where there is a domestic squabble. Ask if you're at the right house, what is going on, if the stepfather is employed, and whether he is armed.

2. You are talking to a battered wife. See if she's hurt and if she needs to go to the hospital. Ask her if she wants to accuse her husband of abuse, and find out if she has a place to spend the night.

3. You go to a house where the parents are suspected of abusing their children. Introduce yourself. Explain that the local doctor suspects abuse because both children are in the hospital again with rather serious injuries. The parents deny everything.

Casos

Act out the following scenarios with a partner.

1. You are a police officer questioning a child about the father's abuse of the mother.

2. Discuss child abuse and counseling with a parent who has been abusing his/her child.

Un paso más

A. Review the *Vocabulario adicional* in this lesson and match the items in column A with those in column B.

	A		*B*
1. _____	hand grenade	a.	mordida
2. _____	punch	b.	puñetazo
3. _____	dagger	c.	bomba de tiempo
4. _____	shotgun	d.	ametralladora
5. _____	bite	e.	nalgada
6. _____	machine gun	f.	explosivo
7. _____	bomb	g.	escopeta
8. _____	time bomb	h.	bomba
9. _____	slap	i.	paliza
10. _____	beating	j.	patada
11. _____	explosive	k.	puñal
12. _____	kick	l.	cuchillo
13. _____	knife	m.	granada de mano
14. _____	spanking	n.	bofetada

B. Read the following brochure about domestic violence. Try to guess the meaning of all cognates. Then, do the exercise items that follow.

¡La violencia doméstica es un delito!

¿Sabía Ud.° que...

- es un crimen amenazar,° golpear,° asaltar sexualmente o en alguna manera causarle daño° a otra persona, aunque sea° un miembro de su familia?
- aproximadamente el 30% de las mujeres que son víctimas de homicidio en los Estados Unidos son matadas por sus esposos o novios°?
- la violencia doméstica afecta por lo menos° a una de cada cuatro familias?
- entre el 75% y el 90% de los niños que son víctimas de abuso sexual conocen a los que cometen el abuso?
- el 33% de los asaltos sexuales ocurren en la casa de la víctima?

Si Ud. es víctima de la violencia doméstica, Ud. debe...

- llamar a la policía.
- no quedarse° en casa si la situación es peligrosa. Salir de la casa y llevar consigo° a los niños y los documentos importantes, como el registro del carro y el certificado de nacimiento.°
- buscar atención médica.
- buscar ayuda profesional para tratar de resolver el problema.

Recuerde...
¡actuando así° Ud. puede poner fin a los maltratos!

¿Sabía... Did you know?
to threaten / to hit
causarle... *to hurt /* **aunque...** *even though it may be*

boyfriends
por... *at least*

no... don't stay
with you
birth

actuando... *by taking action in this way*

---

1. Match each percentage with the fact to which it pertains, according to the information given in the brochure.

a. _____ el por ciento de familias afectadas por la violencia doméstica

b. _____ el por ciento de asaltos sexuales que ocurren en la casa de la víctima

c. _____ el por ciento de mujeres matadas por sus esposos o novios

d. _____ el por ciento de niños víctimas de abuso sexual que conocen a las personas que cometen el abuso.

1. 75%–90%

2. 25%

3. 33%

4. 30%

2. If you were to meet the following Spanish-speaking battered women while responding to domestic violence calls, what would you say to them?

   a. The woman is all black and blue but says she feels fine and will just take an aspirin and get some rest. _____

   _____

   b. The woman has been repeatedly beaten by her spouse but is afraid to involve the police. _____

   _____

   c. The woman feels that her situation is hopeless and that the problems between her and her husband will never be resolved. _____

   _____

   d. The woman is reluctant to leave her home because she has no place to go. _____

   _____

9

🔊 *La prueba del alcohol*

Son las tres de la madrugada. El agente López detiene a un hombre por conducir a cincuenta millas por hora, con las luces apagadas, en una zona residencial. El límite de velocidad es de treinta y cinco millas por hora. El hombre parece estar borracho.

AGENTE LÓPEZ	—Arrime el carro a la acera y apague el motor, por favor.
HOMBRE	—¿Qué pasa, agente?
AGENTE LÓPEZ	—El límite de velocidad en este lugar es de treinta y cinco millas por hora, no de cincuenta.
HOMBRE	—Es que estoy muy apurado.
AGENTE LÓPEZ	—Déjeme ver su licencia de conducir, por favor.
HOMBRE	—Está en mi casa...
AGENTE LÓPEZ	—Muéstreme el registro del coche.
HOMBRE	—No lo tengo. El coche no es mío. Es de mi tío.
AGENTE LÓPEZ	—¿Cómo se llama Ud.?
HOMBRE	—Me llamo Juan Lara.
AGENTE LÓPEZ	—Su dirección y su edad, por favor.
SR. LARA	—Vivo en la calle Quinta, número quinientos veinte. Tengo treinta años.
AGENTE LÓPEZ	—Bájese del carro, por favor.
SR. LARA	—¡Le digo que tengo mucha prisa!
AGENTE LÓPEZ	—Extienda los brazos, así. Cierre los ojos y tóquese la punta de la nariz.
SR. LARA	—No puedo... pero no estoy borracho...
AGENTE LÓPEZ	—Camine por esa línea hasta el final y vuelva por la misma línea.
SR. LARA	—No veo bien la línea.
AGENTE LÓPEZ	—(*Pone una moneda en el suelo.*) Recoja esa moneda del suelo.
SR. LARA	—No la puedo agarrar.
AGENTE LÓPEZ	—Cuente con los dedos, así: uno, dos, tres, cuatro... cuatro, tres, dos, uno...
SR. LARA	—Uno, dos, tres, cuatro, tres... Voy a empezar de nuevo...
AGENTE LÓPEZ	—Recite el abecedario, por favor.
SR. LARA	—A, be, ce, de... efe, jota... ene...
AGENTE LÓPEZ	—Voy a leerle algo, Sr. Lara. Preste atención.

"Por ley estatal Ud. tiene que someterse a una prueba química para determinar el contenido alcohólico de su sangre. Ud. puede elegir si la prueba va a ser de su sangre, orina o aliento. Si Ud. se niega a someterse a una prueba o si no completa una prueba, le vamos a suspender el derecho a manejar por seis meses. Ud. no tiene derecho a hablar con un abogado ni a tener un abogado presente antes de decir si va a someterse a una prueba, antes de decidir cuál de las pruebas va a elegir, ni durante la prueba elegida por Ud. Si Ud. no puede, o dice que no puede, completar la prueba elegida por Ud., debe someterse a cualquiera de las otras pruebas y completarla."

🔊 Vocabulario

COGNADOS

el alcohol alcohol
alcohólico(a) alcoholic
el límite limit
la línea line
el motor engine, motor

la orina urine
residencial residential
la velocidad velocity, speed
la zona zone

NOMBRES

el abecedario, el alfabeto alphabet
la acera, la banqueta (*Méx.*) sidewalk
el aliento breath
el contenido content
el dedo finger
el final end
el límite de velocidad, la velocidad máxima
  speed limit
el lugar place
la madrugada early morning
la milla mile
la moneda coin
la nariz nose
la prueba test
la prueba del alcohol sobriety test
la punta end, tip
la sangre blood
el suelo ground
el (la) tío (tía) uncle (aunt)

VERBOS

agarrar, coger to get hold of, to grab
apagar to turn off
arrimar to pull over, to place nearby
bajarse to get out (off)
cerrar (e:ie) to close, to shut
completar to complete
contar (o:ue) to count
dejar to allow, to let
determinar to determine
elegir (e:i)[1] to choose
empezar (e:ie), comenzar (e:ie) to begin
extender (e:ie) to stretch out, to spread
llamarse to be named, to be called
mostrar (o:ue), enseñar to show
negarse (e:ie) (a) to refuse to
poner[2] to put
recitar to recite
someterse a to submit (oneself) to
tocar to touch

---

[1]First-person present indicative: *yo elijo.*
[2]Irregular first-person present indicative: *yo pongo.*

ADJETIVOS

apagado(a)   out, off (light)
elegido(a)   chosen
estatal   of or pertaining to the state
mismo(a)   same
químico(a)   chemical

OTRAS PALABRAS Y EXPRESIONES

así   like this
conducir a cincuenta millas por hora   to drive
 fifty miles per hour
cualquiera   any (one), either
de nuevo   over, again
Es que...   It's just that . . .
estar apurado(a), tener prisa   to be in a hurry
prestar atención   to pay attention

Vocabulario adicional

VOCABULARIO AUTOMOVILÍSTICO

el aceite   oil
el acelerador   accelerator, gas pedal
el acumulador, la batería   battery
el arranque, el motor de arranque   starter
el asiento   seat
el asiento para el niño   child's car seat
la bomba de agua   water pump
la bujía   spark plug
el cambio de velocidad   gearshift
el capó, la cubierta   hood
el carburador   carburetor
el cinturón de seguridad   safety belt
el filtro   filter
el foco   light
el freno   brake
la gasolina   gasoline
la goma, el neumático   tire
el guardafangos   fender
el indicador   turn signal
el limpiaparabrisas   windshield wiper
la llanta   tire
la llanta pinchada, la goma ponchada   flat tire
el maletero, el portaequipajes, la cajuela (*Méx.*), **el baúl** (*Puerto Rico*)   trunk
la palanca de cambio de velocidades, el embrague   gearshift lever
el portaguantes, la guantera   glove compartment
la rueda   wheel
el silenciador, el amortiguador   muffler
el tanque   tank
la tapicería   upholstery
la ventanilla   window
el volante, el timón (*Cuba*)   steering wheel

Notas culturales

- Alcoholism is stigmatized as a vice in most Hispanic countries, but having several drinks or drinking excessively at social functions is acceptable on occasion. Hispanics generally don't drink alone, but rather in groups, and rarely with the deliberate intention of getting drunk. In some countries, women drink as much as men; in other countries, women hardly drink at all. The frequency of drunkenness among women in Hispanic countries is, overall, much lower than among women in the United States.

- In the majority of Hispanic countries, there is no age limit for the sale and consumption of alcoholic beverages, and, generally, where age limits exist, they are not enforced. Young people generally participate fully in social gatherings and parties, and it is not unusual for them to drink alcoholic beverages.

- The alcoholic beverages most consumed in Hispanic countries are beer, wine, tequila, rum, cognac, and whiskey. Cider, an alcoholic beverage in Hispanic countries, is the preferred beverage for toasts. Upon toasting, Hispanics generally say *¡Salud!* ("To your health!"). In Spain, one frequently says *¡Salud, amor y pesetas,*[1] *y tiempo para gastarlas!* ("Health, love, and pesetas, and the time to spend them!").

¿Recuerdan ustedes?

Answer the following questions, basing your answers on the dialogue.

1. ¿Por qué detiene al hombre el agente López?

   _____

2. ¿Cuál es el límite de velocidad en la zona residencial?

   _____

3. ¿Parece estar borracho el hombre?

   _____

4. ¿Por qué dice el hombre que está manejando a cincuenta millas por hora?

   _____

5. ¿Qué le pide el agente López?

   _____

6. ¿Tiene el hombre el registro del carro?

   _____

7. ¿Cómo se llama el hombre y cuántos años tiene?

   _____

8. ¿Qué no puede hacer bien el hombre?

   _____

_____
[1]Spanish currency

9. ¿Por qué no recoge el hombre la moneda?

_____

10. ¿Por qué debe prestar atención el hombre?

_____

Para conversar

Interview a classmate, using the following questions. When you have finished, switch roles.

1. ¿Para qué es la prueba del alcohol?

_____

2. ¿Cuáles son las tres clases de pruebas?

_____

3. ¿Qué pasa si yo me niego a someterme a la prueba del alcohol?

_____

4. Si yo me someto a la prueba del alcohol, ¿puede estar presente mi abogado(a)?

_____

5. ¿Qué pasa si yo no puedo completar la prueba?

_____

6. ¿Cómo se llama Ud.?

_____

7. ¿Puede Ud. decirme su dirección y su edad?

_____

8. ¿Puede Ud. cerrar los ojos y tocarse la punta de la nariz?

_____

Vamos a practicar

A. Form complete sentences using the words provided in the order given.

1. Ud. / tocarse / la punta de la nariz

_____

2. yo / someterse / prueba del alcohol

_____

3. ella / negarse / completar / la prueba

   _____

4. los criminales / tener que / bajarse / carro

   _____

5. la agente / llamarse / Luisa Delgado

   _____

B. You have just stopped a woman for erratic driving. Say the following to her in Spanish.

1. "Turn off the engine."

   _____

2. "Let me see your license."

   _____

3. "Show me the registration."

   _____

4. "Get out of the car."

   _____

5. "Stretch out your arms."

   _____

6. "Close your eyes."

   _____

You suspect that two men who are creating a disturbance in the street are drunk. Tell them in Spanish to do the following.

7. "Touch your nose."

   _____

8. "Walk."

   _____

9. "Pick up the coins."

   _____

10. "Count on your fingers."

    _____

11. "Recite the alphabet."

_____

12. "Pay attention."

_____

C. **Answer each of the following questions first affirmatively, then negatively.**

Modelo: —¿Se lo digo a ella?

—Sí, **dígaselo.**

—No, **no se lo diga.**

1. ¿Se las doy a Ud.?

Sí, _____

No, _____

2. ¿Lo completo ahora?

Sí, _____

No, _____

3. ¿Le suspendo el derecho a manejar?

Sí, _____

No, _____

4. ¿Me someto a la prueba?

Sí, _____

No, _____

5. ¿Me bajo del carro?

Sí, _____

No, _____

6. ¿Los cierro?

Sí, _____

No, _____

Conversaciones breves

Complete the following dialogue, using your imagination and the vocabulary from this lesson.

Otra prueba del alcohol:

HOMBRE — _____

AGENTE —Lo detengo porque Ud. está manejando sin luz.

HOMBRE — _____

AGENTE —No, no puede irse (*leave*). ¿No sabe Ud. que el límite de velocidad en esta zona es de veinticinco millas por hora?

HOMBRE — _____

AGENTE —Déme su licencia, por favor.

HOMBRE — _____

AGENTE —Ud. debe tener su licencia con Ud. para manejar. Déjeme ver su registro.

HOMBRE — _____

AGENTE —¿El carro no es suyo (*yours*)? ¿De quién es?

HOMBRE — _____

AGENTE —Bájase del carro, por favor.

HOMBRE — _____

AGENTE —Lo siento, pero voy a tener que hacerle la prueba del alcohol.

HOMBRE — _____

AGENTE —Si no se somete a la prueba, le vamos a suspender el derecho a manejar por seis meses.

HOMBRE — _____

En estas situaciones

What would you say in the following situations? What might the other person say?

1. You stop a woman for driving at 60 miles per hour in a 35-mile-per-hour zone. Order her to pull over to the curb, to turn off the engine, and to show you her driver's license and car registration.

2. You are giving a sobriety test to two teenagers caught racing their cars down Main Street. Order them to stretch their arms and touch their noses, to walk a straight line, to pick up a coin from the ground, and to count on their fingers. You find they are not drunk. You decide not to give them a ticket, but remind them about the speed limit.

Casos

Act out the following scenarios with a partner.

1. While on patrol, you spot a reckless driver, whom you pull over. Explain why you have stopped the car and collect the appropriate personal data.

2. You have just pulled over a person suspected of DUI. Administer a field sobriety test.

Un paso más

Review the *Vocabulario adicional* **in this lesson and match the items in column A with those in column B.**

A		B	
1. _____	turn signal	a.	tapicería
2. _____	starter	b.	guardafangos
3. _____	water pump	c.	parabrisas
4. _____	carburetor	d.	maletero
5. _____	oil	e.	rueda
6. _____	tire	f.	silenciador
7. _____	battery	g.	limpiaparabrisas
8. _____	windshield wiper	h.	portaguantes
9. _____	gas pedal	i.	tanque
10. _____	spark plug	j.	ventanilla
11. _____	steering wheel	k.	aceite
12. _____	upholstery	l.	bujía
13. _____	windshield	m.	cambio de velocidades
14. _____	window	n.	carburador
15. _____	glove compartment	o.	acelerador
16. _____	gearshift	p.	capó
17. _____	wheel	q.	volante
18. _____	hood	r.	indicador
19. _____	tank	s.	asiento
20. _____	filter	t.	llanta pinchada
21. _____	flat tire	u.	arranque
22. _____	muffler	v.	filtro
23. _____	trunk	w.	bomba de agua
24. _____	brake	x.	acumulador
25. _____	fender	y.	freno
26. _____	seat	z.	goma

10

📼 *La policía investiga un robo*

Esta mañana la Sra. Ramos llamó por teléfono a la policía para denunciar un robo.
Una hora después llegó a su casa el sargento Nieto, de la Sección de Robos.

El sargento Nieto habla con la Sra. Ramos:

SARGENTO NIETO	—Buenos días, señora. Soy el sargento Nieto, de la Sección de Robos. Aquí está mi identificación.
SRA. RAMOS	—Buenos días, sargento. Llamé porque anoche entraron ladrones en la casa.
SARGENTO NIETO	—¿Qué les robaron, señora?
SRA. RAMOS	—Muchas cosas: dos televisores, una cámara de video, la computadora, el tocadiscos de discos compactos, varias joyas y unos ochenta dólares en efectivo.
SARGENTO NIETO	—¿De qué marca son todos esos equipos?
SRA. RAMOS	—La computadora es de la IBM, los televisores son un Emerson de diecinueve pulgadas y un RCA de veinticuatro pulgadas. Los demás equipos son también de la RCA.
SARGENTO NIETO	—¿Tiene el número de serie de todos los equipos robados?
SRA. RAMOS	—Creo que sí. Nosotros los compramos a plazos y yo tengo guardados los contratos. Un momento.

La señora se va y vuelve con los contratos. El sargento Nieto los revisa.

SARGENTO NIETO	—Aquí falta el contrato de uno de los televisores.
SRA. RAMOS	—Es verdad. Ahora me acuerdo de que lo tiré a la basura cuando terminé de pagarlo.
SARGENTO NIETO	—Y... ¿no anotó el número de serie?
SRA. RAMOS	—No, no lo anoté. Ya sé que fue una tontería.
SARGENTO NIETO	—¿Por dónde entraron los ladrones?
SRA. RAMOS	—Por la ventana del cuarto de mi hijo. Forzaron la cerradura.
SARGENTO NIETO	—¿Limpiaron Uds. la casa después del robo?
SRA. RAMOS	—No, no tocamos nada.
SARGENTO NIETO	—Bien. Luego van a venir los técnicos para ver si dejaron algunas huellas digitales. Ud. no tiene idea de a qué hora fue el robo, ¿verdad?
SRA. RAMOS	—No. Ayer nosotros fuimos a una quinceañera en un pueblo cercano, y nos quedamos allá hasta hoy.
SARGENTO NIETO	—¿Su hijo también fue a la fiesta?
SRA. RAMOS	—Sí, todos fuimos y volvimos juntos.
SARGENTO NIETO	—Bueno, eso es todo, Sra. Ramos. Ahora voy a hablar con los vecinos para continuar las averiguaciones.
SRA. RAMOS	—Yo hablé con los vecinos de al lado y ellos no vieron a nadie sospechoso rondando la casa.

SARGENTO NIETO	—Y le di mi tarjeta, ¿verdad? Llámeme si tiene algo nuevo que decirme.
SRA. RAMOS	—Gracias por su ayuda, sargento. Y, por favor, si Ud. averigua algo, llámeme.
SARGENTO NIETO	—Claro que sí, señora.

📼 Vocabulario

COGNADOS

la cámara de video, la video-cámara video camera	**la idea** idea
el contrato contract	**la serie** series
el disco compacto compact disc	**el (la) técnico(a)** technician
el dólar dollar	

NOMBRES

la averiguación investigation
la basura trash, garbage
la cerradura lock
la computadora, el ordenador (*España*) computer
el cuarto, la habitación room
el equipo equipment
la fiesta party
la huella digital fingerprint
la joya jewelry
la mañana morning
la marca brand
el número de serie serial number
el pueblo town
la quinceañera girl on her fifteenth birthday, party to celebrate a girl's fifteenth birthday
el televisor television set
el tocadiscos record player
la tontería foolishness, nonsense
la ventana window

VERBOS

acordarse (o:ue) (de) to remember
anotar to write down, to take note of
averiguar to find out
comprar to buy
continuar to continue
faltar to be missing, to lack
forzar (o:ue) to force
irse to go away, to leave
limpiar to clean
quedarse to stay
revisar to review, to check
robar to rob, to steal from
rondar to prowl
terminar to finish
tirar, botar to throw away

ADJETIVOS

cercano(a) near, nearby
guardado(a) put away, saved
juntos(as) together
robado(a) stolen, robbed
sospechoso(a) suspicious

OTRAS PALABRAS Y EXPRESIONES

a plazos in installments, on time (payments)
anoche last night
Claro que sí. Of course.
de al lado next-door (neighbor, house)
en efectivo in cash
los demás the remaining (ones)
luego later, afterwards
terminar de + *infinitivo* to finish (doing something)

Vocabulario adicional

**ALGUNOS ARTÍCULOS USADOS PARA
COMETER DELITOS** (*Some crime paraphernalia*)

el cortavidrios   glass cutter
el documento falso   forged document
la escala de soga   rope ladder
la escalera de mano   hand ladder
la identificación falsa   fake identification, forged ID
la jeringuilla   hypodermic syringe
la llave falsa, la ganzúa   skeleton key, picklock
la máscara   mask
la mordaza   gag
la pata de cabra   crowbar
la piedra   stone, rock
la sierra de mano, el serrucho de mano   handsaw
la soga   rope

Nota cultural

In Hispanic cultures, a girl's fifteenth birthday is celebrated with a special party much like a girl's sixteenth birthday party in North America. In both cultures, these celebrations are a rite of passage that mark the transition from girlhood to womanhood. In Mexico, this event is called a *quinceañera*.

¿Recuerdan ustedes?

Answer the following questions, basing your answers on the dialogue.

1. ¿Para qué llamó la Sra. Ramos a la policía?

   _____

2. ¿Para qué fue el agente Nieto a su casa?

   _____

3. ¿Qué les robaron?

   _____

4. ¿De qué marca son los televisores? ¿Y la computadora?

   _____

5. ¿Sabe la Sra. Ramos todos los números de serie? ¿Por qué?

   _____

6. ¿Cómo entraron los ladrones en la casa?

   _____

7. ¿Para qué van a venir los técnicos?

   _____

8. ¿Adónde fueron la Sra. Ramos y su familia ayer?

   _____

9. ¿Qué más va a pasar?

   _____

10. ¿Qué le dio el sargento Nieto a la Sra. Ramos?

    _____

Para conversar

Interview a classmate, using the following questions. When you have finished, switch roles.

1. ¿Adónde fue Ud. ayer?

   _____

2. ¿Se quedó en casa anoche?

   _____

3. ¿Tiene Ud. una computadora en su casa? ¿De qué marca es? Cuando la compró, ¿anotó el número de serie?

   _____

4. ¿Se acuerda Ud. dónde compró su televisor? ¿Lo compró a plazos?

   _____

5. ¿Alguien lo (la) llamó a Ud. esta mañana? ¿Quién fue?

   _____

6. Si Ud. ve a alguien sospechoso rondando una casa, ¿qué hace?

   _____

Vamos a practicar

A. Change the following paragraph to indicate that the actions took place in the past. Pay special attention to the verbs in italics.

Cuando la familia García *sale* de su casa, los ladrones *entran* y le *roban* la computadora. Cuando la familia *regresa*, la Sra. García *llama* a la policía. *Habla* con el sargento Smith y le *da* el número de serie del equipo. El sargento le *promete* investigar el caso. Por la tarde, el sargento *va* a la casa de los García.

_____

_____

_____

_____

_____

B. Fill in the blanks with *por* or *para*, as needed.

1. Los ladrones entraron _____ una ventana.

2. El sargento viene _____ averiguar el robo.

3. Me llamó _____ teléfono _____ decirme tonterías.

4. Ella guarda dinero _____ su fiesta.

5. Compré una computadora _____ mi hija _____ muy poco dinero.

6. No puede identificar la cámara de video _____ no tener el número de serie.

7. _____ entrar en la casa, los ladrones forzaron la ventana.

8. Salimos _____ la mañana, pero la fiesta fue _____ la noche.

9. Nos fuimos de vacaciones _____ dos semanas.

10. La niña es muy pequeña _____ andar sola _____ esta calle.

Conversaciones breves

Complete the following dialogue, using your imagination and the vocabulary from this lesson.

Investigando un robo:

AGENTE —_____

MUJER —Me robaron un televisor y una cámara de video.

AGENTE —_____

MUJER —El televisor es un RCA portátil, de diecinueve pulgadas y la cámara de video, una Sony.

AGENTE —_____

MUJER —Sí, también me robaron una computadora nueva, una IBM.

AGENTE —_____

MUJER —Entraron por la ventana.

AGENTE —_____

MUJER —¡Bah! Mis vecinos nunca ven nada. Siempre están mirando (*watching*) televisión.

AGENTE —_____

En estas situaciones

What would you say in the following situations? What might the other person say?

1. You are investigating a burglary. Ask the victim if he/she called the police, when the burglary took place, what the burglars took, and whether he/she knows how they got in.

2. You are talking to a burglary victim. Say that you are going to talk with the neighbors to try to find out if anybody saw anything. Explain that the technicians are going to come this afternoon to look for fingerprints. The victim asks you to call if you find out anything new.

3. You are talking to the neighbors of a person whose house was robbed. Introduce yourself and explain the reason for your visit. Ask if they saw anyone prowling around last night. They say they saw two suspicious young men in a strange car in front of the house, but they never got out. Tell them to call you if they remember anything new.

Casos

Act out the following scenarios with a partner.

1. You are a police officer talking to a victim of a burglary.

2. You describe to your partner, who was not on duty last night, all you know about the break-in on Cisne Street.

Un paso más

A. Review the *Vocabulario adicional* in this lesson and then list the paraphernalia that you associate with the following crimes.

1. el vandalismo _____

_____

2. el homicidio _____

_____

3. el uso de drogas _____

_____

4. el robo _____

_____

5. el contrabando _____

_____

6. la estafa (*swindle*) _____

_____

B. Write down three precautions you would recommend to someone concerned about preventing a robbery at his/her home.

1. _____

2. _____

3. _____

Now, read the following information about home burglaries. Try to guess the meaning of all cognates. Then do the exercise item that follows.

Seguridad doméstica: Robos

¡Más de seis millones de robos residenciales ocurren en los Estados Unidos cada año: uno cada diez segundos!

Prevención: Cuando Ud. salga° de la casa...

leave

- siempre cierre con llave las puertas y ventanas. (En casi° el 50% de los casos, los ladrones entran en las casas por puertas y ventanas abiertas.°

almost

open

- nunca deje la llave donde se pueda encontrar fácilmente°: bajo un felpudo,° en una maceta de flores,° etc.

find easily

mat / **maceta...** *flower pot*

- use un regulador de encendido para que las luces, el radio y el televisor se prendan y se apaguen automáticamente para dar la impresión de que alguien está en casa.

- en caso de viajes° extensos, acuérdese de suspender la entrega de la correspondencia y de los periódicos o pídale a un(a) vecino(a) que los recoja.

trips

Si Ud. llega a casa y ve indicaciones de que alguien ha forzado la cerradura de la puerta o de la ventana, no entre.
¡Llame a la policía enseguida!

¡Buenos vecinos!
Si ve algo sospechoso en la casa de un vecino, llame a la policía enseguida. Nunca trate de detener° a un delincuente; puede ser peligroso. Recuerde: ¡Una comunidad que trabaja en cooperación con la policía es la mejor protección contra° los delitos!

to stop

against

With a partner, rank the recommendations in the brochure, as well as your
own recommendations, according to their effectiveness.

_____

_____

_____

_____

_____

_____

Repaso

Práctica de vocabulario

A.   Circle the word or phrase that does not belong in each group.

1.   automóvil, carro, dedo

2.   aguja, juzgado, abogada

3.   mano, derecho, brazo

4.   infracción de tráfico, multa, equipo

5.   tragos, corazón, borracho

6.   antes, a plazos, después

7.   peca, puerta, ventana

8.   mentira, cigarrillo, fumar

9.   rubio, lastimado, pelirrojo

10.   hablar, correr, decir

11.   aceptar, abusar, maltratar

12.   volver, pegar, matar

13.   enojada, en este lugar, adentro

14.   agarra, coge, apaga

15.   botan, tiran, averiguan

16.   ordenador, computadora, cerradura

17.   anoche, cercano, de al lado

18.   cámara de video, guantera, televisor

B. Circle the word or phrase that best completes each sentence.

1. No sé quién cometió (el delito, el derecho, la escuela).

2. ¿Dónde está el dinero? ¿En tu (joven, bolsillo, aguja)?

3. (El edificio, La pared, El chofer) está en el carro.

4. El tocadiscos es de ella; ella es (la clienta, la dueña, la estudiante).

5. No (recuerdo, detengo, empiezo) el nombre de este señor...

6. Maneja (dentro del, bajo los efectos del, a cargo del) alcohol.

7. ¿Es gordo o (delgado, amarillo, endrogado)?

8. El coche está (en la licorería, en la navaja, en la zona de estacionamiento).

9. Mide seis pies, cuatro (tatuajes, suelos, pulgadas).

10. Le va a pegar con un (miembro, cinto, aliento).

11. Vienen a las cuatro de la mañana. (¡De madrugada!, ¡Cualquiera!, ¡Durante!)

12. (Las huellas, Las monedas, Los números) digitales están en la ventana.

13. Yo voy con Roberto. Nosotros siempre vamos (cansados, callados, juntos).

14. Con el dinero que robó, el ladrón quiere (vender, limpiar, comprar) drogas.

15. Tenemos (más o menos, a la fuerza, en contra de) cien dólares.

C. **Match the items in column A with the appropriate word or phrase in column B.**

A

1. _____ Muéstreme el registro, por favor.

2. _____ ¿Ellas están muy enojadas con la vecina?

3. _____ ¿De qué país son?

4. _____ ¿Dices que él siempre se entromete?

5. _____ ¿Qué puedo hacer?

6. _____ ¿Cuándo lo viste?

7. _____ ¿Con quién va Teresa?

8. _____ ¿No va a conducir Juan?

9. _____ ¿Cómo está tu tío?

10. _____ ¿Qué tienes en el cuarto?

11. _____ ¿Qué le van a hacer?

12. _____ ¿Dónde está el hospital?

B

a. Sí, porque siempre me dice lo que tengo que hacer.

b. Ayer.

c. Lo siento, pero no lo tengo conmigo.

d. No, porque está borracho.

e. A dos millas de aquí.

f. Un disco compacto.

g. De Colombia.

h. No sé. Tú tienes que decidir.

i. Mejor.

j. Conmigo.

k. Sí, porque ella siempre dice tonterías.

l. La prueba del alcohol.

D. Crucigrama

HORIZONTAL

   4. Quiero ése en _____ de éste.

   5. to forgive, en español

   8. ¿Es por la _____ o por la tarde?

   9. Es el esposo de mi mamá, pero no es mi papá; es mi _____ .

   11. Es muy tarde y no hay _____ tiempo para terminar el informe hoy.

   13. un revólver, por ejemplo

   14. cinto

   18. carro

   19. parecer: yo _____ .

   20. Se puede comprar bebidas alcohólicas en una _____ .

   22. opuesto de con

   23. Escribe con la mano izquierda porque es _____ .

   24. No me hace _____ .

   25. ¿Cuál es la _____ máxima?

   26. coge

VERTICAL

   1. opuesto de dar

   2. con frecuencia

   3. opuesto de gorda

   6. Tóquese la punta de la _____ .

   7. bar

   10. alfabeto

   12. María dice que son de Lima, pero ella está _____ ; son de Santiago.

   13. Perry Mason, por ejemplo.

   15. No es diferente; es el _____ .

   16. El Empire State, por ejemplo.

   17. Tienes que manejar a 25 millas por hora en un distrito _____ .

   18. Tengo prisa: estoy _____ .

   21. mostrar

   24. Ella _____ de uno a diez en español.

📼 Práctica oral

Listen to the following exercise on the audio program. The speaker will ask you some questions. Answer each question, using the cue provided. The speaker will verify your response. Repeat the correct answer.

1. ¿Cuánto mide Ud.? (cinco pies, diez pulgadas)

2. ¿Qué marcas visibles tiene Ud.? (un tatuaje en el brazo izquierdo)

3. ¿Adónde fue Ud. ayer? (a la comisaría)

4. ¿Con quién habló Ud. ayer? (con el técnico)

5. ¿A quién vio Ud. anoche? (a mi familia)

6. ¿A qué hora volvió a su casa anoche? (a las ocho)

7. ¿Hay alguien en su casa en este momento? (no)

8. Cuando Ud. necesita dinero, ¿a quién se lo pide? (a nadie)

9. ¿Le robaron a Ud. algo esta mañana? (sí, mis joyas)

10. ¿De qué marca es su televisor? (Sony)

11. ¿Cuándo compró Ud. su televisor? (en abril)

12. ¿Sabe Ud. el número de serie de su video-cámara? (no)

13. ¿A quiénes llama Ud. si alguien está lastimado? (a los paramédicos)

14. ¿Cómo se llama la doctora? (Luisa Morales)

15. ¿Quién pagó una multa esta tarde? (la señora de al lado)

16. Cuando Ud. sospecha que alguien maneja bajo la influencia del alcohol, ¿qué hace? (la prueba del alcohol)

17. ¿Alguien se negó a someterse a la prueba del alcohol? (sí, la Srta. Silva)

18. Si alguien maneja muy rápido, ¿lo detiene Ud.? (sí)

19. ¿Recuerda Ud. la advertencia Miranda? (claro que sí)

20. ¿Puede leerle la advertencia Miranda a alguien en español? (sí)

21. ¿Puede Ud. interrogar a un detenido en español? (sí)

22. ¿Siempre entiende bien cuando alguien le habla español? (a veces)

23. ¿A quién interrogó Ud. hoy? (el esposo de una mujer maltratada)

24. ¿Ya terminó la averiguación? (sí)

25. ¿Investiga Ud. casos de maltrato a menudo? (sí, frecuentemente)

11

📼 *¡Más robos!*

El Sr. Gómez vino a la comisaría a denunciar el robo de su carro. Ahora está hablando con el sargento Alcalá, de la Sección de Robos.

SARGENTO ALCALÁ	—¿Cuándo le robaron su carro?
SR. GÓMEZ	—Anoche.
SARGENTO ALCALÁ	—¿Dónde estaba estacionado?
SR. GÓMEZ	—Frente a mi casa.
SARGENTO ALCALÁ	—¿El carro estaba cerrado con llave?
SR. GÓMEZ	—No estoy seguro. Mi hijo fue el último que lo manejó y él, a veces, no lo cierra con llave.
SARGENTO ALCALÁ	—Por favor, dígame la marca, el modelo y el año de su carro.
SR. GÓMEZ	—Es un Ford Festiva, azul claro, del año noventa y tres.
SARGENTO ALCALÁ	—¿Cuál es el número de la placa de su carro?
SR. GÓMEZ	—PED 530.
SARGENTO ALCALÁ	—¿Está asegurado su carro?
SR. GÓMEZ	—Sí, señor, contra todo riesgo.
SARGENTO ALCALÁ	—¿Y está totalmente pagado el carro, Sr. Gómez?
SR. GÓMEZ	—No, todavía debo muchos plazos.
SARGENTO ALCALÁ	—¿Está atrasado en los pagos?
SR. GÓMEZ	—La verdad es que no estoy al día. Debo como dos meses.
SARGENTO ALCALÁ	—Muy bien. Voy a entregar las copias del informe a los patrulleros.
SR. GÓMEZ	—A ver si lo encuentran pronto. Muchas gracias, sargento.
SARGENTO ALCALÁ	—No hay de qué, Sr. Gómez.

La Sra. Vega también vino a la comisaría a denunciar un robo. Ahora está hablando con el sargento Rivas.

SRA. VEGA	—¡No puedo creerlo! Hace veinte años que vivo aquí y es la primera vez que hay un robo en el vecindario.
SARGENTO RIVAS	—¿Revisó bien la casa para ver todo lo que le falta?
SRA. VEGA	—Sí. Hice una lista de lo que falta: cubiertos de plata, la videocasetera, una grabadora, una cámara de video y una computadora.
SARGENTO RIVAS	—¿Se llevaron algún arma?
SRA. VEGA	—¡Ah, sí... ! Una pistola de mi esposo.
SARGENTO RIVAS	—Esa pistola, ¿está registrada?
SRA. VEGA	—Creo que sí, pero no estoy segura. Eso tiene que preguntárselo a mi esposo.

SARGENTO RIVAS	—Anóteme la marca, descripción y valor aproximado de todos los objetos robados, por favor.
SRA. VEGA	—Muy bien.
SARGENTO RIVAS	—¿Son todos los objetos robados propiedad de Uds.?
SRA. VEGA	—Sí, señor. Son míos y de mi esposo.
SARGENTO RIVAS	—Bien, vamos a hacer todo lo posible por recobrarlos. (*Al agente Soto*) Lleva a la Sra. Vega a su casa, por favor.

🔲 Vocabulario

COGNADOS

aproximado(a) approximate	**la lista** list
la copia copy	**el modelo** model
la descripción description	**el objeto** object, item

NOMBRES

los cubiertos   silverware (forks, knives, etc.)
la grabadora   tape recorder
el pago   payment
la placa, la chapa   license plate
la plata   silver
el plazo   installment
la propiedad   property
el riesgo   risk
el valor   value
el vecindario   neighborhood
la verdad   truth
la videocasetera, la videograbadora   videocassette recorder (VCR)

VERBOS

deber   to owe
encontrar (o:ue)   to find
entregar   to give, to turn over (i.e., something to someone)
llevarse   to steal (literally, to carry away)
recobrar   to recover

ADJETIVOS

asegurado(a)   insured
atrasado(a)   behind
cerrado(a)   closed, locked
claro(a)   light (in color)
estacionado(a)   parked
pagado(a)   paid (for)
registrado(a)   registered
todo(a)   all
último(a)   last

OTRAS PALABRAS Y EXPRESIONES

al día   up to date
cerrar (e:ie) con llave   to lock
como   about, approximately
contra   against
¿cuándo?   when?
todo lo posible   everything possible
totalmente   totally
No hay de qué.   You're welcome.

Vocabulario adicional

PASADO, PRESENTE Y FUTURO (*Past, present, and future*)

a mediados de mes   about the middle of the month
a mediados de semana   about the middle of the week
a medianoche   at midnight
al mediodía   at noon
al amanecer, de madrugada   at dawn, at daybreak
al anochecer   at dusk
anteanoche, antes de anoche   the night before last
anteayer, antes de ayer   the day before yesterday
durante el día   during the day
durante la noche   during the night
el año pasado   last year
el año que viene, el año próximo   next year
el mes pasado   last month
el mes que viene, el mes próximo   next month
la semana pasada   last week
la semana que viene, la semana próxima   next week
pasado mañana   the day after tomorrow
temprano   early

Nota cultural

Automobile insurance is not mandatory in many Hispanic countries, and thus the habit of insuring cars is not as widespread in Latin America as it is in the United States. Many Hispanics who immigrate to the United States leave their cars uninsured, either out of habit, because they are unaware that automobile insurance is mandatory, or because they cannot afford to pay high insurance premiums.

¿Recuerdan ustedes?

Answer the following questions, basing your answers on the dialogue.

1. ¿Para qué vinieron el Sr. Gómez y la Sra. Vega a la comisaría?

    _____

2. ¿Puede Ud. describir el carro del Sr. Gómez?

    _____

3. ¿Está totalmente pagado el carro del Sr. Gómez?

    _____

4. ¿Cuántos meses debe el Sr. Gómez?

    _____

5. ¿Cuántos años hace que la Sra. Vega vive en su casa?

_____

6. ¿Qué hizo la Sra. Vega después del robo?

_____

7. ¿Qué se llevaron los ladrones?

_____

8. ¿Está registrada la pistola del Sr. Vega?

_____

9. ¿De quién son los objetos robados?

_____

10. ¿Qué va a hacer el agente Soto?

_____

Para conversar

Interview a classmate, using the following questions. When you have finished, switch roles.

1. ¿Cuánto tiempo hace que Ud. trabaja en el Departamento de Policía?

_____

2. ¿Hacen Uds. todo lo posible por recobrar objetos robados?

_____

3. ¿Cuándo fue la última vez que Ud. hizo un informe sobre (*about*) un robo de un carro?

_____

4. ¿Cuál es el número de la chapa de su carro?

_____

5. ¿Está Ud. atrasado(a) en los pagos de su carro?

_____

6. ¿Está asegurado su carro?

_____

7. ¿Cerró Ud. con llave su carro anoche?

_____

Vamos a practicar

A. Create sentences with the elements provided, using
hace + time + *que* + verb.

1. tres años / (yo) tener / carro

   _____

2. dos horas / sargento Alcalá / hablar / Sr. Gómez

   _____

3. ¿Cuántos años / (Ud.) vivir / en esa casa?

   _____

4. quince minutos / (yo) revisar / la casa

   _____

5. veinte años / mi esposo / tener / esas pistolas

   _____

6. media hora / la Sra. Vega / anotar / la marca / objetos robados

   _____

7. dos meses / (nosotros) no estar / al día

   _____

B. Rewrite the following sentences in the preterit tense according to the
cues given.

Modelo: Hoy la agente Rojas viene a entregar el informe.

Ayer la agente Rojas **vino** a entregar el informe.

1. Tengo un Camaro azul claro.

   Hasta este año _____

2. Estamos en la fiesta de una quinceañera.

   Anoche _____

3. No puedo comprar un seguro contra todo riesgo.

   Cuando compré el carro _____

4. Ellos lo saben.

   Anoche _____

5. La Sra. Ramos hace la denuncia en la estación de policía.

   Ayer _____

6. No quiere decir nada.

   Yo le pregunté, pero _____

7. La señora dice la verdad.

Ayer _____

8. Conduzco a toda velocidad.

Anoche _____

C. Change the verbs in the following sentences into the imperfect tense.

1. Yo voy a la comisaría con ellos.

_____

2. Nosotros revisamos el carro.

_____

3. Carlos debe cien dólares.

_____

4. Es la última vez.

_____

5. No tienen la lista de los objetos robados.

_____

6. Yo no sé el valor de la videocasetera.

_____

7. Ella siempre cierra su coche con llave.

_____

8. Son las cuatro y media.

_____

Conversaciones breves

Complete the following dialogues, using your imagination and vocabulary from this lesson.

El sargento Miño habla con la Sra. Paz del robo de su carro.

SARGENTO MIÑO — _____

SRA. PAZ —No, no estoy al día. Debo como cuatro meses.

SARGENTO MIÑO — _____

SRA. PAZ —No, no tengo seguro.

SARGENTO MIÑO — _____

SRA. PAZ —Lo dejé en la calle. No lo puse en el garaje anoche.

SARGENTO MIÑO —_____

SRA. PAZ —No, no las tengo. Las dejé en el coche.

SARGENTO MIÑO —_____

SRA. PAZ —Sí, yo sospecho de mi vecino...

SARGENTO MIÑO —_____

SRA. PAZ —Es un Mazda 1992, de cuatro puertas.

SARGENTO MIÑO —_____

El Sr. Ortega denuncia un robo.

AGENTE BARRIOS —¿Hizo Ud. una lista de lo que falta?

SR. ORTEGA —_____

AGENTE BARRIOS —¿Puede darme la marca, descripción y valor aproximado de los objetos robados?

SR. ORTEGA —_____

_____

_____

AGENTE BARRIOS —¿De quién son los objetos robados, señor?

SR. ORTEGA —_____

En estas situaciones

What would you say in the following situations? What might the other person say?

1. You are speaking to someone who has just come to the police station to report that his/her car was stolen. Question the owner about where he/she left the car, when it was stolen, whether it was locked, and whether it was insured. Ask for a description of the vehicle.

2. You are investigating a burglary. Ask the victim if he/she checked the house carefully to see what is missing. Find out if the burglars took any weapons. Finally, request that he/she write down the description and the approximate value of the tape recorder, the computer, the VCR, and the silverware. Say that you'll let him/her know right away if you find the stolen items.

Casos

Act out the following scenarios with a partner.

1. You are a desk sergeant speaking with a man/woman who is reporting the theft of his/her car.

2. You are an officer speaking with a person whose home has been burglarized.

Un paso más

A. **Review the *Vocabulario adicional* in this lesson and complete the following minidialogues.**

1. —¿Cuándo viene Teresa?

   —El 16 de agosto, creo... A _____ .

   —¿Y Jorge?

   —El viernes al mediodía. Hoy es miércoles. Llega _____ .

2. —¿Van temprano?

   —¡Muy temprano! ¡De _____ !

3. —¡Es muy tarde! ¡Son las once y media de la noche!

   —¡Casi (*almost*) _____ !

4. —¿Qué fecha es hoy?

   —El 12 de noviembre.

   —¿Cuándo regresó Rafael?

   —El 10... ¡ _____ !

   —¿Y Ana María?

   —Ella regresó el _____ . El 20 de octubre, creo.

B. First, read the following list of advice about vehicular security. Then, indicate, in Spanish, the advice you would give the following people, according to what they do wrong.

EVITE EL ROBO DE SU AUTOMÓVIL, HACIENDO LO SIGUIENTE:

1. Cierre su carro con llave y lleve las llaves con Ud.
2. Cierre todas las ventanillas y el maletero del coche.
3. No deje cosas de valor en los asientos; póngalas en el maletero.
4. Si tiene que dejar su carro en un estacionamiento público por mucho tiempo, asegúrese de que esté atendido.
5. No ponga su nombre y domicilio en el llavero.
6. Por la noche, estacione siempre en un lugar bien iluminado.
7. Si es posible, utilice aparatos antirrobos.

---

1. Mario, who works nights, always parks his car in a dark alley.

   _____

   _____

2. Teresa often leaves the car keys in the ignition.

   _____

   _____

3. Daniel's name, address, and phone number appear on his key ring.

   _____

   _____

4. Mrs. Vega likes to leave her car windows open so the car won't be too hot when she comes back to it.

   _____

   _____

5. When Mrs. Torres goes shopping, you can always look inside her car and see store bags full of interesting things.

   _____

   _____

6. Mr. Cota thinks antitheft devices are too expensive and really unnecessary.

_____

_____

7. Antonio doesn't want to pay for parking, so he leaves his car in unattended parking places.

_____

_____

12

▭ Con un agente de la Sección de Tránsito

Con la conductora de un coche que se pasa un semáforo con la luz roja:

AGENTE REYES	—Buenas tardes, señora.
MUJER	—Buenas tardes, señor. ¿Por qué me detiene?
AGENTE REYES	—Porque tengo que imponerle una multa por pasarse un semáforo en rojo.
MUJER	—¡Pero yo empecé a cruzar la calle cuando el semáforo tenía la luz amarilla!
AGENTE REYES	—Pero antes de terminar de cruzarla ya estaba la luz roja.
MUJER	—Bueno, yo no tengo la culpa de eso. La luz cambió muy rápido.
AGENTE REYES	—Ud. sólo debe iniciar el cruce de la calle con luz amarilla si está tan cerca de la línea de parada que no tiene tiempo para parar.
MUJER	—Pero yo no sabía eso... Además, el carro de atrás venía a demasiada velocidad.
AGENTE REYES	—Lo siento, señora, pero tengo que imponerle una multa. Firme aquí, por favor.

En la autopista, con un conductor que cambia de carriles imprudentemente:

AGENTE REYES	—Señor, está cambiando de carriles imprudentemente. En cualquier momento va a causar un accidente.
CONDUCTOR	—Es que tengo mucha prisa. No quiero llegar tarde al trabajo.
AGENTE REYES	—Ésa no es una excusa válida. Ud. está poniendo en peligro su vida y la de los demás.
CONDUCTOR	—Sí, tiene razón. Es mejor llegar tarde que no llegar nunca.
AGENTE REYES	—Bien. Esta vez solamente le voy a dar una advertencia. Aquí la tiene. Buenos días y maneje con cuidado.
CONDUCTOR	—Muchísimas gracias, agente.

Con una señora que dejó a su bebé en un carro cerrado:

SEÑORA	—¿Qué sucede, agente?
AGENTE REYES	—Abra la puerta, por favor. ¿Es Ud. la madre de este bebé?
SEÑORA	—Sí, señor. Lo dejé solamente por un momento.
AGENTE REYES	—Eso es muy peligroso, señora. Alguien puede secuestrar al bebé.

▣ Vocabulario

NOMBRES

la autopista   highway
el bebé   baby
el carril, la vía   lane
el (la) conductor(a)   driver
el cruce   crossing, intersection
la línea de parada   stop line
el semáforo   traffic light

VERBOS

cambiar   to change
causar   to cause
cruzar   to cross
iniciar   to begin
parar   to stop
secuestrar   to kidnap

ADJETIVOS

demasiado(a)   excessive, too much
rojo(a)   red

OTRAS PALABRAS Y EXPRESIONES

atrás   behind
cerca (de)   close
con cuidado   carefully
imponer una multa   to impose a fine, to give a
ticket
imprudentemente   imprudently, recklessly
llegar tarde   to be late
¡Maneje con cuidado!   Drive safely!
mejor   better, best
pasarse la luz roja   to go through a red light
poner en peligro   to endanger
sólo, solamente   only
tan   so
tener la culpa (de), ser culpable (de)   to be at
fault, to be guilty
tener razón   to be right

Vocabulario adicional

SEÑALES DE TRÁNSITO (*Traffic signs*)

Narrow Bridge

Yield

Freeway Begins

Stop

One Way

R.R. Crossing (*ferrocarril*)

Dangerous Curve

Don't Litter

Detour

Danger

No Parking

Pedestrian Crossing

Two-Way Traffic

Slow Traffic Right Lane

Keep to the Right

Private Property
No Trespassing

MÁS SEÑALES DE TRÁNSITO

DESPACIO   Slow

ESCUELA, CRUCE DE NIÑOS   School Crossing

ESTACIONAMIENTO DE EMERGENCIA SOLAMENTE   Emergency Parking Only

MANTENGA SU DERECHA   Keep Right

NO ENTRE   Do Not Enter, Wrong Way

NO PASAR, NO REBASAR (Méx.)   Do Not Pass

PROHIBIDO EL CRUCE DE PEATONES, BICICLETAS Y MOTOCICLETAS   Pedestrians, Bicycles, Motor Driven Cycles Prohibited

PROHIBIDO PASAR   No Trespassing

TERMINA LA DOBLE VÍA   End Divided Road

Notas culturales

- In most Hispanic countries, gasoline and automobiles are much more expensive than they are in the United States. For this reason, motorcycles are very popular, especially among young people.
- The metric system is used in Hispanic countries. One kilometer is equivalent to 0.6 miles; one gallon is equivalent to 3.8 liters.

¿Recuerdan ustedes?

Answer the following questions, basing your answers on the dialogues.

1. ¿Por qué paró el agente Reyes a la mujer?

    _____

2. ¿Por qué le va a imponer una multa?

    _____

3. ¿Cuándo se puede iniciar el cruce de una calle con luz amarilla?

    _____

4. ¿Qué hacía el conductor que venía en el carro de atrás, según (according to) la mujer?

    _____

5. ¿Por qué estaba poniendo en peligro su vida y la de los demás el otro chofer?

    _____

6. ¿Por qué no está manejando con cuidado?

    _____

7. ¿Aceptó el agente esa excusa?

    _____

8. ¿El agente Reyes le impone una multa a este conductor?

_____

9. ¿Qué encontró el agente en un coche cerrado?

_____

10. ¿Por qué es peligroso dejar a un bebé solo en un coche?

_____

Para conversar

Interview a classmate, using the following questions. When you have finished, switch roles.

1. ¿Cuál es la velocidad máxima en la autopista?

_____

2. Si manejo en la autopista a noventa millas por hora, ¿me van a imponer una multa por exceso de velocidad?

_____

3. ¿Maneja Ud. con cuidado siempre? ¿Por qué o por qué no?

_____

4. ¿Tiene Ud. que manejar muy rápido a veces? ¿Cuándo?

_____

5. Generalmente, ¿cuántas multas impone Ud. en un día?

_____

Vamos a practicar

A. Fill in the blanks with the preterit or the imperfect forms of the verbs in parentheses.

1. El coche que yo _____ (ver) _____ (ir) a más de noventa millas por hora.

2. Yo no _____ (saber) que el carro _____ (ir) a esa velocidad.

3. La luz _____ (cambiar) cuando yo _____ (estar) cruzando la calle.

4. Él _____ (venir) a setenta millas por hora cuando el policía lo _____ (detener).

5. _____ (Ser) las tres de la tarde cuando ellas _____ (llegar).

B. **Give the Spanish equivalent of the following sentences.**

1. I wanted to arrive at two, but they refused to come early.

   _____

2. We didn't know her; we met her yesterday.

   _____

3. He didn't know the speed limit on this street. He found it out when the policeman told it to him.

   _____

C. **Complete the following conversational exchanges with the past progressive forms of the verbs in parentheses.**

1. —¿Qué _____ (hacer) él cuando tú llegaste?

   — _____ (Leer) el anuncio.

2. —¿Qué _____ (decir) Uds.?

   — _____ (Decir) que tenías que parar.

3. —¿Qué _____ (escribir) tú?

   — _____ (Escribir) el informe.

Conversaciones breves

Complete the following dialogue, using your imagination and the vocabulary from this lesson.

La agente Nieto, de la Policía de Patrulla, habla con el Sr. Soto.

AGENTE NIETO —Ud. iba manejando a ochenta millas por hora, señor.

SR. SOTO — _____

AGENTE NIETO —Déjeme ver su licencia de conducir, por favor.

SR. SOTO — _____

AGENTO NIETO —También se pasó Ud. una luz roja en la calle Magnolia y cambió de carriles imprudentement.

SR. SOTO — _____

AGENTO NIETO —Ésa no es una excusa válida.

SR. SOTO — _____

AGENTE NIETO —Lo siento, pero voy a tener que darle una multa por exceso de velocidad y por pasarse una luz roja.

En estas situaciones

What would you say in the following situations? What might the other person say?

1. You pull over a car that has just run a red light. The driver says he/she didn't know that there was a light there and didn't see it. Tell the driver that you have to give him/her a ticket. Advise him/her to drive carefully.

2. You stop someone who seems to be driving recklessly. He/She was going more than 90 miles per hour when you stopped him/her and was changing lanes too quickly. The driver explains he/she was going to see his/her mother in the hospital. Say that this time you're issuing a warning, but next time you're going to give him/her a ticket.

Casos

Act out the following scenarios with a partner.

1. Stop someone for running a red light.

2. Give someone a warning for reckless driving.

Un paso más

Review the *Vocabulario adicional* in this lesson and indicate in Spanish which signs the following people are not obeying.

1. A cyclist is trying to enter a highway.

2. A driver is speeding.

3. A driver is trying to park in a zone designated for emergency vehicles.

4. Someone is driving above the speed limit in a school zone.

5. A passenger in a car just threw a paper bag out the window.

6. Someone is going over a fence to get his frisbee.

7. A driver is passing another car illegally.

8. Cars must stop, but this person drives through.

9. A driver just turned the wrong way onto a one-way street.

   _____

10. A car is going 40 miles per hour in the left lane of a highway, holding up
    the cars behind.

   _____

13

🔊 Un accidente

Hubo un accidente en la carretera. Un camión chocó con un carro y una motocicleta. El hombre que manejaba el carro y sus dos pasajeros murieron. El agente Peña, que acaba de llegar, está tratando de ayudar al muchacho que venía en la motocicleta.

AGENTE PEÑA	—No trate de levantarse. Quédese quieto.
MUCHACHO	—¿Qué pasó? Me siento mareado...
AGENTE PEÑA	—Hubo un accidente. ¿Dónde le duele?
MUCHACHO	—La pierna derecha y la mano izquierda...
AGENTE PEÑA	—A ver... voy a ponerle una venda para parar la sangre.
MUCHACHO	—¿Qué le pasó a la chica que venía conmigo?
AGENTE PEÑA	—Se lastimó la cara y los brazos, pero no es serio... Por suerte los dos llevaban puestos sus cascos de seguridad.
MUCHACHO	—¿Y... mi motocicleta?
AGENTE PEÑA	—Está debajo del camión. Por suerte Uds. saltaron a tiempo.

El agente va hacia el camión y ve que hay un incendio en la cabina. Corre y apaga el incendio con un extinguidor de incendios. El hombre que manejaba el camión está a un lado del camino.

AGENTE PEÑA	—¿Cómo se siente?
HOMBRE	—Todavía estoy temblando. Hice todo lo posible para evitar el choque, pero no pude.
AGENTE PEÑA	—¿Qué recuerda del accidente?
HOMBRE	—El chofer del coche trató de rebasar sin darse cuenta de que una motocicleta venía en sentido contrario. Trató de desviarse, pero perdió el control del vehículo, y chocó con mi camión.
AGENTE PEÑA	—Mire, ya vino la ambulancia. Van a llevarlo al hospital a Ud. también.
HOMBRE	—Pero yo no estoy lastimado y no me gustan los hospitales...
AGENTE PEÑA	—Es una precaución. Probablemente le van a tomar radiografías y el médico lo va a examinar. Necesito su nombre y dirección.
HOMBRE	—Rafael Soto, calle La Sierra, 517.
AGENTE PEÑA	—¿Cuál es su número de teléfono?
HOMBRE	—328–9961.

🔲 Vocabulario

COGNADOS

la ambulancia ambulance	**la precaución** precaution
el control control	**serio(a)** serious
la motocicleta motorcycle	**el vehículo** vehicle

NOMBRES

la cabina   cab (of a truck)
el camino   road
el camión   truck
la cara   face
la carretera   highway
el (la) chico(a), el (la) chamaco(a) (*Méx.*)   young boy/girl
el choque   collision, crash
el extinguidor de incendios   fire extinguisher
el lado   side
el (la) pasajero(a)   passenger
la pierna   leg
la radiografía   X-ray
la venda   bandage

VERBOS

apagar   to put out (a fire)
chocar   to collide, to run into, to hit
desviarse   to swerve
doler (o:ue)   to hurt, to ache
evitar   to avoid
examinar, chequear   to examine
gustar   to be pleasing, to like
lastimarse   to get hurt
levantarse   to get up
morir (o:ue)   to die
rebasar (*Méx.*), **pasar**   to pass (a car)
saltar   to jump
sentirse (e:ie)   to feel
temblar (e:ie)   to shake, to tremble, to shiver

ADJETIVOS

derecho(a)   right
mareado(a)   dizzy
quieto(a)   still, quiet, calm

OTRAS PALABRAS Y EXPRESIONES

a tiempo   on time, just in time
acabar de + infinitivo   to have just (done something)
darse cuenta de   to realize, to become aware of
debajo de   under, underneath, below
en sentido contrario   in the opposite direction
hubo   there was, there were
por suerte   fortunately

Vocabulario adicional

LAS PARTES DEL CUERPO (*Parts of the body*)

1. el pelo, el cabello
2. la frente
3. la ceja
4. el ojo
5. la nariz
6. el labio
7. los dientes
8. la barbilla
9. la lengua
10. la boca
11. la mejilla
12. la oreja
13. el oído
14. las pestañas
15. la cabeza
16. la cara
17. el pecho
18. el estómago
19. la cadera
20. la muñeca
21. la mano
22. la rodilla
23. la pierna
24. el tobillo
25. el dedo del pie
26. el pie
27. el cuello
28. el hombro
29. la espalda
30. el brazo
31. el dedo
32. el codo
33. la cintura

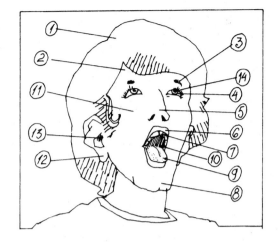

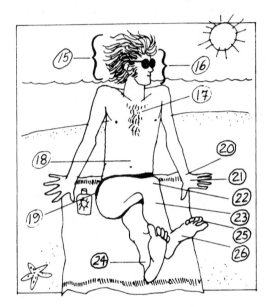

LOS DEDOS DE LA MANO

Los dedos de la mano

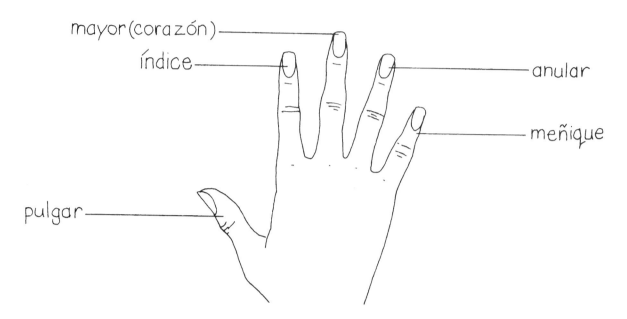

Nota cultural

As a result of the North American Free Trade Agreement (NAFTA), every day more Mexican trucks are traveling U.S. highways, particularly in California, Arizona, New Mexico, and Texas. This poses some challenges and perhaps risks, for although standardized visual traffic signs are used throughout the world, the U.S. highway system relies more extensively on written signs, which truckers who do not speak English cannot understand.

To avoid confusion among Mexican drivers accustomed to the metric system, highway signs near the Mexican border often post speed limits in both miles and kilometers.

¿Recuerdan ustedes?

Answer the following questions, basing your answers on the dialogue.

1. ¿Con qué chocó el camión?

   _____

2. ¿Quiénes murieron?

   _____

3. ¿Qué está haciendo el agente Peña?

   _____

4. ¿Cómo se siente el muchacho que venía en la motocicleta? ¿Qué le duele?

_____

5. ¿Qué le van a hacer al muchacho para parar la sangre?

_____

6. ¿Qué le pasó a la chica que venía con el muchacho?

_____

7. ¿Qué ve el agente cuando va hacia el camión? ¿Qué hace él?

_____

8. ¿Cómo se siente el hombre que manejaba el camión?

_____

9. ¿Cómo ocurrió (*happened*) el accidente?

_____

10. ¿Por qué no quiere ir el hombre al hospital?

_____

11. ¿Qué le van a hacer al hombre en el hospital?

_____

Para conversar

Interview a classmate, using the following questions. When you have finished, switch roles.

1. ¿Qué hace Ud. cuando le duele la cabeza?

_____

2. ¿Cómo se siente Ud.?

_____

3. ¿Le duele algo ahora?

_____

4. ¿Qué tipo de vehículo le gusta manejar?

_____

5. Cuando un(a) policía llega a un accidente en la autopista, ¿qué debe hacer primero?

_____

Vamos a practicar

A. Rewrite the following sentences using the new subjects. Make all necessary changes.

1. Ayer nosotros pedimos un extinguidor de incendios.

   Ayer ellas _____

2. Ella llegó en una ambulancia.

   Yo _____

3. Ellos no murieron en el accidente.

   Ella _____

4. Tú conseguiste (*managed*) controlar el vehículo.

   Él _____

5. Yo no elegí ese camión.

   Uds. _____

6. Él no se acordó del choque.

   Ud. _____

7. Yo me sentí bien.

   Ellos _____

8. Tú serviste de (*served as*) intérprete.

   Carlos _____

B. Indicate whether you like the following things and activities.

1. manejar en la carretera

   _____

2. levantarse tarde

   _____

3. las motocicletas

   _____

4. los carros japoneses

   _____

C. Indicate the aches and pains the following people have, using the cues provided and the verb *doler*.

1. a mí / el brazo derecho

   _____

2. a Ud. / la mano izquierda

   _____

3. al chofer / la cara

   _____

4. a nosotros / las piernas

   _____

5. a Uds. / nada

   _____

Conversaciones breves

Complete the following dialogue, using your imagination and the vocabulary from this lesson.

Hubo un accidente en la autopista.

AGENTE SMITH —Quédese quieto. No trate de levantarse.

HOMBRE —_____

AGENTE SMITH —Un camión chocó con su carro. ¿Dónde le duele?

HOMBRE —_____

AGENTE SMITH —Déjeme ponerle una venda para parar la sangre.

HOMBRE —_____

AGENTE SMITH —¿No recuerda el accidente?

HOMBRE —_____

AGENTE SMITH —Aquí viene la ambulancia para llevarlo al hospital.

HOMBRE —_____

En estas situaciones

What would you say in the following situations? What might the other person say?

1. You are talking to an accident victim. Tell him/her to stay still and ask him/her what hurts. Tell the victim his/her son is hurt, but that it's not serious. Say that the ambulance is coming and they are going to take both of them to the hospital.

2. While on traffic duty, you see a motorcyclist collide with a car. When you question the motorcyclist, the person seems not to feel well and asks what happened. Explain that the motorcycle collided with a car coming in the opposite direction. The motorcyclist was driving too fast to avoid the collision. Luckily he/she had a helmet on, but is injured nevertheless. Unfortunately, the person doesn't want to go to the hospital, and says he/she doesn't like hospitals, ambulances, or doctors.

Casos

Act out the following scenarios with a partner.

1. You are a police officer helping an accident victim who is badly hurt and very scared.

2. You are a police officer talking to someone who witnessed an accident on the highway.

Un paso más

A. **Review the *Vocabulario adicional* in this lesson and name the part of the body that corresponds to each number.**

1. _____
2. _____
3. _____
4. _____
5. _____
6. _____
7. _____
8. _____
9. _____
10. _____
11. _____
12. _____
13. _____
14. _____
15. _____
16. _____
17. _____
18. _____
19. _____
20. _____
21. _____
22. _____
23. _____
24. _____
25. _____
26. _____
27. _____
28. _____
29. _____
30. _____
31. _____
32. _____
33. _____

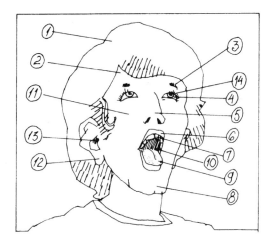

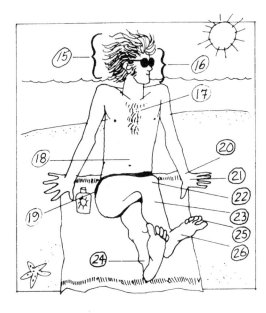

B. Review the *Vocabulario adicional* in this lesson once again, and name the part of the hand that corresponds to each number.

Los dedos de la mano

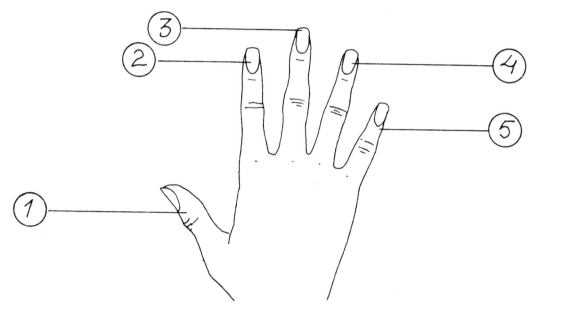

1. _____   4. _____

2. _____   5. _____

3. _____

14

📼 *Interrogatorios*

El sargento Vega acaba de detener a Carlos Guzmán. Le ha leído la advertencia Miranda y ahora empieza a interrogarlo.

SARGENTO VEGA	—¿Entiende Ud. los derechos que le he leído?
SR. GUZMÁN	—Sí, señor, pero yo no necesito un abogado porque soy inocente.
SARGENTO VEGA	—¿Sabe Ud. de qué se le acusa? ¿Entiende Ud. la acusación?
SR. GUZMÁN	—Sí, señor. Se me acusa de un robo que yo no cometí.
SARGENTO VEGA	—Bien, la computadora que Ud. trató de empeñar era robada.
SR. GUZMÁN	—Sí, eso me han dicho, pero yo no lo sabía.
SARGENTO VEGA	—¿Cómo llegó a sus manos esa computadora?
SR. GUZMÁN	—Se la compré a un hombre que me ofreció una ganga.
SARGENTO VEGA	—¿No sospechó Ud. que era robada? Comprar artículos robados es un delito mayor.
SR. GUZMÁN	—Yo no sabía que él la había robado. Me dijo que tenía que venderla urgentemente porque se había quedado sin trabajo.
SARGENTO VEGA	—¿Dónde estaba Ud. la noche del sábado, veinte de abril?
SR. GUZMÁN	—En un bar de la calle Franklin.
SARGENTO VEGA	—¿A qué hora salió de allí?
SR. GUZMÁN	—Después de las doce de la noche.
SARGENTO VEGA	—Sin embargo, yo he hablado con testigos que dicen que lo vieron a eso de las diez de la noche en el edificio donde ocurrió el robo.
SR. GUZMÁN	—No puede ser. El dueño del bar puede decirle que yo estoy allí todas las noches hasta muy tarde.
SARGENTO VEGA	—Sí, pero un empleado me dijo que esa noche Ud. había salido de allí antes de las diez.
SR. GUZMÁN	—Eso es mentira. Es alguien que me quiere perjudicar.

El sargento arresta al hombre.

El detective Rubio interroga al Sr. Darío, un hombre acusado de estafa.

DETECTIVE RUBIO	—Ud. le vendió un collar de perlas a la Sra. Carmen Hernández, ¿verdad?
SR. DARÍO	—Sí, señor. Hace una semana.
DETECTIVE RUBIO	—¿Ud. le dijo a la señora que las perlas eran de cultivo?
SR. DARÍO	—No, señor.
DETECTIVE RUBIO	—Pero Ud. le cobró las perlas como de primera calidad.

| SR. DARÍO | —Bueno, también yo le había dicho que el collar tenía un gran valor sentimental para mí. |
| DETECTIVE RUBIO | —Ud. no le dijo la verdad. Sinceramente, yo creo que Ud. la engañó, pero el jurado va a decidir si la estafó o no. |

Vocabulario

COGNADOS

la acusación   accusation, charge
el artículo   article, thing
el (la) detective   detective
inocente   innocent
sentimental   sentimental

NOMBRES

el collar   necklace
el delito mayor, el delito grave   felony
el (la) empleado(a)   employee, clerk
la estafa   swindle, fraud
la ganga   bargain
el jurado   jury
la perla   pearl
el (la) testigo   witness

VERBOS

cobrar   to charge, to collect
empeñar   to pawn
engañar   to cheat, to deceive
estafar   to swindle
ocurrir   to occur
ofrecer[1]   to offer
perjudicar   to cause damage, to hurt

ADJETIVO

gran   great

OTRAS PALABRAS Y EXPRESIONES

a eso de   about (used with time)
como de   as, like
de cultivo   cultured (pearl)
de primera calidad   first class, top quality
hace una semana   a week ago
para mí   for me
quedarse sin trabajo   to lose one's job
sin embargo   nevertheless, however
sinceramente   sincerely
urgentemente   urgently

---

[1]Irregular first-person present indicative: *yo ofrezco.*

Vocabulario adicional

EL JUICIO (*Trial*)

el (la) abogado(a) defensor(a) counsel for the
   defense
absuelto acquitted
el (la) acusado(a), el (la) reo defendant
la cárcel, la prisión jail, prison
el centro de reclusión de menores juvenile
   hall
el (la) cómplice accomplice
confesar (e:ie) to confess
la confesión confession
culpable guilty

declarar culpable to convict
dictar sentencia, setenciar to sentence
el fallo, el veredicto decision, verdict
el (la) fiscal prosecutor, district attorney
identificar to identify
el (la) perito expert
procesado(a) indicted
la prueba evidence
la sentencia, la condena sentence
el (la) taquígrafo(a) court reporter,
   stenographer

Nota cultural

The justice system in Hispanic countries is very different from that of the United
States. Juries do not exist and the guilt or innocence of the accused is decided by either
a judge or a tribunal. Punishments are determined in accordance with a code that
establishes minimum and maximum sentences for various categories of offense.

¿Recuerdan ustedes?

Answer the following questions, basing your answers on the dialogues.

1. ¿Qué acaba de hacer el sargento Vega?

   _____

2. ¿Por qué dice el Sr. Guzmán que no necesita un abogado?

   _____

3. ¿De qué se le acusa?

   _____

4. ¿Qué dice el sargento Vega de la computadora que el Sr. Guzmán trató de
    empeñar?

   _____

5. Según (*According to*) el Sr. Guzmán, ¿cómo consiguió la computadora?

   _____

6. Según el Sr. Guzmán, ¿dónde estaba la noche del robo? ¿Hasta qué hora
    estuvo allí?

   _____

7. ¿Qué han dicho los testigos?

   _____

8. ¿Qué hizo el Sr. Darío hace una semana?

   _____

9. ¿Por qué cree el detective Rubio que el Sr. Darío no le dijo la verdad a la Sra. Hernández?

   _____

10. ¿Qué va a tener que decidir el jurado?

    _____

Para conversar

Interview a classmate, using the following questions. When you have finished, switch roles.

1. ¿Recuerda Ud. dónde estaba la noche del cuatro de julio?

   _____

2. ¿Ha empeñado Ud. algo?

   _____

3. ¿Cuánto tiempo hace que Ud. compró su carro?

   _____

4. Alguien entró en mi casa y se llevó el televisor. ¿Fue Ud.?

   _____

5. ¿Cómo llegó a sus manos su televisor?

   _____

6. ¿Ha vendido Ud. alguna vez (*ever*) un artículo de gran valor?

   _____

Vamos a practicar

A. **Create sentences using the cues provided and the expression with *hace* meaning "ago."**

Modelo: una semana / esos muchachos / cometer otro robo

Hace una semana **que** esos muchachos **cometieron** otro robo.

1. tres meses / los ladrones / robarse mi coche

    _____

2. varios años / Ud. / no entrar en ese bar

    _____

3. dos días / la empleada / cobrarme demasiado dinero

    _____

4. un momento / yo / empeñar mi computadora

    _____

B. **Rewrite the following sentences, first in the present perfect, then in the past perfect.**

1. Me dice la verdad.

    _____

    _____

2. Lo interrogan.

    _____

    _____

3. Le decimos que no.

    _____

    _____

4. Esa mujer me ofrece una ganga.

    _____

    _____

5. ¿Uds. son testigos?

    _____

    _____

6. Yo no compro artículos robados.

_____

_____

7. Los testigos no pueden hablar con el detective.

_____

_____

8. Empeñan un collar de perlas y otras joyas.

_____

_____

Conversaciones breves

Complete the following dialogue, using your imagination and the vocabulary from this lesson.

El teniente Casas interroga a Juan Luna.

CASAS — _____

LUNA —No, yo no estuve en ese edificio anoche.

CASAS — _____

LUNA —¿Dos testigos dijeron eso? ¡No puede ser!

CASAS — _____

LUNA —¿La videocasetera? Me la dio un amigo...

CASAS — _____

LUNA —Bueno, yo no sabía que era robada.

CASAS —(*Le lee la advertencia Miranda.*) _____

LUNA —Sí, entiendo.

CASAS — _____

LUNA —No. No quiero hablar con un abogado...

CASAS — _____

En estas situaciones

What would you say in the following situations? What might the other person say?

1. You are interrogating a suspect. Ask where he/she was yesterday at 3 P.M. Say that three witnesses saw him/her at the school talking to some children. The suspect claims to have been talking on the phone with a friend. Find out the friend's name, address, and phone number.

2. You are talking to a witness. Ask if he/she is sure about the identification of the person he/she saw in the building the night of the robbery. The man he/she described was not there.

Casos

Act out the following scenarios with a partner.

1. You are an officer interrogating a robbery suspect.

2. You are an officer talking to a suspect about his/her legal rights.

Un paso más

Review the *Vocabulario adicional* in this lesson and complete the following sentences with an appropriate expression from the list.

1. Él fue _____ (*indicted*) por el gran jurado y ahora está esperando el juicio.

2. Si Ud. le dijo al _____ (*defendant*) dónde estaba el dinero, Ud. es

   _____ (*accomplice*) del delito.

3. El _____ (*prosecutor*) dice que el acusado es culpable y el _____
   (*counsel for the defense*) dice que es inocente.

4. Los _____ (*experts*) examinan las pruebas.

5. Ella confesó su delito, pero la _____ (*confession*) no fue aceptada porque no le habían dicho que su abogado podría (*could*) estar presente.

6. La testigo no pudo _____ (*identify*) al acusado.

7. Hoy vamos a saber el _____ (*verdict*) del jurado. Si es culpable, el juez la va a

   _____ (*sentence*) la semana que viene.

8. La _____ (*court reporter*) escribe todo lo que dicen los testigos.

9. La _____ (*sentence*) fue de dos años en un _____ (*juvenile hall*).

15

📼 Con la policía secreta

Isabel Cabrera, agente de la policía secreta, ha sido asignada a la Sección de Servicios Especiales. Se ha matriculado en una escuela secundaria del barrio hispano para infiltrarse en una pandilla que distribuye drogas en la escuela. Ahora, la agente Cabrera habla con María, una estudiante cuyo novio podría ser miembro de una pandilla.

AGENTE CABRERA	—Tú hablas español, ¿verdad?
MARÍA	—Sí, lo aprendí en casa. Soy latina.
AGENTE CABRERA	—Yo no hablo bien el inglés. ¿Podrías ayudarme con mis clases?
MARÍA	—Sí, aunque yo soy muy mala estudiante. ¿De dónde vienes, Isabel?
AGENTE CABRERA	—De Texas. Vinimos a Chicago hace una semana.
MARÍA	—¿Te gusta Chicago?
AGENTE CABRERA	—Sí, pero aquí no tengo amigos.
MARÍA	—Tú verás que pronto encuentras amigos aquí.
AGENTE CABRERA	—Espero que sí. ¿Qué se hace aquí para pasarlo bien?
MARÍA	—No sé, vamos al cine, tenemos fiestas... Ya sabes, hay de todo, si tienes dinero: bebida, yerba, piedra...
AGENTE CABRERA	—Aquí tengo cien dólares que me regaló mi tía.
MARÍA	—Si quieres, mi novio nos conseguirá una botella de tequila, y te presento a algunos de nuestros amigos.
AGENTE CABRERA	—Me gustaría conocerlos. ¿Cómo se llama tu novio?
MARÍA	—Roberto Álvarez.

Esa noche, la agente Rosales, vestida como una prostituta, tiene a su cargo detener hombres que solicitan sexo en una calle de la ciudad. Un hombre que maneja un carro azul se acerca a ella y la saluda.

HOMBRE	—Hola... ¿Quieres pasar un buen rato?
AGENTE ROSALES	—Tú lo pasarás mejor...
HOMBRE	—Eso espero. Sube.
AGENTE ROSALES	—¿Adónde me llevas?
HOMBRE	—Vamos a un motel. Quiero pasar toda la noche contigo.
AGENTE ROSALES	—Bueno, hace falta algo más que querer...
HOMBRE	—Aquí tienes cien dólares y si haces todo lo que yo quiero, te daré más.
AGENTE ROSALES	—No hace falta. Esto es suficiente. Está Ud. detenido. (*Le empieza a leer la advertencia Miranda.*)
HOMBRE	—Por favor, soy un hombre de negocios y esto me perjudicaría muchísimo. Mire, aquí tiene mil dólares.
AGENTE ROSALES	—Eso es un intento de soborno. Su situación se agrava, señor.

▣▣ Vocabulario

COGNADOS

el (la) latino(a), hispano(a)   Latino, Hispanic
el motel   motel
el (la) prostituto(a)   prostitute
el servicio   service
el sexo   sex
suficiente   sufficient, enough
la tequila   tequila

NOMBRES

la botella   bottle
el cine   movie theater, movies
la escuela secundaria   junior high school, high
   school
el hombre (la mujer) de negocios   businessman
   (woman)
el intento   attempt
el (la) novio(a)   boyfriend, girlfriend
la piedra (*coll.*), **el crac**[1]   rock (crack cocaine)
la policía secreta   undercover police
el soborno   bribe
la yerba (*coll.*)   marijuana

VERBOS

agravarse   to get worse, to worsen
aprender   to learn
costar (o:ue)   to cost
distribuir[2]   to distribute
encontrar (o:ue)   to find
hacer falta   to need
infiltrar(se)   to infiltrate
matricularse   to register, to enroll (in a school)
presentar   to introduce
regalar   to give (a gift)
responder   to respond
saludar   to greet
solicitar   to solicit

ADJETIVOS

asignado(a)   assigned
secreto(a)   secret

OTRAS PALABRAS Y EXPRESIONES

aunque   although
contigo   with you (informal)
cuyo(a)   whose
hay de todo   you can find everything
muchísimo   very much
pasarlo bien, pasar un buen rato   to have a
   good time
tener a su cargo   to be in charge of

---

[1]Colloquialisms: *la piedra, la roca, la coca cocinada.*
[2]Present tense: *distribuyo, distribuyes, distribuye, distribuimos, distribuyen.*

Vocabulario adicional

NOMBRES COMUNES DE ALGUNAS DROGAS

el ácido[1]   LSD
la cocaína, la coca[2]   cocaine
el hachich, el hachís[3]   hashish
la heroína[4]   heroin
el leño, la cucaracha, el porro   joint
la mariguana, la marijuana[5]   marijuana
la metadona   methadone
la morfina   morphine
el opio   opium

adicto(a)   addicted
las alucinaciones   hallucinations
el delirium tremens   DT's
la desintoxicación   detoxification
endrogarse   to take drugs, to become addicted to drugs
la jeringuilla, la jeringa hipodérmica   hypodermic syringe
pullar (*Caribe*)   to shoot up
la sobredosis   overdose

Nota cultural

According to the United States Census Bureau, out of a total U.S. population of roughly 259.7 million, approximately 26.6 million are Hispanic. The largest groups are Mexican Americans (62.6%), Puerto Ricans (11.6%), Cubans (5.3%), and Central and South Americans (12.7%). The states with the highest Hispanic populations are California, Texas, New York, Florida, Illinois, Arizona, New Jersey, New Mexico, and Colorado. More than half of all U.S. Hispanics live in California and Texas alone. More than 90% of U.S. Hispanics live in urban areas (often concentrated in Hispanic neighborhoods called *barrios*), compared to 73% of non-Hispanics.

---

[1]Colloquialisms: *el pegao, el sello, la pastilla.*
[2]Colloquialisms: *el perico, el polvo.*
[3]Colloquialisms: *el chocolate, el kif, la grifa.*
[4]Colloquialisms: *el caballo, la manteca (Caribe).*
[5]Colloquialisms: *la yerba, el pito, el pasto, la mota, el zacate.*

¿Recuerdan ustedes?

Answer the following questions, basing your answers on the dialogues.

1. ¿Qué hará la agente Cabrera en la escuela secundaria?

   _____

2. ¿Por qué habla la agente Cabrera con María?

   _____

3. ¿Cuándo dice la agente Cabrera que vino a Chicago?

   _____

4. ¿Qué dice la agente Cabrera de Chicago?

   _____

5. ¿Qué hacen María y sus amigos para pasarlo bien?

   _____

6. ¿Cuánto dinero tiene la agente Cabrera?

   _____

7. ¿Qué dice María que puede hacer su novio?

   _____

8. Describa el trabajo que se le ha asignado a la agente Rosales esta noche.

   _____

9. ¿Por qué detiene su carro un hombre?

   _____

10. ¿Qué le ofrece el hombre a la agente Rosales? ¿Le ofrece algo más?

    _____

11. Cuando la agente Rosales empieza a leerle la advertencia Miranda, ¿cómo responde el hombre?

    _____

12. ¿Por qué le dice la agente Rosales al hombre que su situación se ha agravado?

    _____

Para conversar

Interview a classmate, using the following questions. When you have finished, switch roles.

1. ¿Hay pandillas en la ciudad donde Ud. vive? ¿Son un problema para la policía?

   _____

2. ¿Sabe Ud. si se venden drogas en algunas de las escuelas secundarias de su ciudad?

   _____

3. ¿Cómo podría conseguir drogas o bebidas en su ciudad un(a) estudiante?

   _____

4. ¿Ha trabajado Ud. en la Sección de Servicios Especiales? Describa lo que hizo.

   _____

5. ¿Qué lengua (*language*) habla su familia en casa?

   _____

Vamos a practicar

A. Rewrite the following sentences, replacing the underlined verb phrases with the future tense.

1. Nosotros <u>vamos a tratar</u> de infiltrarnos en la pandilla.

   _____

2. Mi compañera me <u>va a ayudar</u> con el español.

   _____

3. Ellos <u>van a ir</u> a Chicago.

   _____

4. La botella de tequila te <u>va a costar</u> doce dólares.

   _____

5. Yo te la <u>voy a conseguir</u>.

   _____

6. Ella no <u>va a venir</u> a la fiesta.

   _____

7. Nosotros no <u>vamos a poder</u> matricularnos este año.

   _____

B. Answer the following questions, using the cues provided in parentheses.

Modelo: ¿Qué dijo María? (su novio poder conseguirle una botella)

María dijo que su novio **podría** conseguirle una botella.

1. ¿Qué dijo la Sra. Santos? (su hija no poder matricularse mañana)

_____

2. ¿Qué dijo la estudiante? (su amigo salir pronto)

_____

3. ¿Qué creías tú? (mi tía estar en mi casa en dos horas)

_____

4. ¿Qué dijo el hombre de negocios? (eso perjudicarle)

_____

5. ¿Qué pensaba el hombre? (ellos pasar un buen rato)

_____

6. ¿Qué dijo el sargento? (la agente tener que infiltrarse en la pandilla)

_____

7. ¿Qué pensaba la agente? (el acusado no decir la verdad)

_____

Conversaciones breves

Complete the following dialogue, using your imagination and the vocabulary from this lesson.

El agente Gómez, de la Sección de Servicios Especiales, se ha infiltrado en una pandilla que vende drogas en una escuela. Habla con un miembro de la pandilla.

TOMÁS —Me dice Juana que tú querías hablar conmigo...

AGENTE GÓMEZ — _____

TOMÁS —Pues, sí. Puedo venderte eso por cincuenta dólares.

AGENTE GÓMEZ — _____

TOMÁS —¡Hombre, verás que la roca que te voy a conseguir es de primera calidad!

AGENTE GÓMEZ — _____

TOMÁS —Ven a mi casa a las tres.

AGENTE GÓMEZ — _____

TOMÁS —A una cuadra de aquí. Calle Nogales, número 28.

AGENTE GÓMEZ — _____

TOMÁS —Sí, como no. Les diré que vas a traer una botella de tequila para compartirla con nosotros. Nos vemos, ¿eh?

AGENTE GÓMEZ — _____

En estas situaciones

What might you say in the following situations? What might the other person say?

1. You are an undercover agent who has been assigned to infiltrate a gang that has been selling drugs and guns to high school students in the neighborhood. Pretend you just moved to the area and want to get a gun as well as some drugs. Introduce yourself to a gang member at school and ask if he/she could help you get what you want. Mention that money is not a problem, but you're in a hurry to get what you need. Try to arrange to see a dealer later in the day.

2. You are posing as a prostitute in order to arrest people soliciting sex at night in the city. A person approaches you with interest. Ask where he/she wants to take you and discuss price. After you agree on price, identify yourself and announce that the person is under arrest. Say that you will read him/her the Miranda Warning.

Casos

Act out the following scenarios with a partner.

1. You are an undercover agent making a drug deal at the high school with a gang member.

2. You arrest a person who tried to solicit sex from a prostitute and who tries to bribe you.

Un paso más

Review the *Vocabulario adicional* in this lesson and place a 1, 2, 3, 4, or 5 next to each of the following terms according to the definition.

1. marijuana 2. hashish 3. cocaína 4. ácido 5. heroína

_____ chocolate	_____ sello	_____ piedra
_____ zacate	_____ polvo	_____ roca
_____ coca	_____ grifa	_____ yerba
_____ pegao	_____ kif	_____ pito
_____ mota	_____ pastilla	

A "joint" is a _____ , _____ , or _____ .

Repaso

Práctica de vocabulario

A. Circle the word or phrase that does not belong in each group.

1. chapa, placa, plata

2. robar, encontrar, llevarse

3. todo lo posible, de nada, no hay de qué

4. carril, vía, valor

5. pasarse la luz roja, poner en peligro, manejar con cuidado

6. sólo, solo, solamente

7. mejor, atrás, cerca

8. carretera, autopista, venda

9. pierna, cara, choque

10. apagar, chequear, examinar

11. collar, testigo, perla

12. estafar, ofrecer, perjudicar

13. tía, tequila, botella

14. agravarse, necesitar, hacer falta

15. dar, responder, regalar

B. Circle the word or phrase that best completes each sentence.

1. Ud. (inició, cruzó, evitó) la calle cuando la luz estaba roja.

2. Hay muchos (camiones, caminos, cubiertos) en la carretera.

3. El coche estaba (atrasado, pagado, estacionado) frente a mi casa.

4. Me robaron (la verdad, la grabadora, el plazo).

5. No tengo dinero porque (me ofrecieron trabajo, cobré ayer, me quedé sin trabajo).

6. ¿Es Ud. la madre de este (semáforo, bebé, cruce)?

7. Ella no tiene la culpa; es (inocente, asignada, quieta).

8. Lo vende barato. Es (una ganga, una pandilla, un soborno).

9. Se (matriculó, infiltró, lastimó) la pierna.

10. Yo vi el accidente. Todavía estoy (chocando, aprendiendo, temblando).

11. Necesito el extinguidor de (lados, incendios, pasajeros).

12. Estaba en la (estafa, piedra, cabina) del camión.

13. No estoy al día. (Debo, Entrego, Recobro) como dos meses.

14. Es un Chevrolet, azul (rojo, claro, derecho).

15. Es un hombre de (negocios, intento, novios).

C. Match the questions in column A with the appropriate word or phrase in column B.

A	*B*
1. _____ ¿Cómo se siente?	a. Sí, contra todo riesgo.
2. _____ ¿Dónde está la motocicleta?	b. Sí, señor. Pero soy inocente.
3. _____ ¿Qué harán para pasarlo bien?	c. No, por suerte solamente dos días.
4. _____ ¿Adónde me llevarás?	d. Sí, una pistola.
5. _____ ¿Está asegurado tu carro?	e. No, sólo me dio una advertencia.
6. _____ ¿Cuándo le robaron el coche?	f. Debajo del camión.
7. _____ ¿Se llevaron algún arma?	g. A un motel.
8. _____ ¿Son propiedad de Uds.?	h. No, son de cultivo.
9. _____ ¿Sabe Ud. de qué se la acusa?	i. Anoche.
10. _____ ¿Las perlas son de primera calidad?	j. Bien.
11. _____ ¿Hace una semana que lo vio?	k. No, no son nuestros.
12. _____ ¿Te impuso una multa?	l. Iremos a fiestas.

D. Crucigrama

HORIZONTAL

1. mucho, mucho
4. *VCR*, en español
7. ¡Maneje con _____ !
9. chico, en México
13. persona que maneja (*m.*)
14. pasar
15. No es una carretera; es una _____ .
17. *clerk*, en español
18. daría

VERTICAL

2. opuesto de *primero*
3. que tiene valor
5. *X-ray*, en español
6. camión, carro, etc.
8. sin prudencia
10. *jury*, en español
11. Tienes que parar en la línea de _____ .
12. acción de describir
13. vía
16. acción de acusar

📼 Práctica oral

**Listen to the following exercise on the audio program. The speaker will
ask you some questions. Answer each question, using the cue provided.
The speaker will verify your response. Repeat the correct answer.**

1. ¿Cómo se siente Ud. hoy? (bien)

2. ¿Qué hace Ud. para pasarlo bien? (ir al cine)

3. ¿Dónde está estacionado su coche? (frente a la comisaría)

4. ¿Cerró Ud. su coche con llave? (sí)

5. ¿Contra qué está asegurado su coche? (contra todo riesgo)

6. ¿Está Ud. atrasada en los pagos de su coche o está al día? (estoy al día)

7. ¿Llega Ud. tarde al trabajo a veces? (sí)

8. ¿Se pasó Ud. un semáforo con la luz roja alguna vez? (no, nunca)

9. Si alguien cambia de carriles imprudentemente, ¿qué puede causar? (un
   accidente)

10. ¿Cuándo hubo un accidente? (anoche)

11. ¿Dónde ocurrió el accidente? (en la carretera)

12. ¿Cuántas personas murieron en el accidente? (nadie)

13. ¿Se lastimó alguien? (sí, una señora)

14. ¿Qué usa Ud. si hay un incendio? (un extinguidor de incendios)

15. ¿Prefiere Ud. manejar un coche o una motocicleta? (una motocicleta)

16. Cuando Ud. maneja una motocicleta, ¿qué lleva puesto siempre? (el casco
    de seguridad)

17. ¿Perdió Ud. el control de su vehículo alguna vez? (no, nunca)

18. ¿Ud. impone multas frecuentemente o prefiere dar advertencias?
    (dar advertencias)

19. ¿Qué le pasó a la chica que cruzaba la calle? (nada)

20. ¿Qué estaban haciendo muchas pandillas en las escuelas secundarias?
    (distribuir drogas)

21. ¿Hay a veces robos en su vecindario? (sí, frecuentemente)

22. ¿Ha recobrado Ud. algún objeto robado? (sí, muchos)

23. ¿Ha leído Ud. la advertencia Miranda en español alguna vez? (no, nunca)

24. ¿Se ha quedado Ud. sin trabajo alguna vez? (sí, dos veces)

25. ¿Ha empeñado Ud. algo alguna vez? (no, nunca)

16

🔲 *En una celda de detención preventiva*

El Sr. Bravo acaba de llegar, esposado, a la estación de policía. Después de registrarlo, un policía toma las precauciones necesarias antes de encerrarlo en una celda de detención.

POLICÍA	—Quiero que se vacíe los bolsillos por completo y que ponga todas sus cosas en el mostrador.
SR. BRAVO	—Solamente tengo la cartera con el dinero, un pañuelo y un peine.
POLICÍA	—(*Cuenta el dinero a la vista del detenido.*) Ud. tiene aquí setenta y un dólares y treinta y cuatro centavos. ¿Está de acuerdo?
SR. BRAVO	—Sí, señor. Es eso.
POLICÍA	—Ahora quítese el reloj y la cadena que lleva al cuello.
SR. BRAVO	—Por favor, anote ahí que el reloj y la cadena son de oro.
POLICÍA	—Sí. Todas sus pertenencias serán puestas en un sobre sellado.
SR. BRAVO	—¿Pueden entregárselas a mi esposa?
POLICÍA	—Sí, si Ud. lo autoriza por escrito. Ahora lo vamos a retratar y a tomarle las huellas digitales.
SR. BRAVO	—Yo quiero llamar por teléfono a mi señora.
POLICÍA	—Está bien. Ud. tiene derecho a hacer una llamada telefónica. Después de ficharlo le daremos la oportunidad de hacerla.
SR. BRAVO	—Está bien.
POLICÍA	—Párese allí y mire a la cámara. Bien. Ahora mire hacia la derecha. Bien, ahora hacia la izquierda. No se mueva.
SR. BRAVO	—¿Eso es todo?
POLICÍA	—Sí. Ahora el técnico le va a tomar las huellas digitales.
TÉCNICO	—Déme su mano derecha.
POLICÍA	—(*Después de que el técnico terminó de tomarle las huellas digitales*) Ahora quítese el cinto y quíteles los cordones a los zapatos, y me lo entrega todo.
SR. BRAVO	—Para eso necesito que me quite las esposas.
POLICÍA	—Primero voy a encerrarlo en su celda.

Con el oficial investigador:

SR. BRAVO	—¿Qué van a hacer conmigo ahora?
INVESTIGADOR	—Después de terminar todas las investigaciones preliminares, el fiscal lo pondrá a disposición de un juez.
SR. BRAVO	—¿Me dejarán salir en libertad bajo palabra?
INVESTIGADOR	—Es posible. Ud. no está acusado de homicidio.
SR. BRAVO	—Pero me pondrán en libertad bajo fianza, ¿verdad?
INVESTIGADOR	—Eso lo decidirá el juez, y depende, en buena parte, de si tiene o no antecedentes penales.

SR. BRAVO	—Si me ponen una fianza muy alta, yo no voy a tener dinero para pagarla. Entonces me llevarán a la cárcel.
INVESTIGADOR	—Su familia podría comprar un bono pagando una prima.
SR. BRAVO	—¿Puede Ud. recomendarme algún fiancista?
INVESTIGADOR	—Lo siento, pero no nos está permitido hacer eso.

Vocabulario

COGNADOS

la detención   detention
la investigación   investigation
investigador(a)   investigating officer
la oportunidad   opportunity
preliminar   preliminary

NOMBRES

los antecedentes penales   criminal record
el bono   bond
la cadena   chain
la cartera, la billetera   wallet
la celda   cell
el centavo   cent
el cordón (del zapato)   shoelace
el cuello   neck
la derecha   right-hand side
el (la) detenido(a)   person under arrest
las esposas   handcuffs
el (la) fiancista   bailor, bail bondsman
la fianza   bail
el (la) fiscal   prosecutor, district attorney
el homicidio   manslaughter, homicide
el mostrador   counter
el oro   gold
el pañuelo   handkerchief
el peine   comb
las pertenencias   belongings
la prima   premium
el reloj   watch
el sobre   envelope

VERBOS

autorizar   to authorize, to allow
depender   to depend
dudar   to doubt
encerrar (e:ie)   to lock up
mirar   to look at
moverse (o:ue)   to move
pararse   to stand
quitarse   to take off (clothing)
recomendar (e:ie)   to recommend
registrar, fichar   to book, to log in
retratar   to photograph
vaciar   to empty

ADJETIVOS

esposado(a)   handcuffed
permitido(a)   permitted
preventivo(a)   preventive
sellado(a)   sealed

OTRAS PALABRAS Y EXPRESIONES

a la vista de   in the presence of, in front of
ahí   there
en buena parte   to a large extent
en libertad bajo fianza   out on bail
en libertad bajo palabra   out on one's own recognizance
estar de acuerdo   to agree
por completo   completely
por escrito   in writing
tomar las huellas digitales   to fingerprint

Vocabulario adicional

PARA ARRESTAR Y FICHAR

¡Abra las piernas y los brazos!   Spread eagle!
el alias   alias
avisar   to notify
la bala   bullet
el calibre   caliber
la coartada   alibi
¿Cómo se escribe?   How do you spell it?
¡Dése preso(a)!   You're under arrest!
¡Manos arriba!   Hands up!
el motivo   motive
¡Párese! ¡Póngase de pie!   Stand up!
la pista   clue
Ponga las manos en la pared.   Put your hands against the wall.
por poseer drogas   for possession of drugs
la resistencia a la autoridad   resisting arrest
Súbase al carro.   Get in the car.

Nota cultural

In most Hispanic countries, the police by law must either free a person or bring him or her before a judge within 72 hours of the arrest. This law is often not put into practice, especially in the case of political prisoners.

¿Recuerdan ustedes?

Answer the following questions, basing your answers on the dialogue.

1. ¿Dónde está el Sr. Bravo?

   _____

2. ¿Qué quiere el policía que haga el Sr. Bravo con sus pertenencias?

   _____

3. ¿Qué tiene el Sr. Bravo en los bolsillos?

   _____

4. Si el Sr. Bravo desea que el policía le entregue sus cosas a su esposa, ¿qué debe hacer?

_____

5. ¿Por qué no puede llamar el Sr. Bravo a su esposa en este momento?

_____

6. ¿Qué hace el técnico?

_____

7. ¿Dónde encerrará el policía al Sr. Bravo?

_____

8. ¿De qué no está acusado el Sr. Bravo?

_____

9. ¿Qué decidirá el juez?

_____

10. ¿Es un hombre muy rico (*rich*) el acusado? ¿Cómo lo sabe Ud.?

_____

Para conversar

Interview a classmate, using the following questions. When you have finished, switch roles.

1. ¿Qué es lo primero que Ud. hace cuando ficha a una persona detenida?

_____

2. Cuando Ud. arresta a alguien, ¿le toma las huellas digitales?

_____

3. Si un(a) detenido(a) le pide a Ud. que le dé sus pertenencias a un miembro de su familia, ¿qué responde Ud.?

_____

4. Si una persona detenida le pide a Ud. que le recomiende un buen abogado, ¿qué hace Ud.?

_____

5. ¿Dónde conseguiría Ud. el dinero para una fianza?

_____

Vamos a practicar

A. Complete the following verb chart in the subjunctive mood.

INFINITIVO	YO	TÚ	UD., ÉL, ELLA	NOSOTROS(AS)	UDS., ELLOS(AS)
trabajar					
	diga				
		conduzcas			
			venga		
				vayamos	
					entiendan
morir					
	dé				
		estés			
			conozca		
				sepamos	
					sean
mover					
	ponga				
		salgas			
			haga		
				veamos	
					encierren

B. Rewrite the following sentences, beginning each one with the cue given.

Modelo: Él pone sus cosas en el mostrador.

Quiero que él **ponga** sus cosas en el mostrador.

1. Ella paga la prima del bono.

    Queremos que _____

2. Me muestra el sobre con sus pertenencias.

    Necesito que _____

3. Ud. habla con un abogado.

    Le recomiendo que _____

4. Yo deseo entregarle el reloj y la cadena a mi esposa.

    Yo deseo que Ud. _____

5. Le quitan las esposas.

Necesita que _____

6. Ellos van al juzgado.

Yo les pido que _____

7. Me hablas del homicidio.

No quiero que _____

8. Ud. me dice la hora y el lugar del accidente.

Yo le pido que _____

9. Ellos los ponen en libertad bajo fianza.

Deseamos que _____

10. Uds. me dan la información.

Necesito que _____

Conversaciones breves

Complete the following dialogue, using your imagination and the vocabulary from this lesson.

El Sr. Paz está en la cárcel.

SR. PAZ —¿Dónde estoy? ¿Por qué me trajeron a la cárcel?

AGENTE MUÑOZ —_____

SR. PAZ —¿Cuánto tiempo tendré que quedarme aquí?

AGENTE MUÑOZ —_____

SR. PAZ —¿De mis antecedentes... ? ¿Y qué me van a hacer ahora... ?

AGENTE MUÑOZ —_____

_____

SR. PAZ —Esto es todo lo que tengo en los bolsillos... y aquí están mi reloj, mi cinto y los cordones de mis zapatos.

AGENTE MUÑOZ —_____

SR. PAZ —Huellas digitales... fotografía... ¡pero yo no soy un criminal... !

AGENTE MUÑOZ —_____

SR. PAZ —¿Y qué pasa si no consigo el dinero para la fianza?

AGENTE MUÑOZ —_____

En estas situaciones

What would you say in the following situations? What might the other person say?

1. You have just arrested someone. Describe the booking procedure. Explain what to do with personal items.

2. Having booked someone who was arrested, answer his/her questions about the preliminary investigation, the judge, bail, and about being released.

Casos

Act out the following scenarios with a partner.

1. Book someone who has just been charged with homicide.

2. Tell someone who has just been arrested that you need to fingerprint him/her.

Un paso más

Review the *Vocabulario adicional* in this lesson and then translate the following sentences into Spanish.

1. Put your hands against the wall.

   _____

2. Stand up!

   _____

3. Spread eagle!

   _____

4. Hands up! You're under arrest!

   _____

5. How do you spell your last name?

   _____

6. Do you have an alias?

   _____

7. You are under arrest for possession of drugs.

   _____

17

🔊 *Una muchacha se escapa de su casa*

El agente Gómez habla con los Sres. Ruiz, padres de una adolescente que se escapó de su casa.

AGENTE GÓMEZ	—¿Cuándo fue la última vez que vieron a su hija?
SR. RUIZ	—Anoche. Nos dijo que iba a estudiar con una compañera.
AGENTE GÓMEZ	—¿Cuándo se dieron cuenta de que se había escapado?
SRA. RUIZ	—Ya eran las once de la noche y no había regresado. Entonces llamamos a casa de su amiga y supimos que no había estado allí.
AGENTE GÓMEZ	—Su hija puede haber sido víctima de un secuestro. ¿Por qué piensan que se escapó de la casa?
SR. RUIZ	—Su amiga nos dijo que ella estaba pensando en escaparse.
AGENTE GÓMEZ	—¿Qué edad tiene ella?
SR. RUIZ	—Dieciséis años.
AGENTE GÓMEZ	—Es necesario que me den una descripción completa de su hija.
SR. RUIZ	—Se llama María Elena Ruiz Portillo. Es baja —mide cinco pies y dos pulgadas— delgada, de pelo negro y ojos negros. Tiene un lunar cerca de la boca y una cicatriz en la mejilla derecha.
AGENTE GÓMEZ	—¿Qué ropa tenía puesta?
SRA. RUIZ	—Tenía puesta una falda blanca, una blusa roja y un suéter negro... sandalias blancas, y tenía una bolsa blanca.
AGENTE GÓMEZ	—¿Llevaba algunas joyas?
SRA. RUIZ	—Sí, una cadena de oro con una cruz, un anillo de plata y unos aretes rojos.
AGENTE GÓMEZ	—Espero que tengan una fotografía reciente de ella.
SR. RUIZ	—Sí, aquí tengo una en la billetera.
AGENTE GÓMEZ	—Esto debe ser muy difícil para Uds., pero ¿tienen idea de por qué se escapó? ¿Ha tenido algún problema con Uds. o en la escuela?
SR. RUIZ	—Bueno... ella estaba saliendo con un muchacho... y nosotros le dijimos que no nos gustaba... Estuvo preso dos veces.
AGENTE GÓMEZ	—¿Creen que su hija se fue con él?
SRA. RUIZ	—Yo creo que sí.
AGENTE GÓMEZ	—¿Qué edad tiene él?
SRA. RUIZ	—No sé exactamente. Es dos o tres años mayor que ella.
AGENTE GÓMEZ	—¿Saben cómo se llama y dónde vive?
SRA. RUIZ	—Él se llama José Ramírez. No sé dónde vive, pero los dos asisten a la misma escuela secundaria.
AGENTE GÓMEZ	—¿Su hija se había escapado de su casa en alguna otra ocasión?
SRA. RUIZ	—No, nunca. Yo creo que él se la llevó contra su voluntad...

AGENTE GÓMEZ	—¿Saben si tenía dinero?
SRA. RUIZ	—Sí, tenía unos setenta y cinco dólares, por lo menos.
AGENTE GÓMEZ	—¿Tienen alguna idea de dónde puede estar? Es importante que traten de recordar cualquier detalle.
SR. RUIZ	—No, ninguna.
AGENTE GÓMEZ	—¿Tenía carro?
SRA. RUIZ	—No. Nosotros no queremos que maneje. Es muy joven...
AGENTE GÓMEZ	—¿Tiene algún documento de identificación?
SRA. RUIZ	—Creo que lleva la tarjeta de la escuela en la cartera...
AGENTE GÓMEZ	—Bueno. Es necesario que me avisen enseguida si recuerdan algo más o si reciben alguna información.
SRA. RUIZ	—Ojalá que puedan encontrarla pronto.
AGENTE GÓMEZ	—Vamos a hacer todo lo posible, señora.

Vocabulario

COGNADOS

el (la) adolescente adolescent, teenager	**reciente** recent
el documento document	**la sandalia** sandal
importante important	**el suéter** sweater
la ocasión occasion	**la víctima** victim

NOMBRES

el anillo, la sortija ring
el arete earring
la blusa blouse
la boca mouth
la cartera, la bolsa, el bolso purse
la cicatriz scar
el (la) compañero(a) (de clase) classmate
la cruz cross
el detalle detail
la edad age
la falda skirt
el (la) jovencito(a) youth, teenager
el lunar mole
la mejilla, el cachete cheek
el pelo hair
el secuestro kidnapping
la voluntad will

VERBOS

asistir (a) to attend
escaparse, fugarse to run away
estudiar to study
medir (e:i) to measure, to be (*amount*) tall
pensar (e:ie) to think
salir con to go out (with), to date
tener puesto(a), llevar puesto(a) to have on, to wear

ADJETIVOS

bajo(a), bajito(a) (*Cuba*) short
mayor older

OTRAS PALABRAS Y EXPRESIONES

de pelo (negro) with (black) hair
dos veces twice
exactamente exactly
generalmente usually
ojalá I hope
por lo menos at least
los señores (Ruiz) Mr. and Mrs. (Ruiz)

Vocabulario adicional

PARA INVESTIGAR A LAS PERSONAS
DESAPARECIDAS (*To investigate missing persons*)

abandonar los estudios   to drop out of school
el alojamiento, el hospedaje   lodging
el (la) conocido(a)   acquaintance
el (la) delincuente juvenil   juvenile delinquent
desaparecer   to disappear
la estación de ómnibus, la estación de autobuses
  bus station
el (la) maestro(a)   teacher
matar   to kill
mayor de edad   of age, adult
menor de edad   minor
la morgue   morgue
el paradero   whereabouts
pornográfico(a)   pornographic
la prostitución   prostitution
refugiarse   to find refuge, shelter
rescatar   to rescue
el rescate   ransom
el tribunal de menores   juvenile court

Nota cultural

Hispanics in the United States tend to marry within their own groups of origin.
Intermarriage between Hispanics and Anglos is increasing, however, especially among
second-generation Mexican Americans.

¿Recuerdan ustedes?

Answer the following questions, basing your answers on the dialogue.

1. ¿Por qué habla el agente Gómez con los Sres. Ruiz?

   _____

2. ¿Cuándo fue la última vez que el Sr. Ruiz vio a su hija?

   _____

3. ¿Qué les dijo la muchacha a sus padres?

   _____

4. ¿Qué es necesario que hagan los padres de la muchacha?

   _____

5. ¿Cómo se llama la muchacha y cómo es?

_____

6. ¿Qué ropa tenía puesta?

_____

7. ¿Tiene María Elena algunas marcas visibles?

_____

8. ¿Qué espera el agente Gómez?

_____

9. ¿Cuál es el problema que María Elena ha tenido con sus padres?

_____

10. ¿Qué cree la mamá de María Elena? ¿Por qué piensa Ud. que ella cree eso?

_____

11. ¿Por qué no tiene carro María Elena?

_____

12. ¿Qué joyas llevaba María Elena?

_____

Para conversar

Interview a classmate, using the following questions. When you have finished, switch roles.

1. ¿A qué escuela secundaria asistió Ud.?

_____

2. Cuando era estudiante de la escuela secundaria, ¿pensaba en hacerse (*becoming*) policía?

_____

3. Cuando Ud. era adolescente, ¿se escapó alguna vez de su casa?

_____

4. ¿Tiene Ud. una fotografía reciente de su familia?

_____

5. ¿Es importante que una persona siempre traiga consigo (*with him/her*) un documento de identificación?

_____

6. ¿Tiene Ud. algún documento de identificación ahora? ¿Puede mostrármelo?

_____

7. ¿Cuánto dinero tenía Ud. cuando salió de su casa hoy?

_____

Vamos a practicar

A. **Rewrite the following sentences, beginning each one with the cue given.**

Modelo: Ella tiene documentos.

Espero que ella **tenga** documentos.

1. Compran las faldas negras.

Ojalá que _____

2. Ellos nos traen las fotografías.

Nos alegramos de que (*We are glad*) _____

3. No están interrogando al acusado.

Esperamos que _____

4. Ella va a escaparse.

Temo (*I'm afraid*) que _____

B. **Rewrite the following sentences, beginning each one with the cue given. Make the necessary changes.**

1. Ud. nos avisa enseguida.

Es necesario que _____

2. Ella se escapa con su novio.

Es posible que _____

3. Asisten a esa escuela.

Es importante que _____

4. Tú no sales con ese muchacho.

Es mejor que _____

Conversaciones breves

Complete the following dialogue, using your imagination and the vocabulary from this lesson.

El agente Silva y el Sr. Ochoa hablan del hijo del Sr. Ochoa.

AGENTE SILVA —_____

SR. OCHOA —Me di cuenta de que él se había escapado porque no durmió (*didn't sleep*) en casa...

AGENTE SILVA —_____

SR. OCHOA —Lo vi ayer por la tarde antes de ir a la oficina.

AGENTE SILVA —_____

SR. OCHOA —Tengo una fotografía de él, pero no es reciente.

AGENTE SILVA —_____

SR. OCHOA —Llevaba puesto un pantalón azul, pero no recuerdo de qué color era la camisa.

AGENTE SILVA —_____

SR. OCHOA —Solamente un anillo de oro.

AGENTE SILVA —_____

SR. OCHOA —No, no ha tenido problemas conmigo.

AGENTE SILVA —_____

SR. OCHOA —Sí, es escapó una vez cuando tenía diez años, pero regresó a casa al día siguiente (*the next day*).

AGENTE SILVA —_____

SR. OCHOA —No, generalmente no lleva ningún documento.

AGENTE SILVA —_____

_____

SR. OCHOA —Sí, si recuerdo algo más, le aviso enseguida. Ojalá que puedan encontrarlo pronto.

AGENTE SILVA —_____

En estas situaciones

What would you say in the following situations? What might the other person say?

1. You are investigating a runaway. Ask the parents for a description of the child's physical characteristics and the clothing the child was wearing. Question them about his/her friends. Ask for a recent photograph of the child and tell them to notify you immediately if they remember any other details.

2. You are talking to a teenager who ran away from home. Explain that you want to help and ask why he/she ran away. Reassure him/her that if there have been problems with parents or at school, he/she can talk with you.

3. You are investigating a missing person case. Ask the person reporting it to recall when he/she first realized the person wasn't home. Ask for a complete description of the missing person. Promise to do everything possible to find the person.

Casos

Act out the following scenarios with a partner.

1. You are a police officer speaking with the parents of a child who has run away from home.

2. You are speaking with the best friend of a runaway. Ask what the friend knows about the runaway's problems with parents, school, and/or boyfriend/girlfriend. Find out if the friend knows why the child ran away and when he/she last saw the runaway.

Un paso más

Review the *Vocabulario adicional* in this lesson and match the questions in column A with the answers in column B.

	A		*B*
1.	_____ ¿Está muerta (*dead*)?	a.	En la morgue.
2.	_____ ¿Es Ud. mayor de edad?	b.	Cincuenta mil dólares.
3.	_____ ¿No está en la escuela?	c.	No, solamente conocidos.
4.	_____ ¿Se escapó anoche?	d.	Sí, la rescataron anoche.
5.	_____ ¿Dónde está el cadáver?	e.	Sí, y ahora están presos.
6.	_____ ¿Consiguió alojamiento?	f.	En el tribunal de menores.
7.	_____ ¿Son amigos?	g.	No, abandonó los estudios.
8.	_____ ¿No está aquí?	h.	Sí. No conocemos su paradero.
9.	_____ ¿Cuánto piden de rescate?	i.	Sí, está en un motel.
10.	_____ ¿El ladrón tiene 15 años... ?	j.	Sí, es un delincuente juvenil.
11.	_____ ¿Están en la escuela?	k.	Sí, la mató su esposo.
12.	_____ ¿Dónde estaba el hombre?	l.	No... desapareció...
13.	_____ ¿Dónde la van a juzgar (*judge*)?	m.	Sí, con la maestra.
14.	_____ ¿Vendían libros pornográficos?	n.	En la estación de ómnibus.
15.	_____ ¿La víctima del secuestro está en su casa ahora?	o.	No, soy menor de edad.

18

🔊 *Una violación*

Una muchacha hispana de dieciséis años llama a la policía, diciendo que acaban[1] de violarla. La muchacha pide que manden a alguien que hable español, porque ella no habla bien el inglés. La agente Rocha está con la víctima ahora.

VÍCTIMA	—¡Ayúdeme, por favor!
AGENTE ROCHA	—¿Tus padres no están en casa... ?
VÍCTIMA	—No, ellos no llegan hasta mañana.
AGENTE ROCHA	—Bueno, cálmate y cuéntame lo que pasó.
VÍCTIMA	—Yo estaba en mi cuarto, leyendo, cuando tocaron[1] a la puerta... Fui a abrir, y un hombre entró y me empujó... Y me caí... y me golpeó... (*Llora histéricamente.*)
AGENTE ROCHA	—Mira, yo comprendo que esto es muy difícil para ti, pero para poder ayudarte y arrestar al hombre que te violó, necesitamos información.
VÍCTIMA	—Sí, lo sé... pero primero quiero bañarme, quitarme esta ropa... ¡Me siento sucia!
AGENTE ROCHA	—Lo siento, pero es mejor esperar. Primero, tiene que examinarte un médico. Además, un baño puede destruir evidencia necesaria. ¿Conocías al hombre que te atacó?
VÍCTIMA	—No, no, no. Era un extraño.
AGENTE ROCHA	—¿Puedes reconocerlo, si lo ves?
VÍCTIMA	—No creo que pueda olvidar esa cara.
AGENTE ROCHA	—¿De qué raza era?
VÍCTIMA	—Era blanco. Más bien bajo, gordo, de ojos castaños. Tenía barba y bigote, pero era calvo.
AGENTE ROCHA	—¿Nunca lo habías visto antes?
VÍCTIMA	—No, estoy segura de que nunca lo había visto.
AGENTE ROCHA	—¿Qué hora era, más o menos?
VÍCTIMA	—Eran como las nueve y media.
AGENTE ROCHA	—¿Te cambiaste de ropa?
VÍCTIMA	—Todavía no. Llamé en cuanto se fue.
AGENTE ROCHA	—Bien, no te cambies. Un médico debe examinarte enseguida. Tenemos que llevarte al hospital. ¿Dónde están tus padres?
VÍCTIMA	—Están en la casa de mi tía. Su número de teléfono está en aquella libreta.
AGENTE ROCHA	—Ahora, ¿el hombre llegó a violarte? Es decir, ¿hubo penetración?
VÍCTIMA	—Sí. Me amenazó con un cuchillo. Tuve miedo y no hice resistencia.

---

[1]The third person is often used (without a subject) to express an indefinite he, she, or they.

AGENTE ROCHA	—¿Te obligó a realizar algún acto sexual anormal durante la violación?
VÍCTIMA	—No.
AGENTE ROCHA	—¿Se puso un condón?
VÍCTIMA	—No, y eso me tiene aterrorizada. Tal vez tiene SIDA, o una enfermedad venérea...
AGENTE ROCHA	—Trata de tranquilizarte. Se te harán las pruebas necesarias. ¿Qué más recuerdas de él? ¿Tenía alguna marca visible? ¿Un tatuaje?
VÍCTIMA	—Tenía un tatuaje en el brazo izquierdo: un corazón atravesado por una flechita. Además, usaba anteojos.
AGENTE ROCHA	—¿Tenía algún acento? ¿Te dijo algo?
VÍCTIMA	—No, no le noté ningún acento. Sólo me dijo que si gritaba, me mataba.
AGENTE ROCHA	—¿Trataste de luchar con él... de defenderte...?
VÍCTIMA	—No. Tenía tanto miedo...
AGENTE ROCHA	—Comprendo.

🔊 Vocabulario

COGNADOS

el acento accent	**la evidencia** evidence
el acto act	**la penetración** penetration
anormal abnormal	**sexual** sexual
el condón condom	

NOMBRES

los anteojos, los lentes, los espejuelos (*Cuba Puerto Rico*), **las gafas** eyeglasses
el baño bath
la barba beard
el bigote moustache
el cuchillo knife
la enfermedad venérea venereal disease
el (la) extraño(a) stranger
la flecha, la flechita arrow, small arrow
la libreta address book
la raza race
el SIDA (síndrome de inmunodeficiencia adquirida) AIDS
la violación rape

VERBOS

amenazar to threaten
atacar to attack
ayudar to help
bañarse to bathe
caerse[1] to fall
calmarse to calm down
comprender to understand
contar (o:ue) to tell
defender(se) to defend (oneself)
destruir[2] to destroy
empujar to push
golpear to hit, to strike
gritar to scream, to shout
luchar to fight, to struggle
llorar to cry
obligar to obligate, to force
olvidar to forget
ponerse to put on
realizar to perform, to carry out
violar to rape

---

[1]Irregular first-person present indicative: *me caigo.*
[2]Orthographic change in the present indicative, in all forms except the *nosotros* form: *destruyo, destruyes, destruye, destruimos, destruyen.*

ADJETIVOS

aquel, aquella   that
aterrorizado(a)   terrified, frightened
atravesado(a)   pierced
calvo(a), pelado(a)   bald
castaño, café   brown (*ref. to eyes or hair*)
sucio(a)   dirty

OTRAS PALABRAS Y EXPRESIONES

cambiarse de ropa   to change clothes
en cuanto   as soon as
Eran como las (+ *hora*).   It was about (+ time).
es decir...   that is to say . . .
estar seguro(a)   to be certain
hacer resistencia   to resist
Hasta mañana.   (I'll) see you tomorrow.
histéricamente   hysterically
llegar a + *infinitivo*   to succeed in (doing something)
para ti   for you
¿Qué hora era... ?   What time was it . . . ?
tal vez   perhaps
¡Tenía tanto miedo!   I was so scared!

Vocabulario adicional

MÁS DESCRIPCIONES

LA PIEL (*Skin*)

el acné   acne
el grano   pimple
la mancha   spot, mark, blemish
la peca   freckle
la verruga   wart

LOS OJOS

bizco(a)   cross-eyed
el ojo de vidrio   glass eye
los ojos saltones   bulging eyes, bug eyes

EL CUERPO (*Body*)

deformado(a)   deformed
desfigurado(a)   disfigured
embarazada   pregnant
musculoso(a)   muscular

EL PELO

la peluca   wig, hairpiece
el vello   body hair
velludo(a)   hairy

OTRAS PALABRAS

hablar con (la) zeta   to lisp
tartamudear   to stutter

Notas culturales

- Hispanics constitute about 7.9% of the population in the U.S., yet they account for 14% of the reported AIDS cases, nearly 21% of AIDS cases among women, and 22% of all pediatric AIDS cases. Hispanics are at greater risk for HIV infection because of factors such as living in high-prevalence areas and exposure to intravenous drug use, not because of their race and culture. AIDS is most prevalent in large urban centers, with three cities (New York, San Francisco, and Los Angeles) accounting for about 60% of all cases. Nearly half of the Hispanics with AIDS are heterosexuals, and most of the Hispanic AIDS cases in the Northeast are among intravenous drug users. Heterosexual transmission of HIV from intravenous drug users to their sexual partners is more prevalent among Hispanics because of attitudes regarding the use of condoms. A recent survey indicates that Hispanics know less about HIV and AIDS than non-Hispanics. The American Medical Association has recommended that AIDS prevention education programs be tailored to subgroups such as Mexican Americans and Puerto Rican Americans due to cultural and language differences.
- Like many women, Hispanic females may feel uncomfortable or embarrassed discussing matters of sex, especially with a male police officer. This reaction may be due in part to cultural taboos, the patient's level of education, or both. In some cultures, it is not possible or it is considered socially unacceptable to talk about female anatomy or any aspect of sexuality. Therefore, it is important to be sensitive and diplomatic when dealing with these topics.

¿Recuerdan ustedes?

Answer the following questions, basing your answers on the dialogue.

1. ¿Cuántos años tiene la muchacha que llama a la policía?

   _____

2. ¿Qué dice la muchacha y qué pide?

   _____

   _____

3. ¿Dónde estaba la víctima y qué estaba haciendo cuando tocaron a la puerta?

   _____

4. ¿Qué pasó cuando la muchacha abrió la puerta?

   _____

5. ¿Qué quiere hacer la muchacha antes de hablar con la agente?

   _____

6. ¿Por qué dice la agente Rocha que es mejor esperar?

   _____

   _____

7. ¿Conocía la muchacha al hombre que la atacó?

_____

8. Describa al hombre que violó a la muchacha. ¿Tenía alguna marca visible?

_____

9. ¿Se cambió de ropa la muchacha?

_____

10. ¿Esperó mucho tiempo la muchacha antes de llamar a la policía?

_____

11. ¿Llegó a violar el hombre a la muchacha?

_____

12. ¿Trató de defenderse la muchacha? ¿Por qué o por qué no?

_____

Para conversar

Interview a classmate, using the following questions. When you have finished, switch roles.

1. ¿Qué estaba haciendo Ud. anoche cuando tocaron a la puerta?

_____

2. ¿Se cambió Ud. de ropa antes de ir a trabajar?

_____

3. ¿Solamente las mujeres pueden ser víctimas del abuso sexual?

_____

4. En un caso de violación, ¿qué debe hacer el (la) agente de policía para ayudar a la víctima?

_____

5. ¿Ha investigado Ud. casos de violación?

_____

6. ¿Conoce Ud. a alguna mujer que sepa defenderse contra un hombre?

_____

Vamos a practicar

A. **Rewrite the following sentences, beginning each one with the cue given.**

Modelo: Puedo olvidar su cara.

No creo que **pueda** olvidar su cara.

1. Mis padres llegan mañana.

   No creo que _____

2. Él la empuja y la golpea.

   Dudo que _____

3. Esto es muy difícil.

   No es verdad que _____

4. Él tiene bigote y barba.

   No estoy segura de que _____

B. **Rewrite the following sentences, beginning each one with the cue given. Make the necessary changes.**

1. ¿Habla inglés?

   ¿Hay alguien que _____?

2. Un médico puede examinarte.

   Busco a un médico que _____

3. Un testigo está seguro de que lo vio allí.

   Necesito encontrar un testigo que _____

4. La fotografía identifica al ladrón.

   Espero conseguir una fotografía que _____

Conversaciones breves

Complete the following dialogue, using your imagination and the vocabulary from this lesson.

El agente Mena habla con Sara, la víctima de una violación.

AGENTE MENA —_____

SARA —No, nunca lo había visto antes.

AGENTE MENA —_____

SARA —Era blanco... alto... de pelo negro y ojos azules.

AGENTE MENA —_____

SARA	—Tenía bigote, pero no tenía barba.
AGENTE MENA	— _____
SARA	—No recuerdo nada más...
AGENTE MENA	— _____
SARA	—No, no usaba lentes.
AGENTE MENA	— _____
SARA	—Sí, me amenazó con un cuchillo.
AGENTE MENA	— _____
SARA	—Sí, traté de defenderme, pero no pude hacer nada.
AGENTE MENA	— _____
SARA	—Sí, llegó a violarme... hubo penetración...
AGENTE MENA	— _____
SARA	—No, nada anormal...

En estas situaciones

What would you say in the following situations? What might the other person say?

1. You answer a call from a hysterical rape victim. Calm her down and ask her to describe what happened. Explain that you know it is difficult for her to talk about it, but you need to know all the details in order to find the man who raped her.

2. You are with a rape victim. Advise her not to bathe or change clothes, and help to arrange for a medical examination for her at a hospital. Find out from her if there is anyone else you should call.

3. You are investigating a rape. Ask the victim to describe the man. Help her to remember as many details as possible about the rapist by asking questions about his physical characteristics, clothing, accent, etc.

Casos

Act out the following scenarios with a partner.

1. You are an officer trying to calm down a hysterical rape victim.

2. You are talking to a rape victim, trying to get information about the rapist and what happened.

Un paso más

A. Review the *Vocabulario adicional* in this lesson and match the questions in column A with the answers in column B.

A	*B*
1. _____ ¿Es una verruga?	a. Sí, tiene muchos granos...
2. _____ ¿Es gordo?	b. No, habla con zeta.
3. _____ ¿Tiene alguna marca visible?	c. No, no tiene problemas con los ojos.
4. _____ ¿Tiene acné?	d. Algunas, en la nariz.
5. _____ ¿Tartamudea?	e. Saltones.
6. _____ ¿Es velludo?	f. Sí, tiene mucho vello.
7. _____ ¿Tiene pecas?	g. Una es artificial.
8. _____ ¿Está embarazada?	h. Sí, pero usa peluca.
9. _____ ¿Es bizco?	i. No, es musculoso.
10. _____ ¿Cómo son los ojos?	j. Sí, una mancha en la cara.
11. _____ ¿Tuvo un accidente?	k. Sí, y ahora está desfigurada.
12. _____ ¿Es calvo?	l. No, es perfecto.
13. _____ ¿Tiene las dos piernas?	m. No, es un lunar.
14. _____ ¿Es deformado?	n. Sí, va a tener el bebé en octubre.

B. Read the information about sexual abuse in the following brochure.
Then use the information it contains to decide what you would say to
the following people. Work with a partner.

EN CASOS DE ASALTOS° SEXUALES...

assaults

La violación y el abuso sexual

La violación es un delito en que la víctima es dominada por el uso de la fuerza° o la
amenaza.°

force
threat

- Una de cada cuatro mujeres y uno de cada seis hombres serán víctimas de un
asalto sexual durante su vida.
- Cualquier persona puede ser culpable° de un asalto sexual: vecinos,
compañeros, miembros de la familia, desconocidos° o buenos amigos. En más
del 50% de los casos, la víctima conoce al asaltante.

guilty
strangers

- La violación es un acto violento en que una persona usa el sexo para humillar y
controlar a otra. Es una experiencia violenta, aterrorizadora y brutal.

Si Ud. es víctima de una violación o de otro abuso sexual

1. Recuerde que Ud. no tiene la culpa.°
2. Vaya a un lugar seguro.°
3. Busque el apoyo° de su familia o de sus amigos o llame a un centro de ayuda
para víctimas de la violación.
4. Obtenga atención médica.
5. Llame a la policía y recuerde que si se ducha° o se baña,° puede destruir
evidencia importante.
6. Considere la posibilidad de usar los servicios de un consejero profesional.

blame
safe
support

se... shower / se... bathe

¡Recuerde!

Decidir qué hacer después de un asalto es muy difícil. Es normal sentirse confuso.
El centro de ayuda para víctimas de la violación puede ofrecerle información y
apoyo. Los consejeros están a su disposición.

1. Carlos thinks that, since he is not a girl, he never has to worry about being sexually abused.

   _____

   _____

   _____

2. Teresa thinks that she only has to worry about strangers, but that she is safe with friends, classmates, and acquaintances.

   _____

   _____

   _____

3. María was sexually abused, and you are trying to give her some advice about what to do next.

   _____

   _____

   _____

19

📼 *Una tarde cualquiera*

Una tarde en la vida del agente Cabañas de la Cuarta Estación de Policía, en Elizabeth, Nueva Jersey.

Las dos de la tarde:

El agente Cabañas habla con el padre de un menor de edad a quien acaban de arrestar.

PADRE	—Buenos días. Me avisaron que mi hijo estaba detenido aquí.
AGENTE CABAÑAS	—¿Cómo se llama su hijo?
PADRE	—Enrique Fernández.
AGENTE CABAÑAS	—Sí, señor. Está aquí.
PADRE	—¿Por qué lo arrestaron? ¿De qué lo acusan?
AGENTE CABAÑAS	—Su hijo está acusado de venderles drogas a sus compañeros, en su escuela.
PADRE	—¡No es posible! Eso no puede ser cierto. No creo que mi hijo haya hecho tal cosa. ¿Puedo hablar con él?
AGENTE CABAÑAS	—Sí, señor, pero debe esperar hasta que hayan terminado de interrogarlo.

Las tres y cuarto de la tarde:

El agente Cabañas va a la casa de Felipe Núñez para hablar con él. Habla con la mamá del muchacho.

AGENTE CABAÑAS	—Necesito hablar con Felipe Núñez, señora. Es urgente.
SRA. NÚÑEZ	—No está, y no sé a qué hora va a regresar.
AGENTE CABAÑAS	—Bueno, cuando regrese, dígale que me llame a este número, por favor. Dígale que quiero hacerle unas preguntas.
SRA. NÚÑEZ	—Muy bien. Se lo diré tan pronto lo vea.

Las cinco de la tarde:

El agente Cabañas va al apartamento de una muchacha que trató de suicidarse.

AGENTE CABAÑAS	—¿Dónde está la muchacha?
VECINO	—Allí, en la cocina. La encontré con la cabeza metida en el horno.
AGENTE CABAÑAS	—¿Había olor a gas?
VECINO	—Sí, por eso llamé al 911 en cuanto llegué. Ya vienen los paramédicos.

Van a la cocina y el agente habla con la muchacha.

AGENTE CABAÑAS	—¿Puedes oírme? ¿Cómo te sientes?
MUCHACHA	—Mal... Tomé...
AGENTE CABAÑAS	—¿Qué tomaste? ¿Veneno? ¿Qué veneno tomaste... ?
MUCHACHA	—No... calmantes... en el baño... más de diez...

Las seis de la tarde:

El agente Cabañas detiene a una señora que maneja con los faros del carro apagados.

AGENTE CABAÑAS	—La detuve porque los faros de su carro no están prendidos.
SEÑORA	—Sí... parece que están descompuestos...
AGENTE CABAÑAS	—Bueno, no puede manejar este carro a menos que haga arreglar los faros.
SEÑORA	—Muy bien. Mañana, sin falta.
AGENTE CABAÑAS	—Cuando el carro esté listo, llévelo a esta dirección. Ahí le van a firmar el dorso de esta papeleta para confirmar que Ud. hizo arreglar el desperfecto.

Vocabulario

COGNADO	
el gas	gas

NOMBRES

la cabeza head
el calmante, el sedante, el sedativo sedative
el desperfecto (slight) damage, imperfection
el dorso back (of paper)
el faro headlight
el horno oven
el olor smell
la papeleta form
el veneno poison

VERBOS

arreglar to fix
confirmar to confirm
oír[1] to hear
suicidarse to commit suicide

ADJETIVOS

descompuesto(a) broken, not working
listo(a) ready
metido(a) inside, inserted in
prendido(a), encendido(a) lit, turned on (a lamp)

OTRAS PALABRAS Y EXPRESIONES

a menos que unless
en cuanto, tan pronto como as soon as
hacer arreglar to have (something) fixed
hacer una pregunta to ask a question
hasta que until
olor a smell of
sin falta without fail
tal cosa such a thing

---

[1]Irregular present indicative: *oigo, oyes, oye, oímos, oyen.*

Vocabulario adicional

PARA RESPONDER A UNA LLAMADA

la agresión, el ataque   aggression, attack, assault
el (la) agresor(a)   aggressor, assailant
el (la) asesino(a)   murderer, assassin
dar una puñalada   to stab
pegar un tiro, pegar un balazo   to shoot
en defensa propia   in self-defense
la pelea, la riña   fight
la queja   complaint
el ruido   noise

arrancar   to start (a car)
la camilla   stretcher
los primeros auxilios   first aid
respirar   to breathe
la silla de ruedas   wheelchair
tocar la bocina   to honk the horn

Nota cultural

Most Hispanic children are taught from an early age that the family comes first. Knowing one's place in a hierarchical, sometimes authoritarian family structure and showing appropriate deference and respect to older family members are of great importance, as is recognizing the interdependence of family members and the necessity of placing the family's well-being ahead of one's own needs or desires. Within this context, traditional "American" values such as individualism, freedom of choice, and self-sufficiency are of secondary importance.

¿Recuerdan ustedes?

Answer the following questions, basing your answers on the dialogues.

1. ¿Por qué vino a la estación de policía el padre de un menor de edad?

   _____

2. ¿De qué está acusado su hijo?

   _____

3. ¿Qué cree el padre de la acusación?

   _____

4. Si el padre quiere ver a su hijo, ¿hasta cuándo tiene que esperar?

   _____

5. ¿Habla el agente Cabañas con Felipe Núñez? ¿Por qué o por qué no?

_____

6. ¿Para qué quiere hablar con él?

_____

7. ¿Cuándo le va a decir la Sra. Núñez a su hijo que el agente quiere hablar con él?

_____

8. ¿Dónde está la muchacha que trató de suicidarse?

_____

9. ¿Cómo encontró el vecino a la muchacha?

_____

10. ¿Qué olor había?

_____

11. ¿Esperó mucho tiempo el vecino para llamar a la policía?

_____

12. ¿Qué tomó la muchacha?

_____

13. ¿Por qué detiene el agente Cabañas a una señora?

_____

14. ¿Qué tiene que hacer la señora mañana?

_____

15. ¿Qué debe hacer la señora cuando los faros del carro estén listos?

_____

Para conversar

Interview a classmate, using the following questions. When you have finished, switch roles.

1. ¿Qué va a hacer Ud. en cuanto llegue a su casa?

_____

2. ¿A quién quiere Ud. hacerle unas preguntas?

_____

3. ¿Qué le dirá Ud. a su profesor(a) cuando lo (la) vea?

_____

4. ¿Necesita hacer arreglar su coche?

   _____

5. ¿Están prendidos o apagados los faros de su carro en este momento?

   _____

Vamos a practicar

A. Complete the following sentences, using the cue in parentheses.

1. Se lo voy a preguntar cuando _____ (verlos).

2. Yo le avisaré en cuanto _____ (arrestarlas).

3. Lleve el carro a este lugar tan pronto como _____ (arreglar los faros).

4. No me llame hasta que ellas _____ (traer al detenido).

B. Rewrite the following sentences, beginning each one with the cue given.

   Modelo: Le leyeron sus derechos.

   Espero que **le hayan leído** sus derechos.

1. Murieron todos.

   No creo que _____

2. La corte les nombró (*appointed*) un abogado.

   Ojalá que _____

3. Le hicieron algunas preguntas.

   Es posible que _____

4. Se suicidó.

   Ella tiene miedo de que él _____

5. Lo encontraron.

   Espero que _____

6. Los faros estaban prendidos.

   Dudo que _____

Conversaciones breves

Complete the following dialogues, using your imagination and the vocabulary from this lesson.

El agente Ross y el Sr. Soto:

AGENTE ROSS — _____

SR. SOTO —Lo siento, pero en este momento no está.

AGENTE ROSS	—_____
SR. SOTO	—No sé. Sólo me dijo que iba a regresar más tarde.
AGENTE ROSS	—_____
SR. SOTO	—Sí, señor. Se lo diré cuando lo vea.

La agente León y la Sra. Torres:

AGENTE LEÓN	—¿Qué pasa, señora?
SRA. TORRES	—_____
AGENTE LEÓN	—¿Dónde está su hijo ahora?
SRA. TORRES	—_____
AGENTE LEÓN	—¿Llamó Ud. a los paramédicos?
SRA. TORRES	—_____
AGENTE LEÓN	—Voy a llamarlos yo. ¿Qué tomó su hijo, señora?
SRA. TORRES	—_____

La agente Suárez y el Sr. Gil:

AGENTE SUÁREZ	—_____
SR. GIL	—Buenos días. Busco a mi hijo. Me han dicho que está aquí.
AGENTE SUÁREZ	—_____
SR. GIL	—Se llama Alberto Rosas.
AGENTE SUÁREZ	—_____
SR. GIL	—Pero, ¿por qué? Alberto es un buen muchacho.
AGENTE SUÁREZ	—_____
SR. GIL	—¿Cómo? ¿Mi hijo? ¡No puede ser! Quiero verlo ahora mismo.
AGENTE SUÁREZ	—_____
SR. GIL	—Está bien. Voy a esperar, pero primero quiero llamar a mi abogado.
AGENTE SUÁREZ	—_____

En estas situaciones

What would you say in the following situations? What might the other person say?

1. Explain to the parent of a minor who has been arrested that he/she can't speak with the child until they've finished booking him/her. Say that the child was arrested for selling drugs at school and for carrying a gun. Tell the parent to take a seat in the waiting room and try to calm him/her down.

2. You want to speak with Mr. Olmedo. Leave this message with his wife: "When your husband returns, have him call me at this number without fail. It is very urgent, because I want to ask him a few questions."

3. Tell a motorist that he/she has to have his/her car fixed. Tell the motorist also that, after the car is ready, he/she has to take it to 125 Flores Street, where someone will sign the back of the form to confirm that the damage has been fixed.

Casos

Act out the following scenarios with a partner.

1. You are talking with the angry and distraught parent of a minor who has just been arrested.

2. You are having difficulty getting in touch with a young woman you need to interrogate, so you leave several messages with her roommate.

3. You talk to a motorist whose car lights are not on and advise him/her on what to do.

Un paso más

Review the *Vocabulario adicional* in this lesson and translate the following sentences into Spanish.

1. There has been a complaint.

   a. Is there a fight at this party? There's a lot of noise.

   _____

   b. Who was the aggressor?

   _____

   c. She stabbed him.

   _____

   d. He shot her with a gun.

   _____

   e. She's not breathing. (She doesn't breathe.)

   _____

   f. He killed her in self-defense.

   _____

2. There has been an accident on the highway.

   a. Her car wouldn't start.

   _____

   b. He was honking the horn.

   _____

   c. He crashed into her car.

   _____

   d. Do you know anything about first aid?

   _____

   e. We're going to put her on a stretcher.

   _____

   f. Is there a wheelchair for him?

   _____

20

🔊 *Otro día, por la mañana...*

Un día de trabajo para el agente Montero, de la Comisaría Tercera de la ciudad de Albuquerque, Nuevo México.

Las diez y media de la mañana:

El agente Montero investiga un robo en un mercado. Ahora está hablando con el dependiente.

AGENTE MONTERO	—Cuénteme exactamente lo que pasó.
DEPENDIENTE	—A eso de las nueve y media vino un hombre y dijo que quería una botella de vino...
AGENTE MONTERO	—¿Qué pasó entonces?
DEPENDIENTE	—Me apuntó con una pistola y me obligó a que le diera todo el dinero que había en la caja.
AGENTE MONTERO	—¿Podría Ud. reconocerlo, si lo viera otra vez?
DEPENDIENTE	—No sé. Tenía barba y bigote... Si se afeitara, no sé si lo reconocería.
AGENTE MONTERO	—¿Cuánto medía, más o menos? ¿Era como de mi estatura?
DEPENDIENTE	—No, mucho más alto y más grande. Medía como seis pies y dos pulgadas y pesaba unas doscientas cincuenta libras.
AGENTE MONTERO	—¿Cómo estaba vestido?
DEPENDIENTE	—A ver si recuerdo... Pantalón gris oscuro, camisa azul y una chaqueta de pana café.
AGENTE MONTERO	—Ud. le dio todo el dinero. ¿Qué pasó después?
DEPENDIENTE	—Traté de seguirlo, pero me apuntó con la pistola y me dijo que me quedara donde estaba.
AGENTE MONTERO	—¿Puede describir la pistola?
DEPENDIENTE	—Una pistola semiautomática, calibre treinta y dos, posiblemente.

Las once y media:

El agente Montero sospecha que hay drogas en el maletero de un carro. Ahora está hablando con la dueña.

AGENTE MONTERO	—No tengo permiso del juez para registrar su carro, pero me gustaría ver lo que Ud. tiene en el maletero. ¿Quiere darme la llave?
MUJER	—Hay un gato y una llanta en el maletero...
AGENTE MONTERO	—¿Me da Ud. permiso para registrarlo? No la estoy amenazando ni le estoy prometiendo nada. Si Ud. me da permiso, tiene que ser voluntariamente.
MUJER	—Consiga una orden del juez si quiere registrar mi carro.

Las dos y media de la tarde:

El agente Montero arresta a un hombre que atacó a una mujer y trató de robarle la cartera.

AGENTE MONTERO	—Póngase las manos sobre la cabeza y entrelace los dedos. Dése vuelta.
HOMBRE	—¡Hijo de mala madre!
AGENTE MONTERO	—¡Cállese! Camine hacia el carro patrullero. Súbase. ¡Cuidado con la cabeza...!

Las cuatro y media de la tarde:

El agente Montero ve un grupo de personas que están gritando obscenidades y amenazas frente a un consulado y les ordena dispersarse.

AGENTE MONTERO	—Soy el agente Montero, de la Policía. Esta reunión queda declarada ilegal y, por lo tanto, les ordeno que se dispersen inmediatamente.

La multitud empieza a dispersarse y algunos murmuran obscenidades.

Vocabulario

COGNADOS

el calibre caliber	**la obscenidad** obscenity
el consulado consulate	**semiautomático(a)** semiautomatic
el grupo group	**voluntariamente** voluntary

NOMBRES

la amenaza threat
la botella bottle
la caja cash register
la chaqueta, la chamarra (*Méx.*) jacket
el (la) dependiente clerk
la estatura height
el gato, la gata (*Costa Rica*) jack
la libra pound
la llanta, la goma (*Cuba*), **el neumático** tire
el maletero, la cajuela (*Méx.*), **el baúl** (*Puerto Rico*) trunk
el mercado market
la multitud crowd
la pana corduroy
el permiso warrant, permission
la reunión, la congregación, el mitin meeting, assembly
el vino wine

VERBOS

afeitarse to shave
apuntar to point, to aim (a gun)
dispersarse to disperse
entrelazar to intertwine
murmurar to murmur
ordenar to order
pesar to weigh
prometer to promise

ADJETIVO

gris gray

OTRAS PALABRAS Y EXPRESIONES

¡Cállese! Be quiet! Shut up!
¡Cuidado! Careful!
Dése vuelta., Voltéese., Vírese. (*Cuba*) Turn around.
mientras while
por lo tanto therefore, so
queda declarado(a) ilegal is hereby declared illegal
sobre on, on top of

Vocabulario adicional

MANDATOS ÚTILES (*Useful commands*)

¡Acuéstese en el suelo, boca abajo!   Lie down on
the floor (ground), face down!

¡Agáchese!   Bend down!

¡Aléjese de la ventana!   Get away from the window!

¡Bájese de allí!   Get down from there!

¡Levante los brazos!   Lift your arms!

¡Llame al perro!   Call off the dog!

¡No dispare! ¡No tire!   Don't shoot!

¡No salte!   Don't jump!

¡No se mueva!   Don't move!

¡Póngase las manos detrás de la espalda!   Put
your hands behind your back!

¡Póngase de rodillas!   Get on your knees!

¡Salga con las manos en (sobre) la cabeza!
Come out with your hands on top of your head!

¡Sáquese las manos de los bolsillos!   Take your
hands out of your pockets!

¡Separe los pies!   Spread your feet!

¡Siga caminando!   Keep walking!

¡Suelte el arma!   Drop the gun (weapon)!

¡Suéltelo(la)!   Let go of him (her)!

Nota cultural

Until recently, in most Latin American cities, people could walk in the streets late at
night without running the risk of being assaulted or mugged. Holdups were almost
unheard of and there were few incidents like the one described in this lesson.

That is not the case today. Some Latin American big cities have reputations for being
rough. Travellers are warned about the increasing crime in most cities.

¿Recuerdan ustedes?

Answer the following questions, basing your answers on the dialogues.

1. ¿Qué pasó a eso de las nueve y media en el mercado?

    _____

2. ¿Qué hizo el hombre después de apuntarle al dependiente con una pistola?

    _____

3. ¿Cómo era el hombre?

    _____

4. ¿Qué ropa tenía puesta?

    _____

5. ¿Qué hizo el hombre cuando el dependiente trató de seguirlo?

_____

6. ¿Qué clase de pistola tenía el hombre?

_____

7. El agente Montero sospecha que hay drogas en el maletero de un carro. ¿Por qué no le ordena a la dueña que lo abra?

_____

8. ¿Le da la mujer permiso al agente Montero para que abra el maletero y lo registre?

_____

9. El agente Montero arresta a un hombre. ¿Por qué?

_____

10. ¿Qué le ordena el agente Montero al hombre?

_____

11. ¿Qué está haciendo la gente que está frente a un consulado?

_____

12. ¿Qué les ordena el agente Montero?

_____

Para conversar

Interview a classmate, using the following questions. When you have finished, switch roles.

1. Si yo le apuntara con una pistola y le pidiera su dinero, ¿me lo daría?

_____

2. José tiene barba y bigote. Si se afeitara, ¿lo reconocería Ud.?

_____

3. Juana mide cinco pies, nueve pulgadas. ¿Es como de su estatura?

_____

4. ¿Qué ropa tenía Ud. puesta ayer por la tarde?

_____

5. ¿Qué tiene Ud. en el maletero de su coche?

_____

6. ¿Le prometió Ud. algo a su profesor(a) de español?

   _____

7. Yo no tengo permiso del juez para registrar su casa. ¿Me da Ud. permiso
   voluntariamente?

   _____

Vamos a practicar

A. **Rewrite each of the following sentences, using the cue given and the
   appropriate verb tense.**

   Modelo: Es importante que Ud. hable con él.

   Era importante que Ud. **hablara** con él.

   1. Es importante que al agente tenga permiso del juez.

      Era importante _____

   2. Quiero que Ud. abra el maletero.

      Quería _____

   3. Les digo que me den la llave.

      Les diría _____

   4. La mujer no cree que el gato esté en el maletero.

      La mujer no creía _____

   5. Les ordeno que se dispersen.

      Les ordenaría _____

   6. Ella duda que él ataque a las mujeres.

      Ella dudaba _____

   7. La agente nos dice que nos pongamos las manos en la cabeza.

      La agente nos dijo _____

   8. ¡Te he dicho que no me llames así!

      ¡Te dije _____

   9. Es posible que tenga una pistola semiautomática.

      Era posible _____

   10. El agente quiere que el dependiente le diga la verdad.

       El agente quería _____

B. Answer the following questions, using *si* and the appropriate verb forms.

Modelo: ¿Por qué no compras ese carro? (tener dinero)

Si **tuviera** dinero, lo **compraría.**

1. ¿Por qué no me cuentas lo que pasó? (saberlo)

   _____

2. ¿Por qué no le dices qué ropa tenía puesta? (recordarlo)

   _____

3. ¿Por qué no los sigues? (poder)

   _____

4. ¿Por qué no registra el maletero? (tener permiso del juez)

   _____

5. ¿Por qué no les ordenas que se dispersen? (hacer algo ilegal)

   _____

C. Change the following commands into statements, using *si* and the expressions in parentheses.

Modelo: Venga a verme. (tener tiempo, señor)

Si **tengo** tiempo, **vendré** a verlo, señor.

1. Arreste a este hombre. (hacer algo ilegal, señora)

   _____

2. Registre el coche. (Ud. darme la llave, señorita)

   _____

3. Dígale que venga. (verla, señor)

   _____

4. Quédese aquí. (poder hacerlo, señor)

   _____

5. Traiga a los niños. (tener el carro, señora)

   _____

Conversaciones breves

Complete the following dialogue, using your imagination and the vocabulary from this lesson.

El agente Ríos investiga un robo.

AGENTE RÍOS — _____

DEPENDIENTE —Bueno... no recuerdo mucho... un hombre entró y me apuntó con una pistola...

AGENTE RÍOS — _____

DEPENDIENTE —Me dijo que le diera todo el dinero de la caja.

AGENTE RÍOS — _____

DEPENDIENTE —No sé cuánto medía.

AGENTE RÍOS — _____

DEPENDIENTE —No, no era tan alto como Ud. ... y era muy delgado.

AGENTE RÍOS — _____

DEPENDIENTE —Yo creo que pesaba unas ciento treinta libras...

AGENTE RÍOS — _____

DEPENDIENTE —Tenía pantalón blanco y camisa azul... y sombrero.

AGENTE RÍOS — _____

DEPENDIENTE —No, yo no entiendo nada de armas.

AGENTE RÍOS — _____

DEPENDIENTE —Sí, vi el carro que manejaba. Era un Ford azul.

AGENTE RÍOS — _____

DEPENDIENTE —No, no sé el número de la chapa, pero era de otro estado.

En estas situaciones

What would you say in the following situations? What might the other person say?

1. You are investigating the armed robbery of a food store. Ask the employee to tell you exactly what happened and to describe the robber and his weapon. Then ask the employee if he/she would recognize the robber if he came into the store again.

2. You want to search somebody's car, but you don't have a warrant. Ask the owner's permission to search it. Make sure the owner knows that you are not threatening or making any promises.

3. You are arresting a suspect. Tell the person to do the following: "Put your hands on your head. Turn around. Be quiet. Get into the patrol car."

4. You are trying to disperse an unruly crowd. Tell them who you are and order them to disperse immediately.

Casos

Act out the following scenarios with a partner.

1. You are an officer questioning a shopkeeper whose store was just robbed.

2. You are an officer trying to convince someone to let you search his/her car without a warrant.

3. You are an officer arresting a belligerent suspect.

Un paso más

Review the *Vocabulario adicional* in this lesson and respond to each of the following situations with an appropriate command.

1. You are going to handcuff a prisoner.

   _____

2. Someone is near a window, and this might prove dangerous.

   _____

3. Someone is going to jump off a roof.

   _____

4. You want a suspect to drop his gun.

   _____

5. You want a suspect to walk to the police car, but she stops.

   _____

6. You want to stop someone from shooting.

   _____

7. A suspect has his hands in this pockets.

   _____

8. Someone's dog is running toward you with every intention of biting you.

   _____

9. You want a suspect to lift his arms.

   _____

10. Someone is holding a screaming girl, and you want him to let go of her.

_____

11. You need to instruct someone to bend over.

_____

12. You have to tell someone to lie on the floor, face down.

_____

13. You are pointing a gun at a suspect. You don't want her to make any sudden moves.

_____

14. You want a suspect to get on his knees.

_____

15. You want someone to spread his feet.

_____

16. Someone has climbed on a roof, and you want her down.

_____

17. There is a suspect inside a house, but he is ready to give himself up.

_____

Repaso

LECCIONES 16–20

Práctica de vocabulario

A.   Circle the word or phrase that does not belong in each group.

1.   llanta, maletero, neumático

2.   calmante, sedante, cocina

3.   baño, descompuesto, desperfecto

4.   anteojos, faros, lentes

5.   cuchillo, bigote, barba

6.   gritar, llorar, bañarse

7.   pelado, sucio, calvo

8.   anillo, blusa, sortija

9.   cruz, cartera, bolsa

10.   gente, mejilla, cachete

11.   lunar, cicatriz, arete

12.   calmarse, escaparse, fugarse

13.   billetera, celda, cartera

14.   cambiarse de ropa, quitarse, moverse

15.   reloj, voluntad, cadena

B. Circle the word or phrase that best completes each sentence.

1. Todas sus pertenencias serán puestas en un (bono, cuello, sobre) sellado.

2. Lo voy a (retratar, vaciar, mirar) porque necesito su fotografía.

3. Ponga todas sus cosas en el (mostrador, centavo, oro).

4. Es una enfermedad (gris, metida, venérea).

5. Voy a tomarle (la fiscal, el homicidio, las huellas digitales).

6. Su esposa ha sido víctima de (un secuestro, un detalle, una falda).

7. Ponga (las manos, los pies, la cabeza) en la pared.

8. Había (pelo, olor, violación) a gas.

9. Entrelace (la multitud, los dedos, las cajas).

10. Por favor, lea el dorso de (este detenido, esta papeleta, este mercado).

11. Tengo que hacerlo arreglar porque está (listo, prendido, descompuesto).

12. El hombre me (ayudó, afeitó, amenazó) con un revólver.

13. Me caí porque ella me (murmuró, empujó, contó).

14. Tenía (una edad, una cicatriz, una amenaza) en la boca.

15. Ella no tiene (cordones, antecedentes, dependientes) penales.

C. **Match the questions in column A with the appropriate word or phrase in column B.**

	A		*B*
1.	_____ ¿Qué van a hacer con él ahora?	a.	Sí, acaba de llegar.
2.	_____ ¿Le pusieron una fianza muy alta?	b.	Sí, por lo menos cien dólares.
3.	_____ ¿Ud. va a comprar el bono?	c.	Una chaqueta de pana y un suéter negro.
4.	_____ ¿Está el Sr. Bravo?	d.	No, era una extraña.
5.	_____ ¿Necesitas dinero?	e.	No, mi familia.
6.	_____ ¿A quiénes llamaste?	f.	Sí, histéricamente.
7.	_____ ¿Qué ropa tenía puesta?	g.	Blanco.
8.	_____ ¿De qué raza es?	h.	Lo pondrán en libertad bajo palabra.
9.	_____ ¿Lloraba?	i.	Era como de mi estatura.
10.	_____ ¿La conocías?	j.	Mañana, sin falta.
11.	_____ ¿Cuándo arreglarán el horno?	k.	A los Sres. Ruiz.
12.	_____ ¿Cuánto medía?	l.	Sí, y no pudo pagarla.

D. Crucigrama

HORIZONTAL

3. Tengo su dirección en mi _____ .

4. *anteojos*, en Cuba

6. El coche tiene un _____ . Tengo que hacerlo arreglar.

8. En México lo llaman *cajuela*.

9. *arrow*, en español

14. sin obligación

16. bolsa

19. Ella no tiene _____ penales.

21. normalmente

22. Lo necesito para saber la hora.

23. dar autorización

24. Está en _____ bajo fianza.

VERTICAL

1. Tomó _____ para suicidarse.

2. No hable.

5. *chaqueta*, en México

7. sedativo

10. Lo necesito para cambiar una llanta.

11. Quiero comprar una _____ de vino.

12. *test*, en español

13. Él _____ 180 libras.

15. que tiene importancia

17. *belongings*, en español

18. persona que investiga (*m.*)

20. fichar

📼 Práctica oral

Listen to the following exercise on the audio program. The speaker will ask you some questions. Answer each question, using the cue provided. The speaker will verify your response. Repeat the correct answer.

1. ¿Qué tiene Ud. en los bolsillos? (la billetera y un peine)

2. ¿Cuánto dinero tiene Ud. en la cartera? (45 dólares)

3. ¿Se quita Ud. las gafas antes de bañarse? (sí)

4. ¿Tiene todas sus pertenencias con Ud.? (no)

5. ¿Qué lleva Ud. puesto en este momento? (una chaqueta de pana)

6. ¿Necesita Ud. cambiarse de ropa ahora? (no)

7. ¿Qué joya tiene Ud. puesta? (una cadena de oro)

8. ¿Usa Ud. anteojos? (no)

9. ¿Dónde tiene Ud. su libreta de direcciones? (en el bolsillo)

10. ¿De qué calibre es su pistola? (calibre 32)

11. ¿Qué tiene Ud. en el maletero de su carro? (un gato)

12. ¿Ud. necesita hacer arreglar su carro? (sí)

13. ¿Tiene muchos desperfectos su carro? (no)

14. ¿Qué tiene que conseguir Ud. para registrar un carro? (un permiso del juez)

15. Si Ud. viera un grupo de personas gritando obscenidades, ¿qué les ordenaría que hicieran las personas? (dispersarse inmediatamente)

16. ¿Cuándo fue la última vez que Ud. retrató a alguien? (ayer)

17. ¿Le está a Ud. permitido recomendar fiancistas? (no)

18. ¿Dónde vivía Ud. cuando era adolescente? (en California)

19. Cuando Ud. era adolescente, ¿se escapó alguna vez de su casa? (no, nunca)

20. Si Ud. viera a un compañero de clase de la escuela, ¿podría reconocerlo? (sí)

21. ¿Le han tomado a Ud. las huellas digitales? (sí)

22. ¿Le han hecho a Ud. alguna prueba este año? (no)

23. ¿Prefiere Ud. defenderse con un cuchillo o con una pistola? (con una pistola)

24. ¿Tiene Ud. una fotografía reciente de sus padres? (no)

25. ¿Tiene Ud. alguna marca visible? (sí, un lunar en la mejilla)

Appendix A

Introduction to Spanish Sounds and the Alphabet

Sections marked with a cassette icon are recorded on the *Introduction to Spanish Sounds* section of the Cassette Program. Repeat each Spanish word after the speaker, imitating the pronunciation as closely as you can.

The Vowels

1. The Spanish **a** has a sound similar to the English *a* in the word *father*. Repeat:

    Ana   casa   banana   mala   dama   mata

2. The Spanish **e** is pronounced like the English *e* in the word *eight*. Repeat:

    este   René   teme   deme   entre   bebe

3. The Spanish **i** is pronounced like the English *ee* in the word *see*. Repeat:

    sí   difícil   Mimí   ir   dividir   Fifí

4. The Spanish **o** is similar to the English *o* in the word *no*, but without the glide. Repeat:

    solo   poco   como   toco   con   monólogo

5. The Spanish **u** is similar to the English *ue* sound in the word *Sue*. Repeat:

    Lulú   un   su   universo   murciélago

The Consonants

1. The Spanish **p** is pronounced like the English *p* in the word *spot*. Repeat:

    pan   papá   Pepe   pila   poco   pude

2. The Spanish **c** in front of **a, o, u, l,** or **r** sounds similar to the English *k*. Repeat:

    casa   como   cuna   clima   crimen   cromo

3. The Spanish **q** is only used in the combinations **que** and **qui** in which the **u** is silent, and also has a sound similar to the English *k*. Repeat:

    que   queso   Quique   quinto   quema   quiso

4. The Spanish **t** is pronounced like the English *t* in the word *stop*. Repeat:

    toma   mata   tela   tipo   atún   Tito

5. The Spanish **d** at the beginning of an utterance or after **n** or **l** sounds somewhat similar to the English *d* in the word *David*. Repeat:

    día   dedo   duelo   anda   Aldo

    In all other positions, the **d** has a sound similar to the English *th* in the word *they*. Repeat:

    medida   todo   nada   Ana dice   Eva duda

6. The Spanish **g** also has two sounds. At the beginning of an utterance and in all other positions, except before **e** or **i**, the Spanish **g** sounds similar to the English *g* in the word *sugar*. Repeat:

   goma   gato   tengo   lago   algo   aguja

   In the combinations **gue** and **gui**, the **u** is silent. Repeat:

   Águeda   guineo   guiso   ligue   la guía

7. The Spanish **j**, and **g** before **e** or **i**, sounds similar to the English *h* in the word *home*. Repeat:

   jamás   juego   jota   Julio   gente   Genaro   gime

8. The Spanish **b** and the **v** have no difference in sound. Both are pronounced alike. At the beginning of the utterance or after **m** or **n**, they sound similar to the English *b* in the word *obey*. Repeat:

   Beto   vaga   bote   vela   también   un vaso

   Between vowels, they are pronounced with the lips barely closed. Repeat:

   sábado   yo voy   sabe   Ávalos   Eso vale

9. In most Spanish-speaking countries, the **y** and the **ll** are similar to the English *y* in the word *yet*. Repeat:

   yo   llama   yema   lleno   ya   lluvia   llega

10. The Spanish **r (ere)** is pronounced like the English *tt* in the word *gutter*. Repeat:

    cara   pero   arena   carie   Laredo   Aruba

    The Spanish **r** in an initial position and after **l**, **n**, or **s**, and **rr (erre)** in the middle of a word are pronounced with a strong trill. Repeat:

    Rita   Rosa   torre   ruina   Enrique   Israel
    perro   parra   rubio   alrededor   derrama

11. The Spanish **s** sound is represented in most of the Spanish-speaking world by the letters **s**, **z**, and **c** before **e** or **i**. The sound is very similar to the English sibilant *s* in the word *sink*. Repeat:

    sale   sitio   solo   seda   suelo
    zapato cerveza ciudad cena

    In most of Spain, the **z**, and **c** before **e** or **i**, is pronounced like the English *th* in the word *think*. Repeat:

    zarzuela   cielo   docena

12. The letter **h** is silent in Spanish. Repeat:

    hilo   Hugo   ahora   Hilda   almohada   hermano

13. The Spanish **ch** is pronounced like the English *ch* in the word *chief*. Repeat:

    muchacho   chico   coche   chueco   chaparro

14. The Spanish **f** is identical in sound to the English *f*. Repeat:

    famoso   feo   difícil   fuego   foto

15. The Spanish **l** is pronounced like the English *l* in the word *lean*. Repeat:

    dolor   ángel   fácil   sueldo   salgo   chaval

16. The Spanish **m** is pronounced like the English *m* in the word *mother*. Repeat:

    mamá   moda   multa   médico   mima

17. In most cases, the Spanish **n** has a sound similar to the English *n*. Repeat:

    nada   norte   nunca   entra   nene

The sound of the Spanish **n** is often affected by the sounds that occur around it. When it appears before **b, v,** or **p,** it is pronounced like the English *m*. Repeat:

    invierno   tan bueno   un vaso   un bebé   un perro

18. The Spanish **ñ (eñe)** has a sound similar to the English *ny* in the word *canyon*. Repeat:

    muñeca   leña   año   señorita   piña   señor

19. The Spanish **x** has two pronunciations, depending on its position. Between vowels, the sound is similar to the English *ks*. Repeat:

    examen   boxeo   éxito   exigente

Before a consonant, the Spanish **x** sounds like the English *s*. Repeat:

    expreso   excusa   extraño   exquisito

Linking

In spoken Spanish, the various words in a phrase or sentence are not pronounced as isolated elements, but are combined. This is called *linking*.

1. The final consonant of a word is pronounced together with the initial vowel of the following word. Repeat:

    Carlos anda   un ángel   el otoño   unos estudiantes

2. The final vowel of a word is pronounced together with the initial vowel of the following word. Repeat:

    su esposo   la hermana   ardua empresa   la invita

3. When the final vowel of a word and the initial vowel of the following word are identical, they are pronounced slightly longer than one vowel. Repeat:

    Ana alcanza   me espera   mi hijo   lo olvida

The same rule applies when two identical vowels appear within a word. Repeat:

    cooperación   crees   leemos   coordinación

4. When the final consonant of a word and the initial consonant of the following word are the same, they are pronounced as one consonant with slightly longer-than-normal duration. Repeat:

    el lado   un novio   Carlos salta   tienes sed   al leer

Rhythm

Rhythm is the variation of sound intensity that we usually associate with music. Spanish and English each regulate these variations in speech differently, because they have different patterns of syllable length. In Spanish the length of the stressed and unstressed syllables remains almost the same, while in English stressed syllables are considerably longer than unstressed ones. Pronounce the following Spanish words, enunciating each syllable clearly.

es-tu-dian-te	bue-no	Úr-su-la
com-po-si-ción	di-fí-cil	ki-ló-me-tro
po-li-cí-a	Pa-ra-guay	

Because the length of the Spanish syllables remains constant, the greater the number of syllables in a given word or phrase, the longer the phrase will be.

Intonation

Intonation is the rise and fall of pitch in the delivery of a phrase or a sentence. In general, Spanish pitch tends to change less than English, giving the impression that the language is less emphatic.

As a rule, the intonation for normal statements in Spanish starts in a low tone, raises to a higher one on the first stressed syllable, maintains that tone until the last stressed syllable, and then goes back to the initial low tone, with still another drop at the very end.

Tu amigo viene mañana.	José come pan.
Ada está en casa.	Carlos toma café.

Syllable Formation in Spanish

General rules for dividing words into syllables are as follows.

Vowels

1. A vowel or a vowel combination can constitute a syllable.

    a-lum-no   a-bue-la   Eu-ro-pa

2. Diphthongs and triphthongs are considered single vowels and cannot be divided.

    bai-le   puen-te   Dia-na   es-tu-diáis   an-ti-guo

3. Two strong vowels (**a, e, o**) do not form a diphthong and are separated into two syllables.

    em-ple-ar   vol-te-ar   lo-a

4. A written accent on a weak vowel (**i** or **u**) breaks the diphthong, thus the vowels are separated into two syllables.

    trí-o   dú-o   Ma-rí-a

Consonants

1. A single consonant forms a syllable with the vowel that follows it.

    po-der   ma-no   mi-nu-to

    NOTE: **ch, ll,** and **rr** are considered single consonants: **co-che, a-ma-ri-llo, pe-rro.**

2. When two consonants appear between two vowels, they are separated into two syllables.

   al-fa-be-to   cam-pe-ón   me-ter-se   mo-les-tia

   EXCEPTION: When a consonant cluster composed of **b, c, d, f, g, p,** or **t** with **l** or **r** appears between two vowels, the cluster joins the following vowel: **so-bre, o-tros, ca-ble, te-lé-gra-fo.**

3. When three consonants appear between two vowels, only the last one goes with the following vowel.

   ins-pec-tor   trans-por-te   trans-for-mar

   EXCEPTION: When there is a cluster of three consonants in the combinations described in rule 2, the first consonant joins the preceding vowel and the cluster joins the following vowel: **es-cri-bir, ex-tran-je-ro, im-plo-rar, es-tre-cho.**

Accentuation

In Spanish, all words are stressed according to specific rules. Words that do not follow the rules must have a written accent to indicate the change of stress. The basic rules for accentuation are as follows.

1. Words ending in a vowel, **n,** or **s** are stressed on the next-to-the-last syllable.

   hi-jo   **ca**-lle   **me**-sa   fa-**mo**-sos
   flo-**re**-cen   **pla**-ya   **ve**-ces

2. Words ending in a consonant, except **n** or **s,** are stressed on the last syllable.

   ma-**yor**   a-**mor**   tro-pi-**cal**   na-**riz**   re-**loj**   co-rre-**dor**

3. All words that do not follow these rules must have the written accent.

   ca-**fé**   **lá**-piz   **mú**-si-ca   sa-**lón**
   án-gel   **lí**-qui-do   fran-**cés**   **Víc**-tor
   sim-**pá**-ti-co   rin-**cón**   a-**zú**-car   **dár**-se-lo
   sa-**lió**   **dé**-bil   **mé**-di-co   **dí**-me-lo

4. Pronouns and adverbs of interrogation and exclamation have a written accent to distinguish them from relative pronouns.

   —¿**Qué** comes?   *"What are you eating?"*
   —La pera que él dejó.   *"The pear that he left."*

   —¿**Quién** está ahí?   *"Who is there?"*
   —El hombre a quien tú llamaste.   *"The man whom you called."*

   —¿**Dónde** está?   *"Where is he?"*
   —En el lugar donde trabaja.   *"At the place where he works."*

5. Words that have the same spelling but different meanings take a written accent to differentiate one from the other.

el	*the*	él	*he, him*	te	*you*	té	*tea*
mi	*my*	mí	*me*	si	*if*	sí	*yes*
tu	*your*	tú	*you*	mas	*but*	más	*more*

The Alphabet

Letter	Name	Letter	Name	Letter	Name	Letter	Name
a	a	h	hache	ñ	eñe	t	te
b	be	i	i	o	o	u	u
c	ce	j	jota	p	pe	v	ve (uve)
ch	che	k	ka	q	cu	w	doble ve (uve)
d	de	l	ele	r	ere	x	equis
e	e	ll	elle	rr	erre	y	y griega
f	efe	m	eme	s	ese	z	zeta
g	ge	n	ene				

Appendix B

English Translations of Dialogues

Lección preliminar

Brief conversations

A. "Tenth Police Station, good morning. What can I do for you?"
"Good morning. Officer Donoso, please."
"One moment, please."

B. "Good afternoon, ma'am."
"Good afternoon, miss. Come in and take a seat. How are you today?"
"Fine, thank you."
"What can I do for you?"

C. "Good night, sir, and thank you very much for the information."
"You're welcome. At your service. Good-bye."

D. "Hi, Mario. What's new?"
"Nothing, sir."
"Okay, see you later."
"So long."

E. "Name and surname?"
"Roberto Santacruz."
"Address?"
"Number 30 Magnolia Avenue."
"Telephone number?"
"432–0568."

Lección 1

In a police station

Mr. Pérez telephones to report an accident.

MR. PÉREZ:	I don't speak English, but I want to report an accident.
DISPATCHER:	Where? I speak a little Spanish.
MR. PÉREZ:	Here, in front of my house, on Central Street, between Florida and Terracina.
DISPATCHER:	Slowly, please.
MR. PÉREZ:	Central Street, between Florida and Terracina. (*He spells.*) T-e-r-r-a-c-i-n-a.
DISPATCHER:	Very good, thanks. Are there any people injured?
MR. PÉREZ:	Yes, there are two hurt badly: a woman and a girl.
DISPATCHER:	OK. Now I need your personal information. Who's speaking? I need your first and last name, please.
MR. PÉREZ:	José Antonio Pérez.
DISPATCHER:	Address?
MR. PÉREZ:	546 Central Street, apartment 7.
DISPATCHER:	Telephone number?

MR. PÉREZ:	762–5430.
DISPATCHER:	I'll send the paramedics and a patrol car over there right away. Thank you very much for your information.
MR. PÉREZ:	You're welcome.

Mrs. Vera reports a robbery in person.

MRS. VERA:	I don't speak English, but I need help. I wish to speak with a police officer.
DISPATCHER:	Do you speak Spanish? One moment.
OFFICER LÓPEZ:	Good morning, ma'am. What can I do for you?
MRS. VERA:	I want to report a robbery.
OFFICER LÓPEZ:	One moment. You need to speak with Sergeant Viñas of the Robbery Division, but first you need to fill out a (robbery) report.

Mrs. Vera fills out the report.

Lección 2

With a Hispanic officer, on a city street

A lady asks for information.

LADY:	You speak Spanish, right?
OFFICER:	Yes, ma'am. How can I help you?
LADY:	Please, where is Bank of America?
OFFICER:	On Magnolia Street, between Roma and Paris Avenues.
LADY:	How do I get there?
OFFICER:	You should go straight until you reach Magnolia Street. There, you turn left.
LADY:	How many blocks should I go on Magnolia?
OFFICER:	About five or six blocks.
LADY:	Thank you very much for your information.
OFFICER:	At your service, ma'am.

The officer speaks with a boy on a bike.

OFFICER:	Wait a minute, please. Why aren't you wearing your bike helmet?
BOY:	The helmet is very uncomfortable, sir.
OFFICER:	In this state, the law requires the use of a helmet and, besides, helmets save lives. Where do you live?
BOY:	A block from here, on Madison Street.
OFFICER:	Good, you must return home on foot and look for your helmet.
BOY:	And the bike?
OFFICER:	You'll have to walk the bike (by hand).

The officer speaks with a child.

OFFICER:	Little girl, why are you by yourself?
CHILD:	I'm grown-up (big) now.
OFFICER:	No, you're still very small to be walking alone on the street.
CHILD:	It's not very late . . .
OFFICER:	Yes, it's late. Where do you live?

| CHILD: | I live at 267 California Street, apartment 18. |
| OFFICER: | OK, let's go. I need to speak with your mom. |

Later:

MOTHER:	Oh, goodness gracious! What's going on? What's wrong with my little girl?
OFFICER:	Nothing, ma'am, but the child is very small to be walking alone on the street.
MOTHER:	Of course, but she doesn't pay attention to me.

Lección 3

With Officer Smith

Officer Smith is speaking with two members of a gang.

OFFICER SMITH:	(*To one of them*) What are you doing in the street at this hour?
JOSÉ:	Nothing. Why?
OFFICER SMITH:	Because there is a curfew for minors and you must be at your home before midnight.
MARIO:	We are always on this corner with our friends.
OFFICER SMITH:	Let's go to the police station. I am going to call your parents.

The boys protest, but they get into the patrol car without a problem.

Officer Smith speaks with a man who is in the yard of a vacant house.

OFFICER SMITH:	Good day, sir. Why are you in the yard of a vacant house?
MAN:	I'm the gardener.
OFFICER SMITH:	Your identification, please.
MAN:	My green card, is it okay?
OFFICER SMITH:	I need an ID with your photograph.
MAN:	Okay, here's my driver's license.
OFFICER SMITH:	Very well, thank you very much for your cooperation.
MAN:	Any time, officer.

Officer Smith arrests a thief.

| OFFICER SMITH: | Police! Stop! Stop or I'll shoot! Freeze! |

Lección 4

Telephone reports of crimes

The dispatcher at the Fourth Police Station receives an emergency call.

DISPATCHER:	Police Department, good evening.
LADY:	Please! I need help urgently!
DISPATCHER:	What's going on, ma'am?
LADY:	There's a strange man in my yard and I'm alone with my children.
DISPATCHER:	OK. What is your address?

LADY:	709 3rd Avenue, between 11th and 13th Streets. Two blocks from the hospital.
DISPATCHER:	I'll send a patrol car immediately. If the man tries to get in, you should turn on the light.
LADY:	You have to come quick! My husband has a revolver in the house . . .
DISPATCHER:	Are you trained in the use of firearms?
LADY:	No, ma'am.
DISPATCHER:	Then using the revolver is more dangerous for you than for him. What does the man look like? Is he tall or short?
LADY:	He's tall and I believe he's white.
DISPATCHER:	How is he dressed?
LADY:	In dark clothing. His pants are blue or black and his shirt is blue . . . not as dark as his pants.
DISPATCHER:	Is he wearing a hat?
LADY:	A cap.

The dispatcher receives another call.

GENTLEMAN:	I'm calling to let you know that there is a man and a woman in my neighbors' house, and they are on vacation and are not coming home until next week.
DISPATCHER:	The man and the woman, are they inside or outside of the house?
GENTLEMAN:	Inside. The house is dark, but they have a flashlight.
OFFICER:	What do they look like?
GENTLEMAN:	The man is of medium height and the girl is a little bit shorter than he.
OFFICER:	Are they young?
GENTLEMAN:	Yes, but she seems much younger than he. She must be younger than 20 years old.
OFFICER:	Very well. Now I need the address of your neighbor's house.

Lección 5

The Dispatcher Answers the Phone

Tonight the dispatcher of the Fourth Police Station in Los Angeles answers several phone calls.

At seven-thirty:

DISPATCHER:	Fourth Police Station, good evening.
MRS. VALLES ROJAS:	Good evening. I am Isabel Valles Rojas. My husband and I are going to go on vacation, and I want to inform the police.
DISPATCHER:	Very well. What is your complete address and your phone number, ma'am?
MRS. VALLES ROJAS:	596 Fairfax, Los Angeles. My phone number is 232–0649.
DISPATCHER:	How long are you planning to be on vacation?
MRS. VALLES ROJAS:	Two weeks. We're going to be back on January 1.
DISPATCHER:	Are you going to leave a light on?
MRS. VALLES ROJAS:	Yes, we are going to leave the kitchen light on.

DISPATCHER:	Does anybody have the key to your house?
MRS. VALLES ROJAS:	Yes, my neighbor. She lives across the street from our house: 591 Fairfax.
DISPATCHER:	Very well. Is she going to pick up your mail?
MRS. VALLES ROJAS:	No, it's not necessary. We are going to stop the delivery of the mail and newspaper.
DISPATCHER:	Is someone going to mow your lawn?
MRS. VALLES ROJAS:	Yes, and we have an automatic sprinkling system.
DISPATCHER:	Very well, ma'am. Thank you for calling. I am going to communicate this information to the patrol in your district.
MRS. VALLES ROJAS:	Thank you.

At a quarter to eight:

CHILD:	Help! There's a fire in my house, and my mom and dad aren't home . . .
DISPATCHER:	Are you inside the house now?
CHILD:	Yes. I'm scared . . . There's a lot of smoke . . .
DISPATCHER:	You have to get out of the house immediately. You should go to a neighbor's house. Quickly! I am going to call the firefighters.

Lección 6

Officer Chávez reads the Miranda warning

The officer stops two young men who are writing on the wall of a building.

OFFICER CHÁVEZ:	Police! Halt! Don't move! You are under arrest!
YOUNG MAN 1:	Why? We're not doing anything wrong (bad).
OFFICER CHÁVEZ:	You're committing a crime of vandalism. You cannot write on the wall of a building. (*The officer takes a card from his pocket and reads the Miranda warning.*)

MIRANDA WARNING
1. You have the right to remain silent.
2. Anything you say can and will be used against you in a court of law.
3. You have the right to talk to a lawyer and have him present with you during the interrogation.
4. If you cannot afford to hire a lawyer, one will be appointed to represent you before they question you, if you wish.

OFFICER CHÁVEZ:	Do you understand each one of these rights?
YOUNG MEN:	Yes.

| YOUNG MAN 2: | Are you going to arrest us? You're wasting your time on me. I'm under 15 years old; in a few hours I'll be home again. |
| OFFICER CHÁVEZ: | Now you're going to the police station with me. I don't decide the rest. |

Hours later, the officer stops a driver who is committing a traffic violation. When he speaks with him, he notices that the man is drugged.

| OFFICER CHÁVEZ: | Good morning. Your driver's license and car registration, please. |
| DRIVER: | Are you going to give me a ticket (*fine*)? Why? I'm not drunk. Besides, I drive better than ever when I have a couple of drinks. |

The officer notices needle marks on the man's arm and hand. The marks are fresh.

OFFICER CHÁVEZ:	Let me see your arm. Do you have diabetes?
DRIVER:	No.
OFFICER CHÁVEZ:	Do you give blood often?
DRIVER:	Yes, I give blood sometimes.
OFFICER CHÁVEZ:	Where is the blood bank?
DRIVER:	On . . . I don't remember now.
OFFICER CHÁVEZ:	Look here, please. You must try not to blink.
DRIVER:	I can't stop blinking. I'm very sleepy . . .
OFFICER CHÁVEZ:	I'm sorry, but you have to come with me. You're not in a condition to drive.
DRIVER:	Am I under arrest? What's my crime?
OFFICER CHÁVEZ:	Driving under the influence of some drug. (*The officer reads the Miranda warning.*)

Lección 7
Problems of the city

In the morning: Officer Flores speaks with the owner of a liquor store after a burglary.

OFFICER FLORES:	You're saying the burglars are very young? Can you describe them?
OWNER:	Yes. The man is blond, with blue eyes, and the woman is red-haired, with green eyes.
OFFICER FLORES:	What else do you remember?
OWNER:	The man is (measures) about six feet, and she is about five feet, two inches. He's thin. She is rather fat . . .
OFFICER FLORES:	Any visible marks?
OWNER:	He has a tatoo on his left arm. She has freckles.
OFFICER FLORES:	You don't know them, right? They're not customers . . .
OWNER:	No, but I know that I can recognize them if I see them again.
OFFICER FLORES:	What kind of car are they driving?
OWNER:	A two-door yellow Chevrolet. It's an old car.
OFFICER FLORES:	Anything else?
OWNER:	Yes, I think so. He smokes black cigarettes . . . from Mexico . . . and he's left-handed!

| OFFICER FLORES: | If you remember anything else, can you call me at this number? |
| OWNER: | Certainly, sir. |

In the afternoon: Officer Flores sees a man who is standing in front of a school. He suspects that the man has drugs to sell, because there are many students who take drugs.

OFFICER FLORES:	What are you doing here? Are you waiting for someone?
MAN:	No, . . . I'm not doing anything . . .
OFFICER FLORES:	Do you have any identification? Your driver's license, for example?
MAN:	No, not here. I have it at home . . .
OFFICER FLORES:	Do you want to come with me to the car, please? I want to speak to you.

In the evening: Officer Flores leaves the police station to go home. In the parking lot, he sees a man on the ground. He runs toward him.

OFFICER FLORES:	What's wrong? Are you hurt?
MAN:	No, . . . I think . . . a heart attack . . .
OFFICER FLORES:	Do you have any heart medicine?
MAN:	Yes, . . . in the glove compartment of the car . . .
OFFICER FLORES:	(*He brings the medicine.*) Here it is. Now I'm going to call the paramedics.

Lección 8

Cases of abuse of family members

Julia, a young girl, calls the police because her stepfather is hitting her mother. Officer Vera goes to the Aguirre home to investigate the report.

OFFICER VERA:	Good afternoon. Is this the house of the Aguirre family?
JULIA:	Yes. Come in, please. My mom and my stepfather are in their bedroom with the door locked (locked up in their bedroom).
OFFICER VERA:	What's the problem?
JULIA:	My stepfather doesn't have a job now and, instead of looking for other work, he goes to the bar and comes home drunk every day.
OFFICER VERA:	How does he get the money for liquor (drinking)?
JULIA:	He asks my mom for it, and if she doesn't give it to him, he hits her, and takes it from her by force.
OFFICER VERA:	Does he hit her with his fist (hand)?
JULIA:	With his fist and with his belt. Sometimes he tells her that he is going to kill her.
OFFICER VERA:	Does he have any weapons?
JULIA:	Yes, he has a switchblade and a pistol.
OFFICER VERA:	(*He knocks on the door of the bedroom.*) Mr. Aguirre, I'm a police officer and I need to speak with you. Will you come out for a moment, please?
MR. AGUIRRE:	(*From inside*) This is my house. Do you have a warrant? I don't have anything to talk to you about.

MRS. AGUIRRE:	(*Coming out of the bedroom*) He's mad at me because he wants me to give him money for drinks.
MR. AGUIRRE:	(*Coming out also*) That is a matter between my wife and me, and you don't have any reason to butt in.
OFFICER VERA:	Mrs. Aguirre, you're quite injured. You should see a doctor right away. Are you willing to accuse your husband of abuse?
MR. AGUIRRE:	No. She does what I tell her. If you want to know something, you ask me.
MRS. AGUIRRE:	(*She pays no attention to her husband and answers the police officer.*) Yes, officer.
MR. AGUIRRE:	(*To his wife*) You shouldn't do this to me. You know that I treat you well when I am not drunk. Forgive me (I ask you for forgiveness).
MRS. AGUIRRE:	No. This time I won't forgive you. I'm tired of your abuses.

Dr. Andrade notifies the police of his suspicions that the child, Carlos Jiménez, is being abused. Officer Rodríguez, in charge of the case, talks with his parents.

OFFICER RODRÍGUEZ:	Good morning. Are you the father of the child Carlos Jiménez?
MR. JIMÉNEZ:	Yes, I am. What can I do for you?
OFFICER RODRÍGUEZ:	I'm Officer Rodríguez, from the local police. This is my ID.
MR. JIMÉNEZ:	Come in and sit down. How can I help you?
OFFICER RODRÍGUEZ:	Your son has been in (is admitted to) the hospital since yesterday. This is the third time that the boy has been admitted to the hospital with more or less serious injuries, and the doctor suspects that someone is abusing him frequently.
MR. JIMÉNEZ:	What? Who says that? That's a lie. Besides, no one has the authority to tell us how we should discipline our children.
OFFICER RODRÍGUEZ:	You're wrong, Mr. Jiménez. In this country certain forms of child discipline are not accepted.

Lección 9

The Sobriety Test

It's 3:00 in the morning. Officer López stops a man for driving 50 miles per hour, with the lights off, in a residential zone. The speed limit is 35 miles per hour. The man seems to be drunk.

OFFICER LÓPEZ:	Pull over to the curb and turn off the engine, please.
MAN:	What's wrong, officer?
OFFICER LÓPEZ:	The speed limit in this area is thirty-five miles per hour, not fifty.
MAN:	It's just that I'm in a hurry.
OFFICER LÓPEZ:	Let me see your driver's license, please.
MAN:	It's at home . . .
OFFICER LÓPEZ:	Show me your car registration.
MAN:	I don't have it. The car is not mine. It's my uncle's.

OFFICER LÓPEZ:	What's your name?
MAN:	My name is Juan Lara.
OFFICER LÓPEZ:	Your address and your age, please.
MR. LARA:	I live at 520 Fifth Street. I'm thirty years old.
OFFICER LÓPEZ:	Step out of the car, please.
MR. LARA:	I'm telling you, I'm in a big hurry!
OFFICER LÓPEZ:	Stretch your arms, like this. Close your eyes and touch the end of your nose.
MR. LARA:	I can't . . . but I'm not drunk . . .
OFFICER LÓPEZ:	Walk on that line to the end and come back on the same line.
MR. LARA:	I don't see the line well.
OFFICER LÓPEZ:	(*Puts a coin on the ground*) Pick that coin up from the ground.
MR. LARA:	I can't get hold of it.
OFFICER LÓPEZ:	Count on your fingers, like this: one, two, three, four . . . four, three, two, one.
MR. LARA:	One, two, three, four, three . . . I'm going to start over . . .
OFFICER LÓPEZ:	Recite the alphabet, please.
MR. LARA:	A, B, C, D . . . F, J . . . N . . .
OFFICER LÓPEZ:	I'm going to read you something, Mr. Lara. Pay attention.

"You are required by state law to submit to a chemical test to determine the alcohol content of your blood. You have a choice of whether the test is to be of your blood, urine, or breath. If you refuse to submit to a test or fail to complete a test, your driving privilege will be suspended for a period of six months. You do not have the right to talk to an attorney or to have an attorney present before stating whether you will submit to a test, before deciding which test to take, or during the administration of the test chosen. If you are incapable, or state you are incapable, of completing the test you choose, you must submit to and complete any of the remaining tests."

Lección 10

The police investigate a robbery

This morning Mrs. Ramos called the police to report a robbery. An hour later Sergeant Nieto, from the Robbery Division, arrived at her house.

Sergeant Nieto speaks with Mrs. Ramos:

SERGEANT NIETO:	Good morning, ma'am. I'm Sergeant Nieto, of the Robbery Division. Here is my ID.
MRS. RAMOS:	Good morning, Sergeant. I called because thieves broke into (entered) my home last night.
SERGEANT NIETO:	What did they steal from you, ma'am?
MRS. RAMOS:	Many things: two TV sets, a video camera, the computer, the compact disc player, some jewelry, and approximately $80.00 in cash.
SERGEANT NIETO:	What brand name is all that equipment?

MRS. RAMOS:	The computer is an IBM, the TV sets are a 19-inch Emerson and a 24-inch RCA. The rest of the equipment is also RCA.
SERGEANT NIETO:	Do you have the serial numbers for all the stolen equipment?
MRS. RAMOS:	I believe so. We bought them on installments, and I have the contracts put away. Just a moment.

Mrs. Ramos leaves and returns with the contracts. Sergeant Nieto looks them over.

SERGEANT NIETO:	The contract for one of the TV sets is missing here.
MRS. RAMOS:	That's right. Now I remember that I threw it away in the trash when I finished paying for it.
SERGEANT NIETO:	And . . . you didn't write down the serial number?
MRS. RAMOS:	No, I didn't write it down. I see now that that was foolish.
SERGEANT NIETO:	Where did the thieves enter?
MRS. RAMOS:	Through the window in my son's room. They forced the lock.
SERGEANT NIETO:	Did you clean the house after the robbery?
MRS. RAMOS:	No, we didn't touch anything.
SERGEANT NIETO:	Good. Later the technicians are going to come to see if they left any fingerprints. You have no idea when the robbery occurred, right?
MRS. RAMOS:	No. Yesterday we went to a fifteenth birthday party in a nearby town, and we stayed there until today.
SERGEANT NIETO:	Did your son go to the party too?
MRS. RAMOS:	Yes, we all went and returned together.
SERGEANT NIETO:	OK, that's all, Mrs. Ramos. Now I'm going to speak with your neighbors to continue the investigation.
MRS. RAMOS:	I talked to the next-door neighbors and they didn't see anyone suspicious prowling around the house.
SERGEANT NIETO:	I gave you my card, didn't I? Call me if you have anything new to tell me.
MRS. RAMOS:	Thank you for your help, Sergeant. And, please, if you discover something, call me.
SERGEANT NIETO:	Of course, ma'am.

Lección 11

More thefts!

Mr. Gómez came to the police station to notify the police about the theft of his car. Now he is speaking with Sergeant Alcalá of the Robbery Division.

SERGEANT ALCALÁ:	When was your car stolen?
MR. GÓMEZ:	Last night.
SERGEANT ALCALÁ:	Where was it parked?
MR. GÓMEZ:	In front of my house.
SERGEANT ALCALÁ:	Was the car locked?
MR. GÓMEZ:	I'm not sure. My son was the last one to drive it and he sometimes doesn't lock it.
SERGEANT ALCALÁ:	Please tell me the make, model, and year of your car.
MR. GÓMEZ:	It's a '93 light blue Ford Festiva.

SERGEANT ALCALÁ:	What is the license plate number of your car?
MR. GÓMEZ:	PED 530.
SERGEANT ALCALÁ:	Is your car insured?
MR. GÓMEZ:	Yes, sir, I have complete coverage.
SERGEANT ALCALÁ:	Is your car completely paid for now, Mr. Gómez?
MR. GÓMEZ:	No, I still owe many payments.
SERGEANT ALCALÁ:	Are you behind in your payments?
MR. GÓMEZ:	The truth is that I'm not up to date. I owe about two months.
SERGEANT ALCALÁ:	Fine. I will deliver copies of the report to the patrol cars.
MR. GÓMEZ:	Let's see if you find it soon . . . Thank you very much, sergeant.
SERGEANT ALCALÁ:	You're welcome, Mr. Gómez.

Mrs. Vega also comes to the police station to notify the police about a robbery. Now she is speaking with Sergeant Rivas.

MRS. VEGA:	I can't believe it! I've lived here for twenty years, and this is the first time there's been a robbery in the neighborhood.
SERGEANT RIVAS:	Did you search the house carefully to find (see) all that is missing?
MRS. VEGA:	Yes. I made a list of what is missing: silverware, a VCR, a tape recorder, a video camera, and a computer.
SERGEANT RIVAS:	Were any weapons taken?
MRS. VEGA:	Oh, yes . . . ! One of my husband's pistols.
SERGEANT RIVAS:	Is that pistol registered?
MRS. VEGA:	I think so, but I'm not sure. You'll have to ask my husband that.
SERGEANT RIVAS:	Write down for me the brand, description, and approximate value of all the stolen items, please.
MRS. VEGA:	Okay.
SERGEANT RIVAS:	Do all of the stolen items belong to you?
MRS. VEGA:	Yes, sir. They are mine and my husband's.
SERGEANT RIVAS:	We will do everything possible to recover them. (*To Officer Soto*) Take Mrs. Vega home, please.

Lección 12

With an officer of the Traffic Division

With the driver of a car that runs a red light:

OFFICER:	Good afternoon, ma'am.
WOMAN:	Good afternoon, sir. Why are you stopping me?
OFFICER:	Because I have to give you a ticket for going through a red light.
WOMAN:	But I began to cross the intersection when the light was yellow!
OFFICER:	But it was already red before you finished crossing it.
WOMAN:	Well, that's not my fault. The light changed very quickly.
OFFICER:	You should only begin to cross the intersection on a yellow light if you are so close to the stop line that you don't have time to stop.

WOMAN:	But I didn't know that . . . Besides, the car behind me was coming too fast.
OFFICER:	I'm sorry, ma'am, but I have to give you a ticket. Sign here, please.

On the highway with a driver who is changing lanes recklessly:

OFFICER:	Sir, you are changing lanes recklessly. You are going to cause an accident some time (at any moment).
DRIVER:	It's that I'm in a big hurry. I don't want to be late for work.
OFFICER:	That is not a valid excuse. You are endangering your life and that of others.
DRIVER:	Yes, you're right. It's better to arrive late than never.
OFFICER:	Okay. This time I am only going to give you a warning. Here it is. Good day and drive safely.
DRIVER:	Thank you very much, officer.

With a woman who left her baby in a locked car:

WOMAN:	What's happening, officer?
OFFICER:	Open the door, please. Are you the mother of this baby?
WOMAN:	Yes, sir. I only left him alone for a moment.
OFFICER:	That is very dangerous, ma'am. Someone could kidnap the baby.

Lección 13

An accident

There was an accident on the highway. A truck collided with a car and a motorcycle. The man who was driving the car and his two passengers died. Officer Peña, who has just arrived, is trying to help the boy who was riding the motorcycle.

OFFICER PEÑA:	Don't try to get up. Stay still.
BOY:	What happened? I feel dizzy . . .
OFFICER PEÑA:	There was an accident. Where do you hurt?
BOY:	My right leg and my left hand . . .
OFFICER PEÑA:	Let's see . . . I am going to apply a bandage to stop the bleeding.
BOY:	What happened to the girl who was riding (coming) with me?
OFFICER PEÑA:	Her face and her arms were hurt, but it isn't serious . . . luckily both of you were wearing your safety helmets.
BOY:	And . . . my motorcycle?
OFFICER PEÑA:	It's under the truck. Fortunately, both of you jumped off in time.

Officer Peña goes toward the truck and sees that there is a fire in the cab. He runs and puts out the fire with a fire extinguisher. The man who was driving the truck is at the side of the road.

OFFICER PEÑA:	How do you feel?
MAN:	I'm still shaking. I did everything possible to avoid the crash, but I couldn't.
OFFICER PEÑA:	What do you remember about the accident?

MAN:	The driver of the car tried to pass without realizing that a motorcycle was coming in the opposite direction. He tried to swerve, but he lost control of the vehicle, and crashed into my truck.
OFFICER PEÑA:	Look, the ambulance came already. They're going to take you to the hospital, too.
MAN:	But I'm not hurt, and I don't like hospitals . . .
OFFICER PEÑA:	It's just a precaution. They're probably going to take X-rays and the doctor is going to examine you. I need your name and address.
MAN:	Rafael Soto, 517 La Sierra Street.
OFFICER PEÑA:	What is your telephone number?
MAN:	328–9961.

Lección 14

Interrogations

Sergeant Vega has just detained Carlos Guzmán. He has read him the Miranda Warning and is now beginning to interrogate him.

SERGEANT VEGA:	Do you understand the rights that I have read to you?
MR. GUZMÁN:	Yes, sir, but I don't need an attorney because I am innocent.
SERGEANT VEGA:	Do you know what you are accused of? Do you understand the accusation?
MR. GUZMÁN:	Yes, sir. I am accused of a theft that I did not commit.
SERGEANT VEGA:	Well, the computer that you tried to pawn was stolen.
MR. GUZMÁN:	Yes, they have told me that, but I didn't know it.
SERGEANT VEGA:	How did you come into the possession of that computer?
MR. GUZMÁN:	I bought it from a man who offered me a bargain.
SERGEANT VEGA:	You didn't suspect that it had been stolen? Buying stolen property is a felony.
MR. GUZMÁN:	I didn't know that he had stolen it. He told me that he had to sell it urgently because he had been out of work.
SERGEANT VEGA:	Where were you on the night of Saturday, April 20th?
MR. GUZMÁN:	At a bar on Franklin Street.
SERGEANT VEGA:	At what time did you leave?
MR. GUZMÁN:	After 12:00 A.M.
SERGEANT VEGA:	Nevertheless, I have spoken with witnesses who say that they saw you at about 10:00 P.M. in the building where the robbery occurred.
MR. GUZMÁN:	It can't be. The owner of the bar can tell you that I am there every night until very late.
SERGEANT VEGA:	Yes, but an employee told me that that night you had left there before 10:00.
MR. GUZMÁN:	That's a lie. It's someone who wants to get me into trouble (to hurt me).

237

The sergeant arrests the man.

Detective Rubio interrogates Mr. Darío, a man accused of swindling.

DETECTIVE RUBIO:	You sold a pearl necklace to Mrs. Carmen Hernández, right?
MR. DARÍO:	Yes, sir. A week ago.
DETECTIVE RUBIO:	Did you tell her that they were cultured pearls?
MR. DARÍO:	No, sir.
DETECTIVE RUBIO:	But you charged her for the pearls as if (they were) of first quality.
MR. DARÍO:	Well, I also had told her that the necklace had a great sentimental value for me.
DETECTIVE RUBIO:	You did not tell her the truth. I sincerely believe that you deceived her, but the jury is going to decide whether you swindled her or not.

Lección 15

With the undercover police

Isabel Cabrera, an undercover police officer, has been assigned to Special Services. She has enrolled at a high school in a Hispanic neighborhood in order to infiltrate a gang that is distributing drugs at the school. Officer Cabrera is speaking with María, a student whose boyfriend could be a gang member.

OFFICER CABRERA:	You speak Spanish, right?
MARÍA:	Yes, I'm a latina. I learned it at home.
OFFICER CABRERA:	I don't speak English well. Could you help me with my classes?
MARÍA:	Yes, although I am a very bad student. Where are you from, Isabel?
OFFICER CABRERA:	From Texas. We came to Chicago a week ago.
MARÍA:	Do you like Chicago?
OFFICER CABRERA:	Yes, but I don't have any friends here.
MARÍA:	You'll see how soon you'll find friends here.
OFFICER CABRERA:	I hope so. What do people do here to have a good time?
MARÍA:	I don't know, we go to the movies, we have parties . . . You know, you can find anything, if you have money: drinks, pot, rock . . .
OFFICER CABRERA:	I have a hundred dollars that my aunt gave me.
MARÍA:	If you want, my boyfriend will get us a bottle of tequila and I'll introduce you to some of our friends.
OFFICER CABRERA:	I'd like to meet them. What is your boyfriend's name?
MARÍA:	Roberto Álvarez.

Tonight, Officer Rosales, dressed as a prostitute, is responsible for arresting solicitors of prostitution on a street in the city. A man driving a blue car approaches her and greets her.

MAN:	Hello! Do you want to have a good time?
OFFICER ROSALES:	You'll have a better one . . .
MAN:	I hope so. Get in.
OFFICER ROSALES:	Where are you taking me?

MAN:	We're going to a motel. I want to spend the whole night with you.
OFFICER ROSALES:	Well, something more than wanting to is needed.
MAN:	Here's a hundred dollars, and if you do everything I want, I'll give you more.
OFFICER ROSALES:	That's not necessary. This is enough. You're under arrest. (*She begins to read him the Miranda Warning.*)
MAN:	Please, I am a businessman and this would harm me a lot. Look, here is a thousand dollars.
OFFICER ROSALES:	That is an attempt at a bribe. Your situation is getting worse, sir.

Lección 16

In a detention cell

Mr. Bravo has just arrived, handcuffed, at the police station. After logging him in, a policeman takes the necessary precautions before placing him in a detention cell.

POLICEMAN:	I want you to empty your pockets completely and place the contents on the counter.
MR. BRAVO:	I only have my wallet with money, a handkerchief, and a comb.
POLICEMAN:	(*He counts the money in front of the prisoner.*) You have here seventy-one dollars and thirty-four cents. Do you agree?
MR. BRAVO:	Yes, sir. That's it.
POLICEMAN:	Now take off your watch and the chain you're wearing around your neck.
MR. BRAVO:	Please make a note there that the watch and chain are gold.
POLICEMAN:	Okay. All your belongings will be put in a sealed envelope.
MR. BRAVO:	Can you give them to my wife?
POLICEMAN:	Yes, if you authorize it in writing. Now we are going to photograph you and take your fingerprints.
MR. BRAVO:	I want to make a phone call to my wife.
POLICEMAN:	That's fine. You have the right to make one phone call. After we book you, we will give you the opportunity to make a call.
MR. BRAVO:	All right.
POLICEMAN:	Stand over there and look at the camera. Good. Now look toward the right. Good. Now, toward the left. Don't move.
MR. BRAVO:	Is that all?
POLICEMAN:	Yes. Now the technician will take your fingerprints.
TECHNICIAN:	Give me your right hand.
POLICEMAN:	(*After the technician finished taking his fingerprints*) Now take off your belt and take the shoelaces out of your shoes, and give it all to me.
MR. BRAVO:	For that I need you to take off my handcuffs.
POLICEMAN:	First I'm going to lock you in your cell.

With the investigating officer:

MR. BRAVO:	What are you going to do with me now?
INVESTIGATOR:	As soon as they have finished the preliminary investigation, the district attorney will put the case before a judge.
MR. BRAVO:	Will they let me go free on my own recognizance?
INVESTIGATOR:	It's possible. You're not accused of murder.
MR. BRAVO:	But they'll let me go free on bail, right?
INVESTIGATOR:	That the judge will decide, and it depends to a large extent on whether or not you have any previous offenses.
MR. BRAVO:	If they place my bail too high, I won't have enough money to pay it. They'll take me to jail.
INVESTIGATOR:	Your family could post a bond.
MR. BRAVO:	Can you recommend any bail bondsman to me?
INVESTIGATOR:	I'm sorry, but we are not allowed to do that.

Lección 17

A girl runs away from home

Officer Gómez speaks with Mr. and Mrs. Ruiz, the parents of a teenage girl who ran away from home.

OFFICER GÓMEZ:	When was the last time you saw your daughter?
MR. RUIZ:	Last night. She told us that she was going to study with a classmate.
OFFICER GÓMEZ:	When did you realize that she had run away?
MRS. RUIZ:	It was 11:00 P.M. already, and she hadn't returned home. Then we called her friend's house and discovered that she hadn't been there.
OFFICER GÓMEZ:	Your daughter may have been the victim of a kidnapping. Why do you think she ran away from home?
MR. RUIZ:	Her friend told us that she was thinking of running away.
OFFICER GÓMEZ:	How old is she?
MR. RUIZ:	Sixteen.
OFFICER GÓMEZ:	It is necessary that you give me a complete description of your daughter.
MR. RUIZ:	Her name is María Elena Ruiz Portillo. She is short—she's five feet, two inches tall—slim, with black hair and black eyes. She has a mole near her mouth and a scar on her right cheek.
OFFICER GÓMEZ:	What clothes did she have on?
MRS. RUIZ:	She had on a white skirt, red blouse, and a black sweater . . . white sandals, and she had a white purse.
OFFICER GÓMEZ:	Was she wearing any jewelry?
MRS. RUIZ:	Yes, a gold chain with a cross, a silver ring, and some red earrings.
OFFICER GÓMEZ:	I hope you have a recent picture of her.
MR. RUIZ:	Yes, I have one here in my wallet.
OFFICER GÓMEZ:	This must be very difficult for you, but do you have any idea why she ran away? Has she had any problems with you or in school?
MR. RUIZ:	Well, . . . she was going out with a boy . . . and we told her we didn't like him. He was in jail twice.

OFFICER GÓMEZ:	Do you think that your daughter left with him?
MRS. RUIZ:	I think so.
OFFICER GÓMEZ:	How old is he?
MRS. RUIZ:	I don't know exactly. He's two or three years older than she is.
OFFICER GÓMEZ:	Do you know his name and where he lives?
MRS. RUIZ:	His name is José Ramírez. I don't know where he lives but they both attend the same school.
OFFICER GÓMEZ:	Had your daughter run away from home on any other occasion?
MRS. RUIZ:	No, never. I think he took her against her will . . .
OFFICER GÓMEZ:	Do you know whether she had money?
MRS. RUIZ:	Yes, she had about 75 dollars, at least.
OFFICER GÓMEZ:	Do you have any idea where she can be? It is important that you try to remember any detail.
MR. RUIZ:	No, none.
OFFICER GÓMEZ:	Did she have a car?
MRS. RUIZ:	No. We don't want her to drive. She's very young . . .
OFFICER GÓMEZ:	Does she have any ID?
MR. RUIZ:	I think she carries her school ID in her purse . . .
OFFICER GÓMEZ:	Okay. It is necessary that you let me know right away if you remember anything else or if you receive any information.
MRS. RUIZ:	I hope you can find her soon.
OFFICER GÓMEZ:	We are going to do everything possible, ma'am.

Lección 18

A Rape

A sixteen-year-old Hispanic girl calls the police, saying that she has just been raped. The girl asks that they send someone who speaks Spanish, because she does not speak English well. Officer Rocha is with the victim now.

VICTIM:	Help me, please!
OFFICER ROCHA:	Your parents aren't home . . . ?
VICTIM:	No, they won't arrive until tomorrow.
OFFICER ROCHA:	Okay, calm down, and tell me what happened.
VICTIM:	I was in my room, reading, when there was a knock on the door . . . I went to open (it), and a man came in and pushed me . . . And I fell . . . and he hit me . . . (*She cries hysterically.*)
OFFICER ROCHA:	Look, I understand that this is very difficult for you, but to be able to help you and arrest the man that raped you, we need information.
VICTIM:	Yes, I know . . . but first I want to take a bath, take off these clothes . . . I feel dirty!
OFFICER ROCHA:	I'm sorry, but it is better to wait. First, a doctor has to examine you. Besides, a bath can destroy necessary evidence. Did you know the man who attacked you?
VICTIM:	No, no, no. He was a stranger.
OFFICER ROCHA:	Can you recognize him if you see him?
VICTIM:	I don't think I can forget that face.

OFFICER ROCHA:	What race was he?
VICTIM:	He was white . . . Rather short, fat, with brown eyes. He had a beard and a moustache, but he was bald.
OFFICER ROCHA:	You had never seen him before?
VICTIM:	No, I'm sure I had never seen him.
OFFICER ROCHA:	What time was it, more or less?
VICTIM:	It was about 9:30.
OFFICER ROCHA:	Did you change clothes?
VICTIM:	Not yet. I called as soon as he left.
OFFICER ROCHA:	Well, don't change. A doctor should examine you immediately. We have to take you to the hospital. Where are your parents?
VICTIM:	They are at my aunt's house. Her phone number is in that address book.
OFFICER ROCHA:	Now, did the man rape you? I mean, was there penetration?
VICTIM:	Yes. He threatened me with a knife. I was afraid and I didn't resist.
OFFICER ROCHA:	Did he force you to perform any abnormal sexual act during the rape?
VICTIM:	No.
OFFICER ROCHA:	Did he put on a condom?
VICTIM:	No, and that terrifies me. Maybe he has AIDS or a venereal disease.
OFFICER ROCHA:	Try to calm down. They will perform the necessary tests. What else do you remember about him? Did he have any visible marks? A tattoo?
VICTIM:	He had a tattoo on his left arm: a heart with an arrow through it (pierced by an arrow). Also, he wore glasses.
OFFICER ROCHA:	Did he have any accent? Did he say anything to you?
VICTIM:	No, I didn't notice any accent. He only told me that if I screamed, he'd kill me.
OFFICER ROCHA:	Did you try to fight with him . . . to defend yourself?
VICTIM:	No, I was so scared . . .
OFFICER ROCHA:	I understand.

Lección 19

A typical afternoon

An afternoon in the life of Officer Cabañas of the Fourth Police Station in Elizabeth, New Jersey.

2:00 P.M.:

Officer Cabañas is speaking with the father of a minor who has just been arrested.

FATHER:	Good day. Someone informed me that my son was being detained here.
OFFICER CABAÑAS:	What is your son's name?
FATHER:	Enrique Fernández.
OFFICER CABAÑAS:	Yes, sir. He is here.
FATHER:	Why did you bring him in? What is he accused of?

OFFICER CABAÑAS:	Your son is accused of selling drugs to his friends at his school.
FATHER:	It's not possible! That can't be right. I can't believe that my son has done such a thing. Can I speak with him?
OFFICER CABAÑAS:	Yes, sir, but you must wait until they have finished questioning him.

3:15 P.M.:

Officer Cabañas goes to Felipe Núñez's house to speak with him. He speaks with the boy's mother.

OFFICER CABAÑAS:	I need to speak with Felipe Núñez, ma'am. It is urgent.
MRS. NÚÑEZ:	He isn't home, and I don't know what time he is going to return.
OFFICER CABAÑAS:	Well, when he comes back, tell him to call me at this number, please. Tell him I want to ask him some questions.
MRS. NÚÑEZ:	Very well. I'll tell him as soon as I see him.

5:00 P.M.:

Officer Cabañas goes to the apartment of a girl who tried to commit suicide.

OFFICER CABAÑAS:	Where is the girl?
NEIGHBOR:	Over there, in the kitchen. I found her with her head inside the oven.
OFFICER CABAÑAS:	Was there a smell of gas?
NEIGHBOR:	Yes, that's why I called 911 as soon as I arrived. The paramedics are on their way.

They go to the kitchen and the officer speaks with the girl.

OFFICER CABAÑAS:	Can you hear me? How do you feel?
GIRL:	Bad . . . I took . . .
OFFICER CABAÑAS:	What did you take? Poison? What poison did you take . . . ?
GIRL:	No . . . tranquilizers . . . in the bathroom . . . more than ten . . .

6:00 P.M.:

Officer Cabañas stops a woman who is driving her car with its headlights turned off.

OFFICER CABAÑAS:	I stopped you because the headlights of your car are not on.
WOMAN:	Yes, . . . it seems that they are not working . . .
OFFICER CABAÑAS:	Well, you can't drive this car unless you have the lights fixed.
WOMAN:	Okay. Tomorrow, without fail.
OFFICER CABAÑAS:	When the car is ready, take it to this address. There they're going to sign the back of this form to confirm that you had the damage repaired.

Lección 20

Another day, in the morning . . .

A day of work for Officer Montero of the Third Precinct of the City of Albuquerque, New Mexico.

10:30 A.M.:

Officer Montero investigates a robbery at a market. He is talking with the clerk now.

OFFICER MONTERO:	Tell me exactly what happened.
CLERK:	At about 9:30 a man came and said he wanted a bottle of wine . . .
OFFICER MONTERO:	And then what happened?
CLERK:	He pointed at me with a pistol and made me give him all the money (that there was) in the cash register.
OFFICER MONTERO:	Would you be able to recognize him if you saw him again?
CLERK:	I don't know. He had a beard and a moustache . . . If he were to shave, I don't know if I would recognize him.
OFFICER MONTERO:	How tall was he, more or less? Was he about my height?
CLERK:	No, much taller and larger. He was about 6 feet, 2 inches (tall) and weighed about 250 pounds.
OFFICER MONTERO:	How was he dressed?
CLERK:	Let's see if I remember . . . Dark gray pants, blue shirt, and a brown corduroy jacket.
OFFICER MONTERO:	You gave him all the money. What happened then?
CLERK:	I tried to follow him, but he pointed at me with the pistol and told me to stay where I was.
OFFICER MONTERO:	Can you describe the pistol?
CLERK:	A semiautomatic, thirty-two caliber, possibly.

11:30 A.M.:

Officer Montero suspects that there are drugs in the trunk of a car. He's talking with the owner now.

OFFICER MONTERO:	I don't have a warrant from the judge to search your car, but I would like to see what you have in the trunk. Will you give me (do you want to give me) the key?
WOMAN:	There's a jack and a tire in the trunk . . .
OFFICER MONTERO:	Do you give me permission to search it? I'm not threatening you, nor am I promising you anything. If you give me permission, it has to be voluntary.
WOMAN:	Get a warrant from the judge if you want to search my car.

2:30 P.M.:

Officer Montero arrests a man who attacked a woman and tried to steal her wallet.

OFFICER MONTERO:	Put your hands on top of your head and clasp them together (intertwine your fingers). Turn around.
MAN:	Son of a bitch!
OFFICER MONTERO:	Be quiet! Walk toward the police car. Get in. Watch out for your head! . . .

4:30 P.M.:

Officer Montero sees a group of people who are shouting obscenities and threats in front of a consulate, and he orders them to disperse.

OFFICER MONTERO:	I'm Officer Montero of the Albuquerque Police Department. This assembly is hereby declared illegal, and therefore I order you to disperse immediately.

Appendix C

Weights and Measures

Length

la pulgada = inch
el pie = foot
la yarda = yard
la milla = mile
1 pulgada = 2.54 centímetros
1 pie = 30.48 centímetros
1 yarda = 0.9144 metro
1 milla = 1.609 kilómetros
1 centímetro (cm) = .3937 pulgadas (less than $^1/_2$ inch)
1 metro (m) = 39.37 pulgadas (1 yard, 3 inches)
1 kilómetro (km) (1.000 metros) = .6214 millas ($^5/_8$ mile)

Weight

la onza = ounce
la libra = pound
la tonelada = ton
1 onza = 28.35 gramos
1 libra = 0.454 kilogramo
1 tonelada = 0.907 tonelada métrica
1 gramo (g) = .03527 onzas
100 gramos = 3.527 onzas (less than $^1/_4$ pound)
1 kilogramo (kg) (1.000 gramos) = 2.2 libras

Liquid Measure

la pinta = pint
el cuarto (de galón) = quart
el galón = gallon
1 pinta = 0.473 litro
1 cuarto = 0.946 litro
1 galón = 3.785 litros
1 litro (l) = 1.0567 cuartos (de galón) (slightly more than a quart)

Surface Area

el acre = acre
1 hectárea = 2.471 acres

Temperature

°C = Celsius or Centigrade; °F = Fahrenheit
0° C = 32° F (freezing point of water)
37° C = 98.6° F (normal body temperature)
100° C = 212° F (boiling point of water)
Conversión de grados Fahrenheit a grados Centígrados
$°C = ^5/_9 \,(°F - 32)$
Conversión de grados Centígrados a grados Fahrenheit
$°F = ^9/_5 \,(°C) + 32$

Appendix D

Answer Key to the *Crucigramas*

Lecciones 1–5

Horizontal: 2. pequeño   6. fuego   7. español   10. división   11. automático   12. telefonista
14. paramédicos   15. humo   16. estados   18. mujer   19. suceder   21. pistola   22. tarde   24. avisar
26. cooperación   29. tarjeta   31. encendido   33. disparar   34. bajo   35. dentro
Vertical: 1. correspondencia   3. quiero   4. domicilio   5. poco   8. camina   9. doblar   13. izquierda
14. patrullero   17. medianoche   20. desocupada   23. ladrón   25. sin   27. camisa   28. socorro
30. césped   32. joven

Lecciones 6–10

Horizontal: 4. lugar   5. perdonar   8. mañana   9. padrastro   11. bastante   13. arma   14. cinturón
18. automóvil   19. parezco   20. licorería   22. sin   23. zurdo   24. caso   25. velocidad   26. agarra
Vertical: 1. quitar   2. frecuentemente   3. delgada   6. nariz   7. cantina   10. abecedario   12. equivo-
cada   13. abogado   15. mismo   16. edificio   17. residencial   18. apurado   21. enseñar   24. cuenta

Lecciones 11–15

Horizontal: 1. muchísimo   4. videograbadora   7. cuidado   9. chamaco   13. conductora   14. ocurrir
15. autopista   17. empleado   18. entregaría
Vertical: 2. último   3. válido   5. radiografía   6. vehículos   8. imprudentemente   10. jurado
11. parada   12. descripción   13. carril   16. acusación

Lecciones 16–20

Horizontal: 3. libreta   4. espejuelos   6. desperfecto   8. maletero   9. flecha   14. voluntariamente
16. cartera   19. antecedentes   21. generalmente   22. reloj   23. autorizar   24. libertad
Vertical: 1. veneno   2. cállese   5. chamarra   7. calmante   10. gato   11. botella   12. prueba
13. pesa   15. importante   17. pertenencias   18. investigador   20. registrar

Spanish-English Vocabulary

The Spanish-English and English-Spanish vocabularies contain all active and passive vocabulary that appears in this manual. Active vocabulary includes words and expressions appearing in the *Vocabulario* lists. These items are followed by a number indicating the lesson in which each word is introduced in the dialogues. Passive vocabulary consists of words and expressions included in the *Vocabulario adicional* lists and those that are given an English gloss in the readings, exercises, activities, and authentic documents.

The following abbreviations are used in the vocabularies.

adj.	adjective	*inf.*	infinitive
adv.	adverb	*m.*	masculine noun
coll.	colloquialism	*pl.*	plural
f.	feminine noun	*prep.*	preposition
form.	formal		

A

a to, at, on
— **cargo de** in charge of, 8
— **cuadros** plaid
— **eso de** about (with time), 14
— **esta hora** at this time (hour), 3
— **la derecha** to the right, 2
— **la fuerza** by force, 8
— **la izquierda** to the left, 2
— **la vista de** in the presence of, in front of, 16
— **mediados de mes (semana)** about the middle of the month (week)
— **medianoche** at midnight
— **menos que** unless, 19
— **menudo** often, 6
— **pie** on foot, 2
— **plazos** in installments, on time (payments), 10
— **rayas** pinstriped
— **sus órdenes** at your service, 3; any time, 3
— **tiempo** on time, 1; just in time, 13
— **una cuadra de aquí** a block from here, 2
— **veces** sometimes, 2
— **ver** let's see, 6
abandonar los estudios to drop out of school
abecedario (*m.*) alphabet, 9
abierto(a) open
abogado(a) (*m., f.*) lawyer, 6
— **defensor(a)** (*m., f.*) counsel for the defense
abrigo (*m.*) coat
— **de piel** (*m.*) fur coat

abrir las piernas y los brazos to spreadeagle
absuelto(a) acquitted
abuelo(a) (*m., f.*) grandfather; grandmother
abusar to abuse, 8
acabar de (+ *inf.*) to have just (done something), 13
accidente (*m.*) accident, 1
aceite (*m.*) oil
acelerador (*m.*) accelerator
acento (*m.*) accent 18
aceptar to accept, 8
acera (*f.*) sidewalk, 9
ácido (*m.*) LSD
acné (*m.*) acne
acompañar to accompany, to go (come) with, 7
acordarse (o:ue) (de) to remember, 10
acostarse (o:ue) to lie down
actividad (*f.*) activity
acto (*m.*) act, 18
actuar to act
acumulador (*m.*) battery
acusación (*f.*) accusation, 14
acusado(a) (*m., f.*) defendant
acusar to accuse, 8
además besides, 2
adentro inside, 8
adicional additional
adicto(a) addicted
adiós good-bye, P
adjetivo (*m.*) adjective
adolescente (*m., f.*) adolescent, teenager, 17
advertencia Miranda (*f.*) Miranda Warning, 6
afeitarse to shave, 20
agacharse to bend down

agarrar   to get hold of, to grab, 9
agente (*m., f.*)   officer, P
agravarse   to get worse, to worsen, 15
agresión (*f.*)   aggression; attack; assault
agresor(a) (*m., f.*)   aggressor; assailant
aguardiente (*m.*)   a type of liquor
aguja (*f.*)   needle, 6
ahí   there, 16
ahijado(a) (*m., f.*)   godson; goddaughter
ahora   now, 1
al (a + el)
   — amanecer   at dawn; at daybreak
   — anochecer   at dusk
   — contado   in cash, 10
   — día   up to date, 11
   — día siguiente   the next day
   — mediodía   at noon
alcohol (*m.*)   alcohol, 9
alcohólico(a)   alcoholic, 9
alegrarse de   to be glad
alejarse   to get away
alérgico(a)   allergic
alfabeto (*m.*)   alphabet, 9
algo   something, 8; anything, 8
   ¿— más?   Anything else?, 7
alguien   someone, 5
algún (*m.*)   some, 6
alguno(a)   some, 6; any
   alguna vez   ever
alias (*m.*)   alias
aliento (*m.*)   breath, 9
alojamiento (*m.*)   lodging
alto(a)   tall, 4
¡Alto!   Halt!, Stop!, 3
alucinaciones (*f. pl.*)   hallucinations
allá   there, 2
allí   there, 2
amarillo(a)   yellow, 7
ambulancia (*f.*)   ambulance, 13
amenaza (*f.*)   threat, 20
amenazar   to threaten, 18
ametralladora (*f.*)   machine gun
amigo(a) (*m., f.*)   friend, 3
amortiguador (*m.*)   muffler
andar   to walk, 2
anillo (*m.*)   ring, 17
anoche   last night, 10
anormal   abnormal, 18
anotar   to write down, 10; to take note of, 10

anteanoche   the night before last
anteayer   the day before yesterday
antecedente penal (*m.*)   criminal record, 16
anteojos (*m. pl.*)   eyeglasses, 18
antes (de)   before, 3
   — de que lo interroguen before they question you, 6
anular (*m.*)   ring finger
año (*m.*)   year
   el — pasado   last year
   el — próximo   next year
   el — que viene   next year
apagado(a)   out, off (light), 9
apagar   to turn off, 9; to put out (a fire), 13
apartamento (*m.*)   apartment, 1
apellido (*m.*)   last name, surname, P
apoyo (*m.*)   support
aprender   to learn, 15
aproximadamente   approximately
aproximado(a)   approximate, 11
apuntar   to point, to aim, 20
aquel   that, 18
aquello(a)   that, 18
aquí   here, 1
área (*f. but* **el área**)   area
arete (*m.*)   earring, 17
arma (*f. but* **el arma**)   weapon, 8
   — de fuego (*f.*)   firearm, 4
   — blanca (*f.*)   blade
arrancar   to start (i.e., a car)
arranque (*m.*)   starter
arreglar   to fix, 19; to arrange
arrestado(a)   arrested, 6
arrestar   to arrest, 3
arrimar   to pull over (a car), 9; to place nearby, 9
artículo (*m.*)   article, 14
asaltar   to assault; to mug; to hijack
asalto (*m.*)   assault; mugging; hold-up; hijacking, 1
asegurado(a)   insured, 11
asesinar   to murder
asesinato (*m.*)   murder
asesino(a) (*m., f.*)   murderer; assassin
así   like this, 9
asiático(a)   Asian
asiento (*m.*)   seat
   — para el niño (*m.*)   child's car seat
asignado(a)   assigned, 15
asistir(a)   to attend, 17

atacar to attack, 18

ataque (*m.*) aggression; attack; assault
— **al corazón** (*m.*) heart attack, 7

aterrorizado(a) terrified, frightened, 18

atrás behind, 12

atrasado(a) behind, 11

atravesado(a) pierced, 18

aunque although, 15; even though

autobús (*m.*) bus

automático(a) automatic, 5

automóvil (*m.*) automobile, 6

automovilístico(a) car-related

autopista (*f.*) highway, 12

autoridad (*f.*) authority, 8

autorizar to authorize, 16; to allow, 16

¡auxilio! help!

avenida (*f.*) avenue, P

averiguación (*f.*) investigation, 10

averiguar to find out, 10

avisar to inform, to give notice, to report, 1; to notify

¡Ay, Dios mío! Oh, goodness gracious!, 2

ayer yesterday, 8

ayuda (*f.*) help, 1

ayudar to help, 18

azul blue, 4

B

bajarse to get out (off), 9; to get down

bajito(a) (*Cuba*) short, 4

bajo under
— **juramento** under oath
— **los efectos (de)** under the influence (of), 6

bajo(a) short (in height), 4

bala (*f.*) bullet

banco (*m.*) bank, 2
— **de sangre** (*m.*) blood bank, 6

banqueta (*f.*) (*México*) sidewalk, 9

bañadera (*f.*) bathtub

bañarse to bathe, 18

baño (*m.*) bath, 18; bathroom

bar (*m.*) bar, 8

barba (*f.*) beard, 18

barbilla (*f.*) chin

barra (*f.*) bar, 8

barrio (*m.*) neighborhood, district, 5

bastante quite, rather, 8

basura (*f.*) trash, garbage, 10

batería (*f.*) battery

baúl (*m.*) (*Puerto Rico*) trunk, 20

bebé (*m.*) baby, 12

bebida (*f.*) drinking, 8; drink, 8

bicicleta (*f.*) bicycle, 2

bien fine, well, P

bigote (*m.*) moustache, 18

billetera (*f.*) wallet, 16

bizco(a) cross-eyed

blanco(a) white, 4

blusa (*f.*) blouse, 17

boca (*f.*) mouth, 17
— **abajo** face down

bocina (*f.*) horn

bofetada (*f.*) slap

bolsa (*f.*) purse, 17

bolsillo (*m.*) pocket, 6

bolso (*m.*) purse, 17

bomba (*f.*) bomb
— **de agua** (*f.*) water pump
— **de tiempo** (*f.*) time bomb

bombero(a) (*m., f.*) firefighter, 5

bono (*m.*) bond, 16

borracho(a) drunk, 6

bota (*f.*) boot

botar to throw away, 10

botella (*f.*) bottle, 15

botica (*f.*) drugstore

botón (*m.*) button

brazo (*m.*) arm, 6

breve brief

bueno(a) okay, P; good
Buenas noches. Good evening., Good night., P
Buenas tardes. Good afternoon., P
Buenos días. Good morning., Good day., P

bujía (*f.*) sparkplug

buscar to look for, 2

C

caballo (*m.*) heroin (*coll.*)

cabello (*m.*) hair

cabeza (*f.*) head, 19

cabina (*f.*) cab (of a truck), 13

cachete (*m.*) cheek, 17

cada each, 6; every, 6

cadena (*f.*) chain, 16

cadera (*f.*) hip

caerse to fall, 18

café (*adj.*)   brown, 18
caja (*f.*)   cash register, 20
cajero(a) (*m., f.*)   cashier
cajuela (*f.*) (*México*)   trunk (of a car), 20
calibre (*m.*)   caliber, 20
calmante (*m.*)   sedative, 19
calmarse   to calm down, 18
calvo(a)   bald, 18
callado(a)   silent, quiet, 6
callarse   to be quiet
  ¡Cállese!   Be quiet!, Shut up!, 20
calle (*f.*)   street, 1
cámara de video (*f.*)   video camera, 10
cambiar   to change, 12
cambiarse de ropa   to change clothes, 18
cambio de velocidad (*m.*)   gearshift
camilla (*f.*)   stretcher
caminar   to walk, 2
camino (*m.*)   road, 13
camión (*m.*)   truck, 13; bus (*México*)
camisa (*f.*)   shirt, 4
camiseta (*f.*)   T-shirt
canoso(a)   gray-haired
cansado(a)   tired, 8
cantina (*f.*)   bar, 8
capó (*m.*)   hood
capucha (*f.*)   hood
cara (*f.*)   face, 13
característica (*f.*)   characteristic
carburador (*m.*)   carburetor
cárcel (*f.*)   jail
caro(a)   expensive
carretera (*f.*)   highway, 13
carril (*m.*)   lane, 12
carro (*m.*)   car, 6
  — deportivo (*m.*)   sports car
  — patrullero (*m.*)   patrol car, 1
cartera (*f.*)   wallet, 16; purse, 17
casa (*f.*)   house, home, 1
casco de seguridad (*m.*)   safety (bike) helmet, 2
casi   almost
caso (*m.*)   case
castaño(a)   brown, 18
castigo corporal (*m.*)   corporal punishment
causar   to cause, 12
  — daño a   to hurt
ceda el paso   yield
ceja (*f.*)   eyebrow
celda (*f.*)   cell, 16

centavo (*m.*)   cent, 16
central   central, 1
  centro de reclusión de menores (*m.*)   juvenile hall
cerca (de)   close, 12; near
cercano(a)   near, nearby, 10
cerrado(a)   closed, 11; locked, 11
cerradura (*f.*)   lock, 10
cerrar (e:ie)   to close, to shut, 9
  — con llave   to lock, 11
césped (*m.*)   lawn, 5
cicatriz (*f.*)   scar, 17
ciego(a)   blind
cierto(a)   certain, 8
cigarrillo (*m.*)   cigarette, 7
cine (*m.*)   (movie) theatre, 15; movies, 15
cinto (*m.*)   belt, 8
cintura (*f.*)   waist
  nivel de la —   waist-high
cinturón (*m.*)   belt, 8
  — de seguridad (*m.*)   safety belt
ciudad (*f.*)   city, 2
claro(a)   light, 11
  claro que sí   of course, 10
clase (*f.*)   kind, type, 7; class, 7
cliente (*m., f.*)   customer, 7
clínica (*f.*)   clinic
coartada (*f.*)   alibi
cobrar   to charge, 14; to collect, 14
coca (*f.*)   cocaine (*coll.*)
  — cocinada (*f.*)   crack cocaine (*coll.*)
cocaína (*f.*)   cocaine
cocina (*f.*)   kitchen, 5
coche (*m.*)   car, 6
codo (*m.*)   elbow
coger   to get hold of, to grab, 9
cognado (*m.*)   cognate
cojo(a)   lame
colonia (*f.*) (*México*)   neighborhood, district, 5
color (*m.*)   color
colorado(a)   red
collar (*m.*)   necklace, 14
comedor (*m.*)   dining room
cometer   to commit, 6
comisaría (*f.*)   police station, P
como   about, approximately, 11; as, like, 14
¿cómo?   how?, 2
  ¿— es?   What does he/she/you look like?, 4
  ¿— está Ud.?   How are you?, P

¡— no! Certainly!, Gladly!, Sure!, 7

¿— se escribe? How do you spell it?

compañero(a) pal, peer

— de clase (*m., f.*) classmate, 17

completar to complete, 9

completo(a) complete, 5

complexión (*f.*) build

cómplice (*m., f.*) accomplice

comprar to buy, 10

comprender to understand, 18

computadora (*f.*) computer, 10

común common

comunicar to communicate, 5

con with, P

— cuidado carefully, 12

— él with him, 6

condena (*f.*) sentence

condición (*f.*) condition, 6

condón (*m.*) condom, 18

conducir to drive, 6

— a cincuenta millas por hora to drive fifty miles per hour, 9

conductor(a) (*m., f.*) driver, 12

confesar (e:ie) to confess

confesión (*f.*) confession

confirmar to confirm, 19

congregación (*f.*) meeting, assembly, 20

conmigo with me, 6

conocer to know, 7

conocido(a) (*m., f.*) acquaintance

conseguir (e:i) to get, to obtain, 8; to manage

consulado (*m.*) consulate, 20

contar (o:ue) to count, 9; to tell, 18

contenido (*m.*) content, 9

contestación (*f.*) answer

contestar to answer, 5

contigo with you, 15

continuar to continue, 10

contra against, 11

contrabandear to smuggle

contrabando (*m.*) contraband; smuggling

contrato (*m.*) contract, 10

control (*m.*) control, 13

conversación breve (*f.*) brief conversation, P

conversar to talk

cooperación (*f.*) cooperation, 3

copia (*f.*) copy, 11

corazón (*m.*) heart, 7; middle finger

corbata (*f.*) tie

cordón (del zapato) (*m.*) shoelace, 16

correa (*f.*) belt, 8

correo (*m.*) mail, 5

correr to run, 7

correspondencia (*f.*) mail, 5

cortar to mow, to cut, 5

cortavidrios (*m.*) glass cutter

corte (*f.*) court (of law), 6

cortesía (*f.*) courtesy

corto(a) short (in length)

cosa (*f.*) thing, 6

costar (o:ue) to cost, 15

crac (*m.*) crack cocaine

creer to believe, 4; to think, 4

— que sí to think so, 7

crespo(a) curly

criminal criminal

cruce (*m.*) crossing, 12; intersection, 12

— de niños (*m.*) school crossing

cruz (*f.*) cross, 17

cruzar to cross, 12

cuadra (*f.*) block, 2

¿cuál? which?, 4; what?, 4

cualquier(a) any, 6; any (one), 9; either, 9

cualquier cosa que diga anything you say, 6

cuando when, 6

¿cuándo? when?, 11

¿cuánto(a)? how much?

— tiempo? How long?, 5

¿cuántos(as)? how many?, 2

cuarto (*m.*) room, 10

cuarto(a) fourth, 4

cubierta (*f.*) hood

cubiertos (*m. pl.*) silverware, 11

cucaracha (*f.*) joint (*coll.*)

cuchillo (*m.*) knife, 18

cuello (*m.*) neck, 16, collar

cuerpo (*m.*) body

¡Cuidado! Careful!, 20

culpa (*f.*) blame

culpable guilty

cultural cultural

cuñado(a) (*m., f.*) brother-in-law; sister-in-law

cuyo(a) whose, 15

CH

chamaco(a) (*m., f.*) (*México*) boy, 13; girl, 13

chamarra (*f.*) (*México*) jacket, 20
chantaje (*m.*) blackmail
chantajear to blackmail
chapa (*f.*) license plate, 11
chaparro(a) (*México*) short, 4
chaqueta (*f.*) jacket, 20
chequear to examine, 13
chico(a) (*m., f.*) boy, 13; girl, 13
chocar to collide, to run into, to hit, 13
chocolate (*m.*) hashish (*coll.*)
chofer (*m.*) driver, 6
choque (*m.*) collision, crash, 13

D

daga (*f.*) dagger
dar to give, 3
— **fuego** to set on fire
— **un tiro (balazo)** to shoot
— **una puñalada** to stab
darse: — cuenta de to realize, to become aware of, 13
— **vuelta** to turn around, 20
dato personal (*m.*) personal data (information), 1
de of, 1; from, about
— **al lado** next-door (neighbor, house), 10
— **cuadros** plaid
— **cultivo** cultured (pearl), 14
— **la mano** by hand, 2
— **lunares** polka dot
— **madrugada** at dawn; at daybreak
— **nada.** You're welcome., Don't mention it., P
— **nuevo** over, again, 9
— **pelo (negro)** with (black) hair, 17
— **primera calidad** first class, top quality, 14
— **rayas** stripped
— **vacaciones** on vacation
debajo de under, underneath, below, 13
deber must, should, 2; to owe, 11
decidir to decide, 6
décimo(a) tenth, P
decir (e:i) to say, to tell, 7
declaración falsa (*f.*) false statement
declarar culpable to convict
dedo (*m.*) finger, 9
— **del pie** (*m.*) toe

defender(se) to defend (oneself), 18
defensa propia (*f.*) self-defense
deformado(a) deformed
dejar to leave (behind), 5; to allow; to let, 9
— **de** (+ *inf.*) to stop (doing something), 6
deletrear to spell, 1
delgado(a) thin, 7
delincuente juvenil (*m., f.*) juvenile delinquent
delirium tremens (*m.*) DT's
delito (*m.*) crime, 6
— **mayor (grave)** (*m.*) felony, 14
demasiado(a) excessive, too much, 12
dentro inside, 4
— **de** in, within, 6
denuncia (*f.*) report (of a crime), 4
denunciar to report (a crime), 1
departamento (*m.*) department, 4
depender to depend, 16
dependiente(a) (*m., f.*) clerk, 20
derecha (*f.*) right-hand side, 16
derecho (*m.*) right
derecho(a) right, 13
desaparecer to disappear
desaparecido(a) missing
descompuesto(a) broken, not working, 19
desconocido(a) (*m., f.*) stranger
describir to describe, 7
descripción (*f.*) description, 11
desde from, 8
— **luego** of course, 2
¡Dése preso(a)! You're under arrest!
desear to want, to wish, 1
desfigurado(a) disfigured
desintoxicación (*f.*) detoxification
desocupado(a) vacant, empty, 3
despacio slowly, 1; slow
despedida (*f.*) farewell
desperfecto (*m.*) (slight) damage, 19; imperfection, 19
después (de) later, 6; after, 7
destruir to destroy, 18
desviarse to swerve, 13
desvío (*m.*) detour
detalle (*m.*) detail, 17
detective (*m., f.*) detective, 14
detención (*f.*) detention, 16
detener (e:ie) to detain, 6; to stop, 6

detenido(a)   arrested, 6; (*m., f.*) person under arrest, 16
determinar   to determine, 9
detrás de la espalda   behind your back
diabetes (*f.*)   diabetes, 6
diario (*m.*)   newspaper, 5
dictar sentencia   to sentence
diente (*m.*)   tooth
dinamita (*f.*)   dynamite
dinero (*m.*)   money, 8
dirección (*f.*)   address, P
disciplinar   to discipline, 8
disco compacto (*m.*)   compact disc, 10
disparar   to shoot, 3
dispersarse   to disperse, 20
dispuesto(a)   willing, 8
distribuir   to distribute, 15
distrito (*m.*)   area
división (*f.*)   section, 1; division, 1
doblar   to turn, 2
doble   double
— circulación (*f.*)   two-way traffic
— vía (*f.*)   divided road
doctor(a) (*m., f.*)   doctor, 8
documento (*m.*)   document, 17
dólar (*m.*)   dollar, 10
doler (o:ue)   to hurt, to ache, 13
domicilio (*m.*)   address, P; domicile
¿dónde?   where?, 1
dormir (o:ue)   to sleep
dormitorio (*m.*)   bedroom, 8
dorso (*m.*)   back (of paper), 19
dos veces   twice, 17
droga (*f.*)   drug, 6
droguero(a) (*m., f.*)   drug user; drug pusher
ducharse   to shower
dudar   to doubt, 16
dueño(a) (*m., f.*)   owner, 7
durante   during, 6
— el día (la noche)   during the day (night)

E

edad (*f.*)   age, 17
edificio (*m.*)   building, 6
elegido(a)   chosen, 9
elegir (e:i)   to choose, 9
embarazada   pregnant

embrague (*m.*)   gearshift lever
emergencia (*f.*)   emergency, 4
empeñar   to pawn, 14
empezar (e:ie)   to begin, 9
empleado(a) (*m., f.*)   employee, 14; clerk, 14
empujar   to push, 18
en   in, 1; on, 1; at, 1
— bicicleta   on a bike, 2
— buena parte   to a large extent, 16
— contra de   against, 6
— cuanto   as soon as, 18
— efectivo   in cash, 10
— libertad bajo fianza   out on bail, 16
— libertad bajo palabra   out on one's own recognizance, 16
— lugar de   instead of, 8
— persona   personally, in person, 1
¿— qué puedo (podemos) servirle?   What can I (we) do for you?, P
— sentido contrario   in the opposite direction, 13
encender (e:ie)   to turn on (a light), 5
encendido(a)   on (a light, a TV set), 5
encerrado(a)   locked up, 8; closeted, 8
encerrar (e:ie)   to lock up, 16
encontrar (o:ue)   to find, 11
endrogado(a)   on drugs, 6
endrogarse   to take drugs; to become addicted to drugs
enfermedad (*f.*)   disease
— venérea (*f.*)   venereal disease, 18
enfrente de   across the street from, 5
engañar   to cheat, to deceive, 14
enojado(a)   angry, 8
enseguida   right away, 1
enseñar   to show, 9
entender (e:ie)   to understand, 6
entonces   then, 4
entrada (*f.*)   entrance
entrar (en)   to go in, 4
no entre   do not enter; wrong way
entre   between, 1; among
entrega (*f.*)   delivery, 5

255

entregar to give, 11; to turn over (something to someone), 11
entrelazar to interlace, 20
entremeterse to meddle, to butt in, 8
entrenado(a) trained, 4
entrometerse to meddle, to butt in, 8
epiléptico(a) epileptic
equipo (*m.*) equipment, 10
es it is
  — decir... That is to say . . . , 18
  — que... It's just that . . . , 9
escala de soga (*f.*) rope ladder
escalera de mano (*f.*) hand ladder
escaparse to run away, 17
escopeta (*f.*) shotgun
escribir to write, 6
escuela (*f.*) school, 7
  — secundaria (*f.*) junior high school, 15; high school, 15
escusado (*m.*) (*México*) bathroom
ése(a) (*m., f.*) that one, 8
eso (*m.*) that, 8
espalda (*f.*) back
español (*m.*) Spanish (language), 1
espejo (*m.*) mirror
espejuelos (*m.*) (*Cuba, Puerto Rico*) eyeglasses, 18
esperar to wait (for), 7
esposado(a) handcuffed, 16
esposas (*f. pl.*) handcuffs, 16
esposo(a) (*m., f.*) husband, 4; wife
esquina (*f.*) corner, 3
esta (*f.*) this
  — noche tonight, 5
  — vez this time, 8
ésta this one, 8
estación (*f.*) station
  — de bomberos (*f.*) fire department
  — de correos (*f.*) post office
  — de ómnibus (autobuses) (*f.*) bus station
  — de policía (*f.*) police station, P
  — de servicio (*f.*) gas station
estacionado(a) parked, 11
estacionamiento de emergencia solamente emergency parking only
estado (*m.*) state, 2
estafa (*f.*) swindle, fraud, 14
estafar to swindle, 14

estampado(a) print
estar to be, 3
  — a la vista to be visible
  — apurado(a) to be in a hurry, 9
  — bien to be okay, 3
  — de acuerdo to agree, 16
  — de regreso to be back, 5
  — de vuelta to be back, 5
  — en condiciones de (+ *inf.*) to be in a condition to (do something), 6
  — equivocado(a) to be wrong, 8
  — preso(a) to be under arrest, to be in jail
  — seguro(a) to be certain, 18
estatal of or pertaining to the state, 9
estatua (*f.*) statue
estatura (*f.*) height, 20
  de — mediana medium height, 4
este(a) this, 2
éste(a) (*m., f.*) this one, 8
estómago (*m.*) stomach
estos(as) these, 6
estudiante (*m., f.*) student, 7
estudiar to study, 17
evidencia (*f.*) evidence, 18
evitar to avoid, 13
exactamente exactly, 17
examinar to examine, 13
excusa (*f.*) excuse, 12
excusado (*m.*) (*México*) bathroom
exigir to demand, 2
explosivo (*m.*) explosive
expresión (*f.*) expression
extender (e:ie) to stretch out, 9; to spread, 9
extinguidor de incendios (*m.*) fire extinguisher, 13
extraño(a) strange, 4; (*m., f.*) stranger, 18

F

fácilmente easily
falda (*f.*) skirt, 17
falsificación (*f.*) falsification; counterfeit; forgery
falsificar to falsify; to counterfeit; to forge
falso(a) forged; fake
faltar to be missing, 10
fallo decision; verdict

familia (*f.*) family, 8
farmacia (*f.*) pharmacy
faro (*m.*) headlight, 19
felpudo (*m.*) mat
ferrocarril (*m.*) railroad
fiancista (*m., f.*) bailor, bail bondsman, 16
fianza (*f.*) bail, 16
fichar to book, 16; to log in, 16
fiesta (*f.*) party, 10
filtro (*m.*) filter
final (*m.*) end, 9
fiscal (*m., f.*) prosecutor, 16; district attorney, 16
flaco(a) thin; skinny
flecha, flechita (*f.*) arrow, 18
floreado(a) flowered
foco (*m.*) light
fondo (*m.*) back
  en el — in the back
forma (*f.*) way, 8
forzar (o:ue) to force, 10
fotografía (*f.*) photograph, 3
frecuentemente frequently, 8
freno (*m.*) brake
frente (*f.*) forehead
  — a in front of, 1
fuego (*m.*) fire, 5
  — intencional (*m.*) arson
fuera outside, 4
fugarse to run away, 17
fumar to smoke, 7
futuro (*m.*) future

G

gafas (*f.*) eyeglasses, 18
galleta (*f.*) (*Cuba*) slap
ganga (*f.*) bargain, 14
ganzúa (*f.*) skeleton key; picklock
garaje (*m.*) garage
gas (*m.*) gas, 19
gasolina (*f.*) gasoline
gasolinera (*f.*) gas station
gata (*f.*) (*Costa Rica*) jack, 20
gato (*m.*) jack, 20
generalmente generally, 17
gente (*f.*) people, 20
golpear to hit, to strike, 18
goma (*f.*) tire, 20
  — ponchada (*f.*) flat tire
gordo(a) fat, 7
gorra (*f.*) cap, 4
grabadora (*f.*) tape recorder, 11

gracias thank you, P
grafiti (*m.*) graffiti
gran great, 14
granada de mano (*f.*) hand grenade
grande big, large, 2
grano (*m.*) pimple
grave serious, 1
grifa (*f.*) hashish (*coll.*)
gris gray, 20
gritar to scream, to shout, 18
grueso(a) fat
grupo (*m.*) group, 20
guagua (*f.*) (*Cuba*) bus
guante (*m.*) glove
guantera (*f.*) glove compartment, 7
guardado(a) put away, saved, 10
guardafangos (*m.*) fender
guardar to keep
güero(a) (*México*) blonde, 7
gustar to be pleasing, to like, 13

H

habitación (*f.*) room, 10
hablar to speak, to talk, 1
  — con (la) zeta to lisp
hace una semana a week ago, 14
hacer to do, 3; to make, 3
  — arreglar to have (something) fixed, 19
  — caso to pay attention, 2
  — falta to need, 15
  — resistencia to resist, 18
  — una pregunta to ask a question, 19
hacerse to become
hacia toward, 7
hachich, hachís (*m.*) hashish
hasta until, 2
  — luego. So long., See you later., P
  — que until, 19
hay there is (are), 1
  — de todo. You can find everything., 15
  No — de qué. You're welcome., Don't mention it., P
herido(a) hurt, injured, 1
hermano(a) (*m., f.*) brother; sister
heroína (*f.*) heroin
hijastro(a) (*m., f.*) stepson; stepdaughter
hijo(a) (*m., f.*) son; daughter

hijos (*m. pl.*) children, 4; sons
hispánico(a) Hispanic
hispano(a) Hispanic, 2
histéricamente hysterically, 18
hola hello, hi, P
hombre (*m.*) man, 3
 — de negocios (*m.*) business-man, 15
hombro (*m.*) shoulder
homicidio (*m.*) manslaughter, 16; homicide, 16
hora (*f.*) time, 3; hour, 3
horno (*m.*) oven, 19
hospedaje (*m.*) lodging
hospital (*m.*) hospital, 4
hotel (*m.*) hotel
hoy today, P
hubo there was, 13
huella digital (*f.*) fingerprint, 10
humo (*m.*) smoke, 5

I

idea (*f.*) idea, 10
identificación (*f.*) identification, ID, 3
identificar to identify
iglesia (*f.*) church
impermeable (*m.*) raincoat
imponer una multa to impose a fine, to give a ticket, 12
importante important, 17
imprudentemente imprudently, recklessly, 12
incendio (*m.*) fire, 5
 — intencional (*m.*) arson
incómodo(a) uncomfortable, 2
indicador (*m.*) turn signal
índice (*m.*) index finger
infiltrar(se) to infiltrate, 15
información (*f.*) information, P
informe (*m.*) report, 1
infracción de tránsito (*f.*) traffic violation, 6
inglés (*m.*) English (language), 1
ingresado(a) admitted (to), 8
ingresar to be admitted (to), 8; to enter, 8
iniciar to begin, 12
inmediatamente immediately, 8
inocente innocent, 14
intento (*m.*) attempt, 15
interrogar to question, to interrogate, 6

interrogatorio (*m.*) interrogation, questioning, 6
inválido(a) disabled; crippled
investigación (*f.*) investigation, 16
investigador(a) investigating, 16
investigar to investigate, 8
ir to go, 3
 — a (+ *inf.*) to be going (to do something), 5
irse to go away, 10; to leave, 10
izquierdo(a) left

J

jardín (*m.*) garden
jardinero(a) (*m., f.*) gardener, 3
jefatura de policía (*f.*) police station, P
jeringa hipodérmica (*f.*) hypodermic syringe
jeringuilla (*f.*) hypodermic syringe
joven young, 4; (*m., f.*) young man, young woman, 6
jovencito(a) (*m., f.*) adolescent, teenager, 17
joya (*f.*) jewel, 10
juez (*m., f.*) judge, 8
juicio (*m.*) trial
juntos(as) together, 10
jurado (*m.*) jury, 14
juramento (*m.*) oath
jurar to take an oath; to swear
juzgado (*m.*) court (of law), 6
juzgar to judge

L

labio (*m.*) lip
lacio(a) straight (hair)
lado (*m.*) side, 13
ladrón(ona) (*m., f.*) thief, 3
largo(a) long
lastimado(a) hurt, injured, 7
lastimarse to get hurt, 13
latino(a) Latin, 15; Hispanic
leer to read, 6
lengua (*f.*) tongue; language
lentes (*m. pl.*) eye glasses, 18
leño (*m.*) joint (*coll.*)
lesión (*f.*) injury, 8
lesionado(a) injured, 8
levantar to lift
levantarse to get up, 13
ley (*f.*) law, 2
libra (*f.*) pound, 20

librería (*f.*) bookstore
libreta de teléfonos (*f.*) address book, 18
licencia (*f.*) license
  — de conducir (*f.*) driver's license, 3
  — para manejar (conducir) (*f.*) driver's license, 3
licorería (*f.*) liquor store, 7
límite (*m.*) limit, 9
  — de velocidad (*m.*) speed limit, 9
limpiaparabrisas (*m.*) windshield wiper
limpiar to clean, 10
línea (*f.*) line, 9
  — de parada (*f.*) stop line, 12
linterna (*f.*) flashlight, 4
lista (*f.*) list, 11
listo(a) ready, 19
lo you, 6; him, 6
  — demás the rest, 6
  — que what, 8
  — siento. I'm sorry., 6
local local, 8
luchar to fight, to struggle, 18
luego later, 10; afterwards, 10
lugar (*m.*) place, 9
lunar (*m.*) mole, 17
  de lunares polka dot
luz (*f.*) light, 4

K

kif (*m.*) hashish

LL

llamada (*f.*) call, 4
  — telefónica (*f.*) phone call, 5
llamar to call, 1
  — al perro to call off the dog
llamarse to be named, to be called, 9
llanta (*f.*) tire, 20
  — pinchada (*f.*) flat tire
llave (*f.*) key, 5
  — falsa (*f.*) skeleton key; picklock
llegar (a) to arrive (at), 2; to reach, 2
  — a (+ *inf.*) to succeed in (doing something), 18
  — tarde to be late, 12
llenar to fill out, 1

llevar to take, 2; to carry, 2; to wear, 2
  — puesto(a) to wear, 2
llevarse to steal, 11
llorar to cry, 18

M

maceta de flores (*f.*) flower pot
madrastra (*f.*) stepmother
madre (*f.*) mother, mom, 2
madrina (*f.*) godmother
madrugada (*f.*) early morning, 9
maestro(a) (*m., f.*) teacher
maletero (*m.*) trunk (of a car), 20
malo(a) bad, 6
maltratar to abuse, 8
maltrato (*m.*) abuse, 8
mamá (*f.*) mom, mother, 2
mancha (*f.*) spot: mark; blemish
mandar to send, 1
manejar to drive, 6
  ¡Maneje con cuidado! Drive safely!, 12
mangas (*f. pl.*) sleeves
  de — cortas short-sleeved
  de — largas long-sleeved
  sin — sleeveless
mano (*f.*) hand, 6
  ¡Manos arriba! Hands up!
manteca (*f.*) (*Caribe*) heroin (*coll.*)
mantener (e:ie) to keep
  mantenga su derecha keep right
mañana (*f.*) morning, 10; (*adv.*) tomorrow
máquina (*f.*) (*Cuba*) car, 6
marca (*f.*) mark, 6; brand, 10; make (car)
mareado(a) dizzy, 13
marido (*m.*) husband, 4
mariguana, marijuana (*f.*) marijuana
más more
  — bien rather, 7
  — o menos more or less, 8
  —... que (de) more . . . than, 4
  — tarde later, 2
máscara (*f.*) mask
matar to kill, 8
matricularse to register, 15; to enroll (in a school), 15
mayor older, 17
  — de edad of age; adult
  dedo — (*m.*) middle finger

mediano(a) medium; average
medianoche (*f.*) midnight, 3
medicina (*f.*) medicine, 7
médico (*m., f.*) doctor, 8
medio (*adv.*) rather, 7
medir (e:i) to measure, 7; to be (amount) tall, 17
mejilla (*f.*) cheek, 17
mejor better, 12; best, 12
  que nunca better than ever, 6
menor younger, 4; minor
  — de edad (*m., f.*) minor, 3
menos de less than, 4; fewer than, 4
mentira (*f.*) lie, 8
meñique (*m.*) little finger
mercado (*m.*) market, 20; super-market
  — al aire libre (*m.*) open-air market
mes (*m.*) month
  el — pasado (próximo) last (next) month
mestizo(a) mixed (any of two or more races)
metadona (*f.*) methadone
metido(a) inside, inserted in, 19
mi my, 1
miembro (*m., f.*) member, 3
mientras while, 20
milla (*f.*) mile, 9
mirando watching
mirar to look at, 16
Mire. Look., 6
mismo(a) same, 9
  por sí mismo(a) by himself; by herself
mitin (*m.*) meeting, assembly, 20
modelo (*m.*) model, 11
momento (*m.*) moment, P
moneda (*f.*) coin, 9
monumento (*m.*) monument
mordaza (*f.*) gag
mordida (*f.*) bite
morfina (*f.*) morphine
morgue (*f.*) morgue
morir (o:ue) to die, 13
mostrador (*m.*) counter, 16
mostrar (o:ue) to show, 9
mota (*f.*) marijuana (*coll.*)
motel (*m.*) motel, 15
motivo (*m.*) motive
motocicleta (*f.*) motorcycle, 13; motor-driven cycle

motor (*m.*) engine, motor, 9
  — de arranque (*m.*) starter
mover(se) (o:ue) to move, 16
  ¡No se mueva(n)! Don't move!, Freeze!, 6
muchacho(a) (*m., f.*) boy, 2; girl, 2
muchísimo very much, 15
mucho (*adv.*) much, 4
muchos(as) many, 2
  Muchas gracias. Thank you very much., P
mujer (*f.*) woman, 1; wife
  — de negocios (*f.*) business-woman, 15
mulato(a) mixed race (black and white)
multa (*f.*) ticket, fine, 6
multitud (*f.*) crowd, 20
muñeca (*f.*) wrist
murmurar to murmur, 20
musculoso(a) muscular
muy very, 1

N

nacimiento (*m.*) birth
nada nothing, P
nadie nobody, 8
nalgada (*f.*) spanking; slap on the buttocks
nariz (*f.*) nose, 9
navaja (*f.*) switchblade, 8; razor, 8
necesario(a) necessary, 5
necesitar to need, 1
negarse (e:ie) to refuse to, 9
negro(a) black, 4
neumático (*m.*) tire, 20
nieto(a) (*m., f.*) grandson; grand-daughter
ninguno(a) not any
niño(a) (*m., f.*) child, 3
noche (*f.*) night, 5
nombrar to appoint
nombre (*m.*) name, P; noun
nota (*f.*) note
notar to notice, 6
notificar to inform, to give notice, to report, 1
novio(a) (*m., f.*) boyfriend, 15; girlfriend, 15
nuera (*f.*) daughter-in-law
nuestro(a) our, 5
nuevo(a) new, 6; fresh, 6
número (*m.*) number

— de serie (*m.*)   serial number, 10
— de teléfono (*m.*)   phone number, P
nunca   never, 6

O

o   or, 3
objeto (*m.*)   object, item, 11
obligar   to obligate, to force, 18
obscenidad (*f.*)   obscenity, 20
ocasión (*f.*)   occasion, 17
ocurrir   to occur, 14; to happen
oficina (*f.*)   office
— de correos (*f.*)   post office
ofrecer   to offer, 14
oído (*m.*)   inner ear
oír   to hear, 19
ojalá   I hope, 17
ojo (*m.*)   eye
— de vidrio (*m.*)   glass eye
de ojos (azules) (*m.*)   with (blue) eyes, 7
ojos saltones (*m. pl.*)   bulging eyes; bug eyes
olor (*m.*)   smell, 19
— a   smell of, 19
olvidar   to forget, 18
ómnibus (*m.*)   bus
operador(a) (*m., f.*)   telephone operator, dispatcher, 1
opio (*m.*)   opium
oportunidad (*f.*)   opportunity, 16
orden (*f.*)   warrant, order, 8
ordenador (*m.*) (*España*)   computer, 10
ordenar   to order, 20
oreja (*f.*)   outer ear
orina (*f.*)   urine, 9
oro (*m.*)   gold, 16
oscuro(a)   dark, 4
otro(a)   other, another, 4
otra vez   again, once again, 6

P

padrastro (*m.*)   stepfather, 8
padre (*m.*)   father, dad, 5
padres (*m. pl.*)   parents, 3
padrino (*m.*)   godfather
pagado(a)   paid (for), 11
pagar   to pay (for), 6
pago (*m.*)   payment, 11
país (*m.*)   country, 8

palabra (*f.*)   word
palanca de cambio de velocidades (*f.*)   gearshift lever
paliza (*f.*)   beating
pana (*f.*)   corduroy, 20
pandilla (*f.*)   gang, 3
pantalón, pantalones (*m.*)   pants, trousers, 4
pañuelo (*m.*)   handkerchief, 16
papá (*m.*)   dad, father, 5
papeleta (*f.*)   form, 19
par: un — de   a couple of, 6
para   for, 1
— allá   there, over there, 1
— mí   for me, 14
— que   so that
— servirle.   At your service., P
— ti   for you, 18
parada de autobuses (*f.*)   bus stop
paradero (*m.*)   whereabouts
parado(a)   standing, 7
paramédico (*m., f.*)   paramedic, 1
parar   to stop, 12
¡Pare!   Stop!
pararse   to stand, 16
¡Párese!   Stand up!
parecer   to seem, 4
pared (*f.*)   wall, 6
pariente (*m., f.*)   relative
—s políticos (*m. pl.*)   in-laws
parpadear   to blink, 6
parque (*m.*)   park
parte (*f.*)   part
pasado (*m.*)   past
pasado(a)   last
— mañana   the day after tomorrow
pasajero(a) (*m., f.*)   passenger, 13
pasar   to come in, P; to happen, 2; to pass (a car), 13; to spend (time)
no—   do not pass
no pase   wrong way; do not enter
— un buen rato   to have a good time, 15
pasarlo bien   to have a good time, 15
pasarse la luz roja   to go through a red light, 12
pasillo (*m.*)   hallway
paso de peatones   pedestrian crossing
pastilla (*f.*)   LSD (*coll.*)
pasto (*m.*)   marijuana (*coll.*)
pata de cabra (*f.*)   crowbar

patada (*f.*)   kick
patio (*m.*)   yard, 3
patrulla (*f.*)   patrol, 5
patrullero(a) (*adj.*)   patrol
peatón (*m., f.*)   pedestrian
peca (*f.*)   freckle, 7
pecho (*m.*)   chest
pedir (e:i)   to ask (for), 8
pegao (*m.*)   LSD (*coll.*)
pegar   to beat, 8
   — fuego   to set on fire
   — un tiro   to shoot
peine (*m.*)   comb, 16
pelado(a)   bald, 18
pelea (*f.*)   fight
peligroso(a)   dangerous, 4
pelirrojo(a)   red-haired, 7
pelo (*m.*)   hair, 17
pelón(ona)   bald
peluca (*f.*)   wig; hairpiece
penetración (*f.*)   penetration, 18
pensar (e:ie)   to think, 17
   — (+ *inf.*)   to plan (to do something), 5
pequeño(a)   small, little, 2
perder (e:ie)   to lose, 6
perdido(a)   lost, 2
perdón (*m.*)   pardon, 8; forgiveness, 8
perdonar   to forgive, 8
perico (*m.*)   cocaine (*coll.*)
periódico (*m.*)   newspaper, 5
perito (*m., f.*)   expert
perjudicar   to cause damage, to hurt, 14
perla (*f.*)   pearl, 14
permanecer   to stay, to remain, 6
permiso (*m.*)   permission, 20; warrant, 20
permitido(a)   permitted, 16
pero   but, 1
persona (*f.*)   person, 3
pertenencias (*f. pl.*)   belongings, 16
pesar   to weigh, 20
peso (*m.*)   weight
pestaña (*f.*)   eyelash
pie (*m.*)   foot, 7
piedra (*f.*)   rock (crack cocaine) (*coll.*), 15; stone, rock
piel (*f.*)   skin
pierna (*f.*)   leg, 13
pista (*f.*)   clue
pistola (*f.*)   pistol, 4
pito (*m.*)   marijuana (*coll.*)

placa (*f.*)   license plate, 11
plata (*f.*)   silver, 11
plazo (*m.*)   installment, 11
poco   little
   un — de   a little, 1
poder (o:ue)   can, 6; to be able, 6
   No se puede escribir...   You (one) cannot write . . . , 6
   puede usarse   can be used, 6
policía (*f.*)   police (force), 1; (*m., f.*) police officer, 1
   — secreta (*f.*)   undercover police, 15
polvo (*m.*)   cocaine (*coll.*)
poner   to put, 9
   — en peligro   to endanger, 12
   — las manos en la pared   to put one's hands against the wall
ponerse   to put on, 18
   — de rodillas   to get on one's knees
por   for, P; on (by way of), 2; through, 2
   — completo   completely, 16
   — ejemplo   for example, 7
   — escrito   in writing, 16
   — favor   please, P
   — la mañana   in the morning, 7
   — la noche   in the evening, at night, 7
   — la tarde   in the afternoon, 7
   — lo menos   at least, 17
   — lo tanto   therefore, so, 20
   — poseer drogas   for possession of drugs
   ¿— qué?   why?
   — suerte   fortunately, 13
   — teléfono   on the phone, by phone, 1
pornográfico(a)   pornographic
por que   because, 3
porqué (*m.*)   reason, 8
porro (*m.*)   joint (*coll.*)
portaequipajes (*m.*)   trunk (of a car)
portaguantes (*m.*)   glove compartment
portal (*m.*)   porch
practicar   to practice
precaución (*f.*)   precaution, 13
pregunta (*f.*)   question
preguntar   to ask, 8
preliminar   preliminary, 16
prender   to arrest, 3; to turn on (a light), 4

prendido(a) on (a light, a TV set), 5; lit, 19
presentar to introduce, 15
presente present, 6
preso(a) arrested, 6
prestar to lend
— **atención** to pay attention, 9
prevenir to prevent
preventivo(a) preventive, 16
prima (*f.*) premium, 16
primero (*adv.*) first, 1
primero(a) first, 5
primeros auxilios (*m. pl.*) first aid
primo(a) (*m., f.*) cousin
prisión (*f.*) prison, jail
problema (*m.*) problem, 3
procesado(a) indicted
prohibido(a) prohibited
— **pasar** no trespassing
prometer to promise, 20
propiedad (*f.*) property, 11
prostitución (*f.*) prostitution
prostituto(a) (*m., f.*) prostitute, 15
protestar to complain, to protest, 3
próximo(a) next, 4
prueba (*f.*) test, 9; evidence
— **del alcohol** (*f.*) sobriety test, 9
pueblo (*m.*) town, 10
puerta (*f.*) door, 7
pulgada (*f.*) inch, 7
pulgar (*m.*) thumb
pullar (*Caribe*) to shoot up (drugs)
punta (*f.*) end, tip, 9
puñal (*m.*) dagger
puñalada: dar una — to stab
puñetazo (*m.*) punch

Q

que that, 3
¿qué? what?, 1
¿— hay de nuevo? What's new?, P
¿— hora era (es)? What time was (is) it?, 18
¿— más? What else?, 7
¿— tiene? What's wrong?, 7
¿— se le ofrece? What can I (we) do for you?, P
quedar to be located, 2
— **declarado(a) ilegal** to be hereby declared illegal, 20
quedarse to stay, 10

— **callado(a)** to remain silent, 6
— **sin trabajo** to lose one's job, 14
queja (*f.*) complaint
querer (e:ie) to want, 5; to wish, 5
¿quién? who?, 1
quieto(a) still, 13
¡Quieto(a)! Freeze!, 3
químico(a) chemical, 9
quinceañera (*f.*) girl on her fifteenth birthday, 10; party to celebrate a girl's fifteenth birthday, 10
quitar to take away, 8
quitarse to take off (clothing), 16

R

radiografía (*f.*) X-ray, 13
rápido quick, quickly, fast, 5
raza (*f.*) race, 18
realizar to perform, to carry out, 18
rebasar (*México*) to pass (a car), 13
recámara (*f.*) (*México*) bedroom, 8
recibir to receive, 4
reciente recent, 17
recitar to recite, 9
recobrar to recover, 11
recoger to pick up, 5
recomendar (e:ie) to recommend, 16
reconocer to recognize, 7
recordar (o:ue) to remember, 6
refugiarse to find refuge (shelter)
regalar to give (a gift), 15
registrado(a) registered, 11
registrar to book, 16; to log in, 16
registro (*m.*) registration, 6
regresar to return, 2
reloj (*m.*) watch, 16
reo(a) (*m., f.*) defendant
reporte (*m.*) report, 1
representar to represent
rescatar to rescue
rescate (*m.*) ransom
residencial residential, 9
resistencia a la autoridad (*f.*) resisting arrest
respirar to breathe
responder to respond, 15
respuesta (*f.*) answer
restaurante (*m.*) restaurant
retratar to photograph, 16
reunión (*f.*) meeting, assembly, 20

revisar to review, 10; to check, 10
revólver (*m.*) revolver, 4
rico(a) rich
riego (*m.*) watering, 5
riesgo (*m.*) risk, 11
rifle (*m.*) rifle
riña (*f.*) fight
rizado(a) curly
rizo(a) curly
robado(a) stolen, 10
robar to rob, to steal from, 10
robo (*m.*) robbery, 1
roca (*f.*) crack cocaine (*coll.*)
rodilla (*f.*) knee
rojo(a) red, 12
rondar to prowl, 10
ropa (*f.*) clothes, 4
rubio(a) blond(e), 7
rueda (*f.*) wheel
ruido (*m.*) noise

S

saber to know, 7
sacar to take out, 6
saco (*m.*) jacket
sala (*f.*) living room
— **de estar** (*f.*) family room
salir to get out, 5; to leave, 5; to come out
— **con** to go out with, 17; to date, 17
saltar to jump, 13
¡Salud! To your health!
saludar to greet, 15
saludo (*m.*) greeting
salvar to save, 2
sandalia (*f.*) sandal, 17
sargento (*m.*) sergeant, 1
sección (*f.*) section, division, 1
secreto(a) secret, 15
secuestrar to kidnap, 12
secuestro (*m.*) kidnapping, 17
sedante (*m.*) sedative, 19
sedativo (*m.*) sedative, 19
seguir (e:i) to follow
— **caminando** to keep walking
— **derecho** to go straight ahead, 2
según according to
seguro(a) safe
sellado(a) sealed, 16
sello (*m.*) LSD (*coll.*)
semáforo (*m.*) traffic light, 12

semana (*f.*) week, 4
la — pasada (próxima) last (next) week
la — que viene next week
semiautomático(a) semiautomatic, 20
sentarse (e:ie) to sit down
Siéntese. Sit down., 8
sentencia (*f.*) sentence
sentenciar to sentence
sentimental sentimental, 14
sentirse (e:ie) to feel, 13
señal de tránsito (*f.*) traffic sign
señor (Sr.) (*m.*) Mr., sir, gentleman, P
los señores (Ruiz) (*m. pl.*) Mr. and Mrs. (Ruiz), 17
señora (Sra.) (*f.*) Mrs., lady, Ma'am, Madam, P
señorita (Srta.) (*f.*) Miss, young lady, P
separar los pies to separate (spread) your feet
ser to be, 2
— **como las** (+ *time*) to be about (+ time), 18
— **culpable (de)** to be at fault, to be guilty (of), 12
serie (*f.*) series, 10
serio(a) serious, 13
serrucho de mano (*m.*) handsaw
servicio (*m.*) service, 15
servir (e:i) to serve
sexo (*m.*) sex, 15
sexual sexual, 18
shorts (*m. pl.*) shorts
si if, 4
sí yes, 1
sí mismo(a) yourself; himself; herself
SIDA (síndrome de inmunodeficiencia adquirida) (*m.*) AIDS, 18
siempre always, 3
sierra de mano (*f.*) handsaw
siguiente following
silenciador (*m.*) muffler
silla de ruedas (*f.*) wheelchair
sin without, 3
— **embargo** nevertheless, however, 14
— **falta** without fail, 19
sinceramente sincerely, 14
sistema (*m.*) system, 5

situación (*f.*) situation
soborno (*m.*) bribe, 15
sobre (*m.*) envelope, 16
sobre (*prep.*) on, on top of, 20
sobredosis (*f.*) overdose
sobrino(a) (*m., f.*) nephew; niece
¡Socorro! Help!, 5
soga (*f.*) rope
solamente only, 12
solicitar to ask for, 2; to solicit, 15
solo(a) alone, 2
sólo only, 12
soltar (o:ue) to let go of
  — **el arma** to drop the gun (weapon)
sombrero (*m.*) hat, 4
someterse a to submit (oneself) to, 9
sordo(a) deaf
sortija (*f.*) ring, 17
sospecha (*f.*) suspicion, 8
sospechar to suspect, 7
sospechoso(a) suspicious, 10
sótano (*m.*) basement
su your, 1; his, 3; her, 3
subir to get in (a car, etc.), 3
  Súbase al carro. Get in the car.
suceder to happen, 2
sucio(a) dirty, 18
suegro(a) (*m., f.*) father-in-law; mother-in-law
suelo (*m.*) floor, 7
suéter (*m.*) sweater, 17
suficiente sufficient, enough, 15
suicidarse to commit suicide, 19
supermercado (*m.*) supermarket, market
suspender to stop, 5
suyo(a) yours

T

tal such
  — **cosa** such a thing, 19
  — **vez** perhaps, 18
tamaño (*m.*) size
también also, too, 8
tan so, 12
  — **...como** as . . . as, 4
tanque (*m.*) tank
tapicería (*f.*) upholstery
taquígrafo(a) (*m., f.*) court reporter; stenographer
tarde (*f.*) afternoon; (*adv.*) late, 2

tarjeta (*f.*) card, 3
tartamudear to stutter
tatuaje (*m.*) tattoo, 7
teatro (*m.*) (movie) theater
técnico(a) (*m., f.*) technician, 10
techo (de tejas) (*m.*) (tile) roof
telefonista (*m., f.*) operator, 1; dispatcher, 1
teléfono (*m.*) telephone, 1
televisor (*m.*) television set, 10
temblar (e:ie) to shake, to tremble, to shiver, 13
temer to fear
temprano early
tener to have, 4
  — **a su cargo** to be in charge of, 15
  — **...años** to be . . . years old, 4
  — **el derecho de** to have the right to, 6
  — **la culpa (de)** to be at fault, 12; to be guilty, 12
  — **miedo** to be afraid, 5
  — **(mucho) sueño** to be (very) sleepy, 6
  — **prisa** to be in a hurry, 9
  — **puesto(a)** to have on, to wear, 17
  — **que** (+ *inf.*) to have to (do something), 4
  — **razón** to be right, 12
  — **tanto miedo** to be so scared, 18
tequila (*f.*) tequila, 15
tercero(a) third, 8
terminar to finish, 10; to end
  — **de** (+ *inf.*) to finish (doing something), 10
terraza (*f.*) terrace
testigo (*m., f.*) witness, 14
tianguis (*m.*) (*México*) open-air market
tiempo (*m.*) time, 6
tienda (*f.*) store
timón (*m.*) (*Cuba*) steering wheel
tío(a) (*m., f.*) uncle, 9; aunt, 15
tirar to throw away, 10; to shoot
título (*m.*) title
tobillo (*m.*) ankle
tocadiscos (*m.*) record player, 10
tocar to touch, 9
  — **a la puerta** to knock at the door, 8
  — **la bocina** to honk the horn

todavía   still, yet, 2
todo (*m.*)   everything
— **lo posible**   everything possible, 11
todo(a)   all, 11
— **el (la)...**   the whole . . .
todos(as)   all, every
todos los días   every day, 8
tomar   to drink, 6; to take, 6
— **asiento**   to take a seat, P
— **las huellas digitales**   to fingerprint, 16
tontería (*f.*)   foolishness, nonsense, 10
toque de queda (*m.*)   curfew, 3
totalmente   totally, 11
trabajo (*m.*)   work, 8; job, 8
traer   to bring, 7
trago (*m.*)   drink, 6
traje (*m.*)   suit
tránsito (*m.*)   traffic
tratar (de)   to try (to), 4; to treat, 8
tribunal (*m.*)   court
— **de menores** (*m.*)   juvenile court
trompada (*f.*)   punch
tu   your, 2

U

últimamente   last
último(a)   last, 11
unos(as)   about, around, 2
urgente   urgent, 4
urgentemente   urgently, 14
usado(a)   used
usar   to use, 4
se usará   will be used, 6
uso (*m.*)   use, 2

V

vacaciones (*f. pl.*)   vacation
de —   on vacation, 4
vaciar   to empty, 16
válido(a)   valid, 12
valor (*m.*)   value, 11
Vamos.   Let's go., 2
vandalismo (*m.*)   vandalism, 6
varios(as)   several, 5
vecindario (*m.*)   neighborhood, 11
vecino(a) (*m., f.*)   neighbor, 4
vehículo (*m.*)   vehicle, 13
velocidad (*f.*)   speed, 9
— **máxima** (*f.*)   speed limit, 9
vello (*m.*)   body hair
velludo(a)   hairy
venda (*f.*)   bandage, 13

vender   to sell, 7
veneno (*m.*)   poison, 19
venir (e:ie)   to come, 4
ventana (*f.*)   window, 10
ventanilla (*f.*)   window (of a car)
ver   to see, 7
verbo (*m.*)   verb
verdad (*f.*)   truth, 11
¿verdad?   right?, true?, 2
verde   green, 3
veredicto (*m.*)   verdict, 14
verruga (*f.*)   wart
vestido (*m.*)   dress
vestido(a)   dressed, 4
vez (*f.*)   time, 8
vía (*f.*)   lane, 12
viaje (*m.*)   trip
víctima (*f.*)   victim, 17
vida (*f.*)   life, 2
video-cámara (*f.*)   video camera, 10
videocasetera (*f.*)   videocassette recorder (VCR), 11
videograbadora (*f.*)   videocassette recorder (VCR), 11
viejo(a)   old, 7
vino (*m.*)   wine, 20
violación (*f.*)   rape, 18
violar   to rape, 18
virarse (*Cuba*)   to turn around, 20
visible   visible, 7
visto(a)   seen
vivir   to live, 2
vocabulario (*m.*)   vocabulary
volante (*m.*)   steering wheel
voltearse   to turn around, 20
voluntad (*f.*)   will, 17
voluntariamente   voluntarily, 20
volver (o:ue)   to come (go) back, to return, 8

Y

y   and, P
ya   already, 2; at last, finally, 8
yerba (*f.*)   marijuana (*coll.*), 15
yerno (*m.*)   son-in-law

Z

zacate (*m.*) (*México*)   lawn, 5; marijuana (*coll.*)
zapato de tenis (*m.*)   tennis shoe
zona (*f.*)   zone, 9
— **de estacionamiento** (*f.*)   parking lot, 7
zurdo(a)   left-handed, 7

English-Spanish Vocabulary

A

a little un poco, 1
a week ago hace una semana, 14
abnormal anormal, 18
about unos(as), 2; como, 11; (*with time*) a eso de, 14
abuse maltrato (*m.*), 8; maltratar, abusar, 8
accelerator acelerador (*m.*)
accent acento (*m.*), 18
accept aceptar, 8
accident accidente (*m.*), 1
accompany acompañar, 7
accomplice cómplice (*m., f.*)
according to según
accusation acusación (*f.*), 14
accuse acusar, 8
ache doler (o:ue), 13
acid (LSD) pegao (*m.*) (*coll.*)
acne acné (*m.*)
acquaintance conocido(a) (*m., f.*)
acquitted absuelto(a)
across the street from enfrente de, 5
act acto (*m.*), 18; actuar
activity actividad (*f.*)
addicted adicto(a)
additional adicional
address dirección (*f.*), P; domicilio (*m.*), P
  — book libreta de direccíones (*f.*), 18
adjective adjetivo (*m.*), 1
admitted (to) ingresado(a), 8
adolescent adolescente (*m., f.*), jovencito(a) (*m., f.*), 17
adult mayor de edad
after después (de), 7
afternoon tarde (*f.*)
  in the — por la tarde, 7
afterwards luego, 10
again otra vez, 6; de nuevo, 9
against en contra de, 6; contra, 11
age edad (*f.*), 17
ago: a week — hace una semana, 14
agree estar de acuerdo, 16
aggression agresión (*f.*); ataque (*m.*)
aggressor agresor(a) (*m., f.*)
AIDS SIDA (síndrome de inmunodeficiencia adquirida) (*m.*), 18

aim (a gun) apuntar, 20
alcohol alcohol (*m.*), 9
alcoholic alcohólico(a), 9
alias alias (*m.*)
alibi coartada (*f.*)
all todo(a), 11; todos(as)
allergic alérgico(a)
allow dejar, 9; autorizar, 16
almost casi
alone solo(a), 2
alphabet abecedario (*m.*), 9; alfabeto (*m.*), 9
already ya, 2
also también, 8
although aunque, 15
always siempre, 3
ambulance ambulancia (*f.*), 13
among entre
and y, P
angry enojado(a), 8
ankle tobillo (*m.*)
another otro(a), 4
answer contestar, 5; respuesta (*f.*), contestación (*f.*)
any cualquier, alguno(a) 6
  — one cualquier(a)
  — time a sus órdenes, 3
  not — ninguno(a)
anything algo (*m.*), 8; cualquier cosa (*f.*)
  — else? ¿Algo más?, 7
  — you say cualquier cosa que diga, 6
apartment apartamento (*m.*), 1
appoint nombrar
approximate aproximado(a), 11
approximately como, 11; aproximadamente
area distrito (*m.*), área (*f. but* el área)
arm brazo (*m.*), 6
around unos(as), 2
arrange arreglar
arrest arrestar, prender, 3; llevar preso(a)
  person under — detenido(a) (*m., f.*), 16
arrested arrestado(a), detenido(a), preso(a), 6
arrive (at) llegar (a), 2
arrow flecha (*f.*), 18
arson fuego intencional (*m.*), incendio intencional (*m.*)
article artículo (*m.*), 14

as   como, 14

— **(big, small, etc.) as**   tan (grande, pequeño, etc.) como, 4

— **soon as**   en cuanto, 18

Asian   asiático(a)

ask (a question)   preguntar, 8

— **a question**   hacer una pregunta, 19

— **for**   solicitar, 2; pedir (e:i), 8

assailant   agresor(a) (*m., f.*)

assassin   asesino(a) (*m., f.*)

assault   asaltar, asalto (*m.*); agresión (*f.*), ataque (*m.*)

assembly   reunión (*f.*), congregación (*f.*), mitin (*m.*), 20

assigned   asignado(a), 15

at   en, 1; a, 2

— **dawn (daybreak)**   al amanecer; de madrugada

— **dusk**   al anochecer

— **least**   por lo menos, 17

— **midnight**   a medianoche

— **night**   por la noche

— **noon**   a mediodía

— **this time (hour)**   a esta hora, 3

— **your service**   para servir, P; a sus órdenes, 3

attack   atacar, 18; ataque (*m.*), agresión (*f.*)

attempt   intento (*m.*), 15

attend   asistir, 17

aunt   tía (*f.*), 15

authority   autoridad (*f.*), 8

authorize   autorizar, 16

automatic   automático(a), 5

automobile   automóvil (*m.*), 6

avenue   avenida (*f.*), P

average   mediano(a)

avoid   evitar, 13

B

baby   bebé (*m.*), 12

back   (*of paper*) dorso (*m.*); (*part of body*) espalda (*f.*)

in the — (of)   en el fondo (de)

bad   malo(a), 6

bail   fianza (*f.*), 16

— **bondsman**   fiancista (*m., f.*), 16

bailor   fiancista (*m., f.*), 16

bald   calvo(a), pelado(a), 18; pelón(ona)

bandage   venda (*f.*), 13

bank   banco (*m.*), 2

bar   bar (*m.*), cantina (*f.*), barra (*f.*), 8

bargain   ganga (*f.*), 14

basement   sótano (*m.*)

bath   baño (*m.*), 18

bathe   bañarse, 18

bathroom   baño (*m.*); escusado (excusado) (*m.*) (*México*)

bathtub   bañadera (*f.*), tina (*f.*) (*Mex.*)

battery   batería (*f.*), acumulador (*m.*)

be   ser, 2; estar, 3

— **able to**   poder (o:ue), 6

— **about** (+ *time*)   ser como las (+ *time*), 18

— **admitted (to)**   ingresar, 8

— **afraid**   tener miedo, 5; temer

— **at fault**   tener la culpa (de), ser culpable (de), 12

— **back**   estar de vuelta, estar de regreso, 5

— **called**   llamarse, 9

— **certain**   estar seguro(a), 18

— **free on bail**   estar en libertad bajo fianza

— **glad**   alegrarse

— **going (to do something)**   ir a (+ *inf.*), 5

— **guilty**   tener la culpa (de), ser culpable (de), 12

— **hereby declared illegal** quedar declarado(a) ilegal, 20

— **in a condition to (do something)**   estar en condiciones de (+ *inf.*), 6

— **in a hurry**   estar apurado(a), tener prisa, 9

— **in charge**   tener a su cargo, 15

— **in jail**   estar preso(a)

— **late**   llegar tarde, 12

— **located**   quedar, 2

— **missing**   faltar, 10

— **named**   llamarse, 9

— **okay**   estar bien, 3

— **pleasing**   gustar, 13

— **quiet!**   ¡Cállese!, 20

— **right**   tener razón, 12

— **(very) sleepy**   tener (mucho) sueño, 6

— **so scared**   tener tanto miedo, 18

— (*amount*) **tall**   medir (e:i) (*amount*), 17

— **under arrest**   darse preso(a)

— **visible**   estar a la vista

— **wrong**   estar equivocado(a), 8

— **. . . years old**   tener... años, 4

beard   barba (*f.*), 18

beat   pegar, 8

beating   paliza (*f.*)

because   porque, 3

become   hacerse

— **addicted to drugs**   endrogarse

— **aware of**   darse cuenta de, 13

bedroom   dormitorio (*m.*), recámara (*f.*) (*México*), 8

before   antes (de), 3

— **they question you**   antes de que lo interroguen, 6

begin   empezar (e:ie), 9; iniciar, 12

behind   atrasado(a), 11; atrás, 12

— **your back**   detrás de la espalda

believe   creer, 4

belongings   pertenencias (*f. pl.*), 16

below   debajo de, 13

belt   cinto (*m.*), cinturón (*m.*), correa (*f.*), 8

bend down   agacharse

besides   además, 2

best   mejor, 12

better   mejor, 12

— **than ever**   mejor que nunca, 6

between   entre, 1

bicycle   bicicleta (*f.*), 2

big   grande, 2

birth   nacimiento (*m.*)

bite   mordida (*f.*)

black   negro(a), 4

blackmail   chantaje (*m.*); chantajear

blade   arma blanca (*f. but* el arma blanca)

blame   culpa (*f.*); culpar

blemish   mancha (*f.*)

blind   ciego(a)

blink   parpadear, 6

block   cuadra (*f.*), 2

a — from here   a una cuadra de aquí, 2

blonde   rubio(a), güero(a) (*México*), 7

blood   sangre (*f.*)

— **bank**   banco de sangre (*m.*), 6

blouse   blusa (*f.*), 17

blue   azul, 4

body   cuerpo (*m.*); (*corpse*) cadáver (*m.*)

— **hair**   vello (*m.*)

bomb   bomba (*f.*)

time —   bomba de tiempo (*f.*)

bond   bono (*m.*), 16

book   registrar, fichar, 16

bookstore   librería (*f.*)

boot   bota (*f.*)

bottle   botella (*f.*), 15

boy   muchacho (*m.*), 2; chico (*m.*), chamaco (*m.*), 13

boyfriend   novio (*m.*), 15

brake   freno (*m.*)

brand   marca (*f.*), 10

breath   aliento (*m.*), 9

breathe   respirar

bribe   soborno (*m.*), 15

brief   breve

— **conversation**   conversación breve (*f.*), P

bring   traer, 7

broken   descompuesto(a), 19

brother   hermano (*m.*)

— **-in-law**   cuñado (*m.*)

brown   (*hair, eyes*) castaño(a), 18; café, 18

bug-eyes (bulging eyes)   ojos saltones (*m. pl.*)

build   complexión (*f.*)

building   edificio (*m.*), 6

bullet   bala (*f.*)

bus   ómnibus (*m.*), autobuses (*m.*), guagua (*f.*) (*Cuba*)

— **station**   estación de ómnibus (autobuses) (*f.*)

— **stop**   parada de autobuses (*f.*)

businessman(woman)   hombre (mujer) de negocios (*m., f.*), 15

but   pero, 1

butt in   entremeterse, entrometerse, 8

button   botón (*m.*)

buy   comprar, 10

by force   a la fuerza, 8

by hand   de la mano, 2

by phone   por teléfono, 1

C

cab   (*of a truck*) cabina (*f.*), 13

caliber   calibre (*m.*), 20

call   llamar, 1; llamada (*f.*), 4

— **off the dog**   llamar al perro

calm   quieto(a), 13

269

— **down**   calmarse, 18
can   poder (o:ue), 6
cannot: You (One) — write . . .
   No se puede escribir... , 6
cap   gorra (f.), 4
car   carro (m.), coche (m.), máquina
   (f.) (Cuba), 6
— **-related**   automovilístico(a)
carburetor   carburador (m.)
card   tarjeta (f.), 3
Careful!   ¡Cuidado!, 20
carefully   con cuidado, 12
carry   llevar, 2
— **out**   realizar, 18
case   caso (m.)
cash: in —   en efectivo, 10
— **register**   caja (f.), 20
cashier   cajero(a) (m., f.)
cause   causar, 12
— **damage**   perjudicar, 14
cell   celda (f.), 16
cent   centavo (m.), 16
central   central, 1
certain   cierto(a), 8
Certainly!   ¡Cómo no!, 7
chain   cadena (f.), 16
change   cambiar, 12
— **clothes**   cambiarse de ropa, 18
characteristic   característica (f.)
charge   acusación (f.), 14;
   cobrar, 14
cheat   engañar, 14
check   revisar, 10
cheek   mejilla (f.), cachete (m.), 17
chemical   químico(a), 9
chest   pecho (m.)
child   niño(a) (m., f.), 1
—**'s car seat**   asiento para el
   niño (m.)
children   hijos (m. pl.), 4
chin   barbilla (f.)
choose   elegir (e:i), 9
chosen   elegido(a), 9
church   iglesia (f.)
cigarette   cigarrillo (m.), 7
city   ciudad (f.), 2
class   clase (f.), 7
classmate   compañero(a) de clase
   (m., f.), 17
clean   limpiar, 10
clerk   empleado(a) (m., f.), 14;
   dependiente (m., f.), 20
clinic   clínica (f.)
close   cerrar (e:ie), 9; cerca (de), 12

closed   cerrado(a), 11
closeted   encerrado(a), 8
clothes   ropa (f.), 4
clothing   ropa (f.), 4
clue   pista (f.)
coat   abrigo (m.)
cocaine   coca (f.), cocaína (f.); coll.:
   perico (m.), polvo (m.)
cognate   cognado (m.)
coin   moneda (f.), 9
collar   cuello (m.)
collect   cobrar, 14
collide   chocar, 13
collision   choque (m.), 13
color   color (m.)
comb   peine (m.), 16
come   venir (e:ie), 4
— **back**   volver (o:ue), 8
— **in**   pasar, P; entrar (en)
— **out**   salir
— **with**   acompañar, 7
commit   cometer, 6
— **suicide**   suicidarse, 19
common   común
communicate   comunicar, 5
compact disc   disco
   compacto (m.), 10
complain   protestar, 3
complaint   queja (f.)
complete   completo(a), 5;
   completar, 9
completely   por completo, 16
computer   computadora (f.),
   ordenador (m.) (España), 10
condition   condición (f.), 6
condom   condón (m.), 18
confess   confesar (e:ie)
confession   confesión (f.)
confirm   confirmar, 19
consulate   consulado (m.), 20
content   contenido (m.), 9
continue   continuar, 10
contraband   contrabando (m.)
contract   contrato (m.), 10
control   control (m.), 13
conversation   conversación (f.)
convict   declarar culpable
cooperation   cooperación (f.), 3
copy   copia (f.), 11
corduroy   pana (f.), 20
corner   esquina (f.), 3
corporal punishment   castigo
   corporal (m.)
cost   costar (o:ue), 15

270

counsel for the defense abogado(a) defensor(a) (*m., f.*)

count contar (o:ue), 9

counter mostrador (*m.*), 16

counterfeit falsificar; falsificación

country país (*m.*), 8

couple: a — of un par de, 6

court (of law) corte (*f.*), 6; tribunal (*m.*), juzgado (*m.*), 6

— reporter taquígrafo(a) (*m., f.*)

courtesy cortesía (*f.*)

cousin primo(a) (*m., f.*)

crack cocaine crac (*m.*); *coll.:* piedra (*f.*), roca (*f.*), coca cocinada (*f.*)

crash choque (*m.*), 13

crime delito (*m.*), 6

criminal criminal

— record antecedentes penales (*m. pl.*), 16

crippled inválido(a)

cross cruzar, 12; cruz (*f.*), 17

cross-eyed bizco(a)

crossing cruce (*m.*), 12

crowbar pata de cabra (*f.*)

crowd multitud (*f.*), 20

cry llorar, 18

cultural cultural

curfew toque de queda (*m.*), 3

curly rizado(a), rizo(a), crespo(a)

customer cliente (*m., f.*), 7

cut cortar, 5

D

dad papá (*m.*), 5

dagger puñal (*m.*); daga (*f.*)

damage: slight — desperfecto (*m.*), 19

dangerous peligroso(a), 4

dark oscuro(a), 4

date fecha (*f.*); salir con, 17

daughter hija (*f.*)

— -in-law nuera (*f.*)

day día (*m.*)

during the — durante el día

the — after tomorrow pasado mañana

the — before yesterday anteayer, antes de ayer

deaf sordo(a)

deceive engañar, 14

decide decidir, 6

decision fallo (*m.*)

defend (oneself) defender(se), 18

defendant acusado(a) (*m., f.*), reo(a) (*m., f.*)

deformed deformado(a)

delivery entrega (*f.*), 5

demand exigir, 2

department departamento (*m.*), 4

depend depender, 16

describe describir, 7

description descripción (*f.*), 11

destroy destruir, 18

detail detalle (*m.*), 17

detain detener (e:ie), 6

detective detective (*m., f.*), 14

detention detención (*f.*), 16

determine determinar, 9

detour desvío (*m.*)

detoxification desintoxicación (*f.*)

diabetes diabetes (*f.*), 6

die morir (o:ue), 13

dining room comedor (*m.*)

dirty sucio(a), 18

disabled inválido(a)

disappear desaparecer

discipline disciplinar, 8

disease enfermedad (*f.*)

disfigured desfigurado(a)

dispatcher operador(a) (*m., f.*), telefonista (*m., f.*), 1

disperse dispersar(se), 20

distribute distribuir, 15

district barrio (*m.*), colonia (*f.*) (*México*), 5

— attorney fiscal (*m., f.*), 16

divided road doble vía (*f.*)

division división (*f.*), 1; sección, 1

dizzy mareado(a), 13

do hacer, 3

doctor médico(a) (*m., f.*), doctor(a) (*m., f.*), 8

document documento (*m.*), 17

dollar dólar (*m.*), 10

domicile domicilio (*m.*)

door puerta (*f.*), 7

double doble

doubt dudar, 16

dress vestido (*m.*)

dressed vestido(a), 4

drink trago (*m.*), 6; bebida (*f.*), 8; tomar, 6

drinking bebida (*f.*), 8

drive manejar, conducir, 6

— fifty miles per hour conducir a cincuenta millas por hora, 9

— safely! ¡Maneje con cuidado!, 12

driver chofer (*m.*), 6; conductor(a) (*m., f.*), 12

—'s license licencia para manejar (*f.*), licencia de conducir (*f.*), 3

drop soltar (o:ue)

— out of school abandonar los estudios

— the gun (weapon) soltar el arma

drug droga (*f.*), 6

— pusher droguero(a) (*m., f.*)

— user droguero(a) (*m., f.*)

on drugs endrogado(a), 6

drugstore farmacia (*f.*), botica (*f.*)

drunk borracho(a), 6

DT's delirium tremens (*m.*)

during durante, 6

dynamite dinamita (*f.*)

E

each cada, 6

ear (inner) oído (*m.*); (outer) oreja (*f.*)

early temprano

earring arete (*m.*), 17

easy fácil

either cualquiera, 9

elbow codo (*m.*)

emergency emergencia (*f.*), 4

— parking only estacionamiento de emergencia solamente

employee empleado(a) (*m., f.*), 14

empty desocupado(a), 3; vaciar, 16

end final (*m.*), punta (*f.*), 9; terminar

endanger poner en peligro, 12

engine motor (*m.*), 9

English (language) inglés (*m.*), 1

enough suficiente, 15

enroll (in a school) matricularse, 15

enter ingresar, 8

do not — no entre; no pase

entrance entrada (*f.*)

envelope sobre (*m.*), 16

epileptic epiléptico(a)

equipment equipo (*m.*), 10

even though aunque

evening noche (*f.*)

in the — por la noche, 7

ever alguna vez

every cada, 6, todos(as)

— day todos los días, 8

everything possible todo lo posible, 11

evidence evidencia (*f.*), 18; prueba (*f.*)

exactly exactamente, 17

examine examinar, chequear, 13

example: for — por ejemplo, 7

excessive demasiado(a), 12

excuse excusa (*f.*), 12

expensive caro(a)

expert perito(a) (*m., f.*)

explosive explosivo (*m.*)

expression expresión (*f.*)

— of courtesy expresión de cortesía (*f.*)

extent: to a large — en buena parte, 16

eye ojo (*m.*)

with (blue) eyes de ojos (azules), 7

eyebrow ceja (*f.*)

eyeglasses anteojos (*m.*), lentes (*m.*), espejuelos (*m.*) (*Cuba, Puerto Rico*), gafas (*f.*), 18

eyelashes pestañas (*f. pl.*)

F

face cara (*f.*), 13

— down boca abajo

fake falso(a)

fall caerse, 18

false statement declaración falsa (*f.*)

falsification falsificación (*f.*)

falsify falsificar

family familia (*f.*), 8

— room sala de estar (*f.*)

farewell despedida (*f.*)

fast rápido, 5

fat gordo(a), 7; grueso(a)

father padre (*m.*), papá (*m.*), 5

— -in-law suegro (*m.*)

fear temer

feel sentir(se) (e:ie), 13

felony delito mayor (*m.*), delito grave (*m.*), 14

fender guardafangos (*m.*)

fewer than menos de, 4

fight luchar, 18; pelea (*f.*); riña (*f.*)

fill out llenar, 1

filter filtro (*m.*)

finally ya, 8
find encontrar (o:ue), 11; hallar
— **out** averiguar, 10
— **refuge (shelter)** refugiarse
fine (*adv.*) bien, P; multa (*f.*), 6
finger dedo (*m.*), 9
fingerprint huella digital (*f.*), 10;
tomar las huellas digitales, 16
finish terminar, 10
— **(doing something)** terminar
de (+ *inf.*), 10
fire fuego (*m.*), incendio (*m.*), 5
— **department** estación de
bomberos (*f.*)
— **extinguisher** extinguidor de
incendios (*m.*), 13
—**fighter** bombero(a) (*m., f.*), 5
firearm arma de fuego (*f. but* el
arma de fuego), 4
first (*adv.*) primero, 1; (*adj.*)
primero(a)
— **aid** primeros auxilios (*m. pl.*)
— **class** de primera calidad, 14
fix arreglar, 19
flashlight linterna (*f.*), 4
flat tire goma ponchada (*f.*), llanta
pinchada (*f.*)
floor piso (*m.*), 7
flower flor (*f.*)
— **pot** maceta de flores (*f.*)
flowered floreado(a)
following siguiente
foolishness tontería (*f.*), 10
foot pie (*m.*), 7
for por, P; para, 1
— **me** para mí, 14
— **possession of drugs** por
poseer drogas
— **you** para ti, 18
force forzar (o:ue), 10; obligar, 18;
fuerza (*f.*)
by — a la fuerza, 8
forehead frente (*f.*)
forge falsificar
forged falso(a)
forgery falsificación (*f.*)
forget olvidar, 18
forgive perdonar, 8
forgiveness perdón (*m.*), 8
form papeleta (*f.*), 19
fortunately por suerte, 13
fourth cuarto(a), 4
fraud estafa (*f.*), 14
freckle peca (*f.*), 7

Freeze! ¡Quieto(a)!, 3; ¡No se
mueva(n)!, 6
frequently frecuentemente, 8
fresh nuevo(a), 6
friend amigo(a) (*m., f.*), 3
frightened aterrorizado(a), 18
from desde, 8
front: in — of frente a, 1
fur coat abrigo de piel (*m.*)
future futuro (*m.*)

G

gag mordaza (*f.*)
gang pandilla (*f.*), 3
garage garaje (*m.*)
garbage basura (*f.*), 10
garden jardín (*m.*)
gardener jardinero(a) (*m., f.*), 3
gas gas (*m.*), 19
— **station** gasolinera (*f.*),
estación de servicio (*f.*)
— **pedal** acelerador (*m.*)
gasoline gasolina (*f.*)
gearshift cambio de velocidades
(*m.*)
— **lever** palanca de cambio de
velocidades (*f.*), embrague (*m.*)
generally generalmente, 17
gentleman señor (Sr.) (*m.*), P
get conseguir (e:i), 8
— **away** alejarse
— **down** bajarse
— **hold of** agarrar, coger, 9
— **hurt** lastimarse, 13
— **in (a car, etc.)** subir, 3
— **off** bajarse, 9
— **on one's knees** ponerse de
rodillas
— **out** salir, 5; bajarse, 9
— **up** levantarse, 13
— **worse** agravarse, 15
girl muchacha (*f.*), 2
girlfriend novia (*f.*), 15
give dar, 3; entregar, 11
— **a gift** regalar, 15
— **a ticket** imponer una
multa, 12
— **notice** avisar de, 1
Gladly! ¡Cómo no!, 7
glass vidrio (*m.*)
— **cutter** cortavidrios (*m.*)
— **eye** ojo de vidrio (*m.*)
glove guante (*m.*)

— **compartment** guantera (*f.*), 7; portaguantes (*m.*)

go ir, 3

  — **away** irse, 10

  — **in** entrar, 4

  — **out (with)** salir (con), 17

  — **through a red light** pasarse la luz roja, 12

  — **with** acompañar, 7

goddaughter ahijada (*f.*)

godfather padrino (*m.*)

godmother madrina (*f.*)

godson ahijado (*m.*)

gold oro (*m.*), 16

good bueno(a)

  — **afternoon.** Buenas tardes., P

  — **evening.** Buenas noches., P

  — **morning (day).** Buenos días., P

  — **night.** Buenas noches., P

good-bye adiós, P

grab agarrar, coger, 9

graffiti grafiti (*m.*)

granddaughter nieta (*f.*)

grandfather abuelo (*m.*)

grandmother abuela (*f.*)

grandson nieto (*m.*)

gray gris, 20

gray-haired canoso(a)

great gran, 14

green verde, 3

greet saludar, 15

greeting saludo (*m.*)

ground suelo (*m.*)

group grupo (*m.*), 20

guilty culpable

H

hair pelo (*m.*), 17; cabello (*m.*)

  body — vello (*m.*)

hairpiece peluca (*f.*)

hairy velludo(a)

hall pasillo (*m.*)

hallucinations alucinaciones (*f. pl.*)

Halt! ¡Alto!, 3

hand mano (*f.*), 6

  — **grenade** granada de mano (*f.*)

  Hands up! ¡Manos arriba!

handcuffed esposado(a), 16

handcuffs esposas (*f. pl.*), 16

handkerchief pañuelo (*m.*), 16

handsaw sierra de mano (*f.*), serrucho de mano (*m.*)

happen pasar, suceder, 2; ocurrir

hashish hachich (*m.*), hachís (*m.*), *coll.:* chocolate (*m.*), kif (*m.*), grifa (*f.*)

hat sombrero (*m.*), 4

have tener, 4

  — **a good time** pasarlo bien, pasar un buen rato, 15

  — **(something) fixed** hacer arreglar, 19

  — **just (done something)** acabar de (+ *inf.*)

  — **on** tener puesto(a), llevar puesto(a), 17

  — **the right to** tener el derecho de, 6

  — **to (do something)** tener que (+ *inf.*), 4

head cabeza (*f.*), 19

headlight faro (*m.*), 19

health salud (*f.*)

  To your —! ¡Salud!

hear oír, 19

heart corazón (*m.*), 7

  — **attack** ataque al corazón (*m.*), 7

height estatura (*f.*), 20

  of medium — de estatura mediana, 4

hello hola, P

helmet casco (*m.*) de seguridad, 2

help ayuda (*f.*), 1; ayudar, 18

Help! ¡Socorro!, ¡Auxilio!, 5

her su, 3

here aquí, 1

heroin heroína (*f.*); *coll.:* caballo (*m.*), manteca (*f.*) (*Caribe*)

herself: by — por sí misma

hi hola, P

high school escuela secundaria (*f.*), 15

highway autopista (*f.*), 12; carretera (*f.*), 13

hijack asaltar

hijacking asalto (*m.*)

him lo, 6

himself: by — por sí mismo

hip cadera (*f.*)

his su, 3

Hispanic hispano(a), 2; hispánico(a), latino(a)

hit chocar, 13; golpear, 18

hold-up asalto (*m.*)
home casa (*f.*), 1
homicide homicidio (*m.*), 16
honk the horn tocar la bocina
hood capucha (*f.*); (car) capó (*m.*); cubierta (*f.*)
hope: I — ojalá, 17
horn bocina (*f.*)
hospital hospital (*m.*), 4
hotel hotel (*m.*)
hour hora (*f.*), 3
house casa (*f.*), 1
how? ¿cómo?, 2
   — are you? ¿Cómo está Ud.?, P
   — do you spell it? ¿Cómo se escribe?
   — long? ¿cuánto tiempo?, 5
   — many? ¿cuántos(as)?, 2
however sin embargo, 14
hurt herido(a), 1; lastimado(a), 7; doler (o:ue), 13; perjudicar, 14; causarle daño a
husband esposo (*m.*), marido (*m.*), 4
hypodermic syringe jeringuilla (*f.*), jeringa hipodérmica (*f.*)
hysterical histérico(a)
hysterically histéricamente, 18

I

ID identificación (*f.*), 3
idea idea (*f.*), 10
identification identificación (*f.*), 3
identify identificar
indicted procesado(a)
if si, 4
immediately inmediatamente, 8
imperfection desperfecto (*m.*), 19
important importante, 17
impose a fine imponer una multa, 12
imprudently imprudentemente, 12
in en, 1; dentro (de), 6
   — charge of a cargo de, 8
   — front of a la vista de, 16
   — installments a plazos, 5
   — the afternoon por la tarde, P
   — the evening por la noche, P
   — the morning por la mañana, P
   — the presence of la vista de, 16
   — writing por escrito, 16
inch pulgada (*f.*), 7

index finger (dedo) índice (*m.*)
indicted procesado(a)
infiltrate infiltrar, 15
inform avisar de, notificar, 1
information información (*f.*), P
   personal — dato personal (*m.*), 1
injured herido(a), 1; lastimado(a), 7; lesionado(a), 8
injury lesión (*f.*), 8
in-laws parientes políticos (*m. pl.*)
innocent inocente, 14
inserted in metido(a), 19
inside dentro, 4; adentro, 8; metido(a), 19
installment plazo (*m.*), 11
   in —s a plazos, 10
instead of en lugar de, 8
insured asegurado(a), 11
interlace entrelazar
interrogate interrogar, 6
interrogation interrogatorio (*m.*), 6
interview entrevista (*f.*)
introduce presentar, 15
investigate investigar, 8
investigating investigador(a), 16
investigation averiguación (*f.*), 10; investigación (*f.*)
item objeto (*m.*), 11

J

jack gato (*m.*), gata (*f.*) (*Costa Rica*), 20
jacket chaqueta (*f.*), chamarra (*f.*) (*México*), 20; saco (*m.*)
jail cárcel (*f.*), prisión (*f.*)
jewelry joya (*f.*), 10
   — store joyería (*f.*)
job trabajo (*m.*), 8
joint *coll.:* cucaracha (*f.*), leño (*m.*), porro (*m.*) (drugs)
judge juez (*m., f.*), 8; juzgar
jump saltar, 13
junior high school escuela secundaria (*f.*), 15
jury jurado (*m.*), 14
just: It's — that . . . Es que... , 9
just in time a tiempo
juvenile juvenil
   — court tribunal de menores (*m.*)
   — delinquent delincuente juvenil (*m., f.*)

— **hall**   centro de reclusión de menores (*m.*)

K

keep   guardar; mantener (e:ie)
  — **right**   mantenga su derecha
  — **walking**   seguir (e:i) caminando
key   llave (*f.*), 5
kick   patada (*f.*)
kidnap   secuestrar, 12
kidnapping   secuestro (*m.*), 17
kill   matar, 8
kind   clase (*f.*), 7
kitchen   cocina (*f.*), 5
knee   rodilla (*f.*)
knife   cuchillo (*m.*), 18
knock at the door   tocar a la puerta, 8
know   conocer, saber, 7

L

ladder   escalera (*f.*)
  rope —   escala de soga (*f.*)
  hand —   escalera de mano (*f.*)
lady   señora (*f.*), P
lame   cojo(a)
lane   carril (*m.*), 12
language   lengua (*f.*)
large   grande, 2
last   último(a), 11, pasado(a)
  at —   ya, 8
  — **month**   el mes pasado
  — **name**   apellido (*m.*), P
  — **night**   anoche, 10
  — **week**   la semana pasada
  — **year**   el año pasado
late   tarde, 2
later   más tarde, 2; después, 6; luego, 10
Latin   latino(a), 15
law   ley (*f.*), 2
lawn   césped (*m.*), zacate (*m.*) (*México*), 5
lawyer   abogado(a) (*m., f.*), 6
learn   aprender, 15
leave   salir, 5; irse, 10
  — **behind**   dejar, 5
left   izquierdo(a), 7
left-handed   zurdo(a), 7
leg   pierna (*f.*), 13
lend   prestar
less than   menos de, 4

let   dejar, 9
  — **go of**   soltar (o:ue)
let's (do something)   vamos a (+ *inf.*)
  — **go.**   Vamos., 2
  — **see**   a ver, 6
license plate   placa (*f.*), chapa (*f.*), 11
lie   mentira (*f.*), 8
  — **down**   acostarse (o:ue)
life   vida (*f.*), 2
lift   levantar
light   luz (*f.*), 4; foco (*m.*); (*light in color*) claro(a), 11
like   como, 14
  — **this**   así, 9
limit   límite (*m.*), 9
line   línea (*f.*), 9
lip   labio (*m.*)
liquor store   licorería (*f.*), 7
lisp   hablar con (la) zeta
list   lista (*f.*), 11
lit   prendido(a), 19
little   (*quantity*) poco; (*size*) pequeño(a), 2
  a —   un poco de, 1
  — **finger**   meñique (*m.*)
live   vivir, 2
living room   sala (*f.*)
local   local, 8
lock   cerradura (*f.*), 10; cerrar (e:ie) con llave, 11
  — **up**   encerrar (e:ie), 16
locked   cerrado(a), 11
  — **up**   encerrado(a), 8
lodging   alojamiento (*m.*), hospedaje (*m.*)
log in   registrar, fichar, 16
long   largo(a)
long-sleeved   de mangas largas
Look.   Mire., 6
  — **at**   mirar, 16
  — **for**   buscar, 2
  What is he/she/you — like?   ¿Cómo es?, 4
lose   perder (e:ie), 6
  — **one's job**   quedarse sin trabajo, 14
lost   perdido(a), 2
LSD   ácido (*m.*); *coll.*: pastilla (*f.*), pegao (*m.*), sello (*m.*)

M

Ma'am   señora (Sra.) (*f.*), P
machine gun   ametralladora (*f.*)

Madam señora (Sra.) (*f.*), P
mail correo (*m.*), correspondencia (*f.*), 5
make hacer, 3; (car) marca (*f.*)
man hombre (*m.*), 3
manage conseguir (e:i)
manslaughter homicidio (*m.*), 16
many muchos(as), 2
marijuana yerba (*f.*) (*coll.*), 15; mariguana (*f.*), marijuana (*f.*); *coll.:* mota (*f.*), pasto (*m.*), pito (*m.*), zacate (*m.*)
mark marca (*f.*), 6; mancha (*f.*)
market mercado (*m.*), 20
  open-air — mercado al aire libre (*m.*), tianguis (*m.*) (*México*)
mask máscara (*f.*)
mat felpudo (*m.*)
measure medir (e:i), 7
meddle entremeterse, 8; entrometerse, 8
medication medicina (*f.*), medicamento (*m.*)
medicine medicina (*f.*), 7
medium mediano(a)
meeting reunión (*f.*), congregación (*f.*), mitin (*m.*), 20
member miembro (*m.*, *f.*), 3
mention: Don't — it. De nada., No hay de qué., P
methadone metadona (*f.*)
middle medio (*m.*)
  about the — of the month (week) a mediados de mes (semana)
  — finger dedo mayor (*m.*), dedo corazón (*m.*)
midnight medianoche (*f.*), 3
mile milla (*f.*), 9
minor menor de edad (*m.*, *f.*), 3; menor
Miranda Warning advertencia Miranda (*f.*), 6
mirror espejo (*m.*)
miss señorita (Srta.) (*f.*), P
missing desaparecido(a)
mixed race (*black and white*) mulato(a); (*any of two or more races*) mestizo(a)
model modelo (*m.*), 11
mole lunar (*m.*), 17
mom mamá (*f.*), madre (*f.*), 2
moment momento (*m.*), P
money dinero (*m.*), 8

month mes (*m.*)
monument monumento (*m.*)
more más
  — or less más o menos, 8
  — . . . than más... que, 4
morgue morgue (*f.*)
morning mañana (*f.*), 10
  early — madrugada (*f.*), 9
  in the — por la mañana, 7
morphine morfina (*f.*)
motel motel (*m.*), 15
mother madre (*f.*), mamá (*f.*), 2
  — -in-law suegra (*f.*)
motive motivo (*m.*)
motor motor (*m.*), 9
motorcycle motocicleta (*f.*), 13
motor-driven cycle motocicleta (*f.*)
moustache bigote (*m.*), 18
mouth boca (*f.*), 17
move moverse (o:ue), 16
  Don't—! ¡No se mueva(n)!, 6
movie theatre cine (*m.*), 15
movies cine (*m.*), 15
mow cortar, 5
Mr. señor (Sr.) (*m.*), P
  — and Mrs. (Ruiz) los señores (Ruiz) (*m. pl.*), 17
Mrs. señora (Sra.) (*f.*), P
much (*adv.*) mucho, 4
muffler silenciador (*m.*)
mug asaltar
mugging asalto (*m.*)
murder asesinar; asesinato (*m.*)
murderer asesino(a) (*m.*, *f.*)
murmur murmurar, 20
muscular musculoso(a)
must deber, 2
my mi, 1

N

name nombre (*m.*), P
near cercano(a), 10; (*prep.*) cerca de
nearby cercano(a), 10
necessary necesario(a), 5
neck cuello (*m.*), 16
necklace collar (*m.*), 14
need necesitar, 1; hacer falta, 15
needle aguja (*f.*), 6
neighbor vecino(a), 4
neighborhood barrio (*m.*), colonia (*f.*) (*México*), 5; vecindario (*m.*), 11
nephew sobrino (*m.*)

never   nunca, 6

nevertheless   sin embargo, 14

new   nuevo(a), 6

newspaper   periódico (*m.*), diario (*m.*), 5

next   próximo(a), 4; siguiente
— **month (year)**   el mes (año) que viene, el mes (año) próximo
— **week**   la semana que viene, la semana próxima
the — **day**   al día siguiente

next-door   (*neighbor, house*) de al lado, 10

niece   sobrina (*f.*)

night   noche (*f.*), 5
the — **before last**   anteanoche

nobody   nadie, 8

noise   ruido (*m.*)

nonsense   tontería (*f.*), 10

nose   nariz (*f.*), 9

note   nota (*f.*)
take — **of**   anotar, 10

nothing   nada, P

notice   notar, 6

notify   avisar

noun   nombre (*m.*)

now   ahora, 1

number   número (*m.*)

O

oath   juramento (*m.*)
to take an —   jurar
under —   bajo juramento

object   objeto (*m.*), 11

obligate   obligar, 18

obscenity   obscenidad (*f.*), 20

occasion   ocasión (*f.*), 17

occur   ocurrir, 14

of   de, 1
— **age**   mayor de edad
— **course**   desde luego, 2; claro que sí, 10

off   (*light*) apagado(a), 9

offer   ofrecer, 14

officer   agente (*m., f.*), P

often   a menudo, 6

Oh, goodness gracious!   ¡Ay, Dios mío!, 2

oil   aceite (*m.*)

okay   bueno, P

old   viejo(a), 7

older   mayor, 17

on   en, 1; a, 2; (*by way of*) por, 2; (*a*

light) encendido(a), prendido(a), 5; sobre, 20
— **a bike**   en bicicleta, 2
— **foot**   a pie, 2
— **time**   a tiempo
— **time payments**   a plazos, 10
— **top of**   sobre, 20
— **vacation**   de vacaciones, 4

once again   otra vez, 6

only   sólo, solamente, 12

open   abierto(a)

opium   opio (*m.*)

opportunity   oportunidad (*f.*), 16

opposite: in the — **direction**   en sentido contrario, 13

or   o, 3

order   orden (*f.*), 8; ordenar, 20

other   otro(a), 4

our   nuestro(a), 5; nuestros(as), 15

out   (*light*) apagado(a), 9
— **on bail**   en libertad bajo fianza, 16
— **on one's own recognizance**   en libertad bajo palabra, 16

outside   fuera, 4

oven   horno (*m.*), 19

over there   para allá, 1

overdose   sobredosis (*f.*)

owe   deber, 11

owner   dueño(a) (*m., f.*), 7

P

paid (for)   pagado(a), 11

pants   pantalón (*m.*), pantalones (*m. pl.*), 4

paramedic   paramédico(a) (*m., f.*), 1

pardon   perdón, 8

parents   padres (*m.*), 3

park   parque (*m.*)

parked   estacionado(a), 11

parking lot   zona de estacionamiento (*f.*), 7

part   parte (*f.*)

party   fiesta (*f.*), 10

pass (a car)   pasar, rebasar (*México*), 13
do not —   no pasar; no rebasar (*México*)

passenger   pasajero(a) (*m., f.*), 13

patrol   patrulla (*f.*), 5
— **car**   carro patrullero (*m.*), 1

pawn   empeñar, 14

pay   pagar, 6

— **attention**   hacer caso, 2; prestar atención, 9
— attention (to someone) hacerle caso a, 8
payment   pago (*m.*), 11
pearl   perla (*f.*), 14
   cultured —   perla de cultivo (*f.*), 14
pedestrian   peatón(ona) (*m., f.*)
penetration   penetración (*f.*), 18
people   gente (*f.*), 20
perform   realizar, 18
perhaps   tal vez, 28
permission   permiso (*m.*), 20
permitted   permitido(a), 16
person   persona (*f.*), 3
   in —   en persona, 1
personal data   dato personal (*m.*), 1
personally   en persona, 1
phone   teléfono (*m.*)
   by —   por teléfono, 1
   on the —   por teléfono, 1
   — call   llamada telefónica (*f.*), 5
   — number   número de teléfono (*m.*), P
photograph   fotografía (*f.*), 3; retratar, 16
pick up   recoger, 5
picklock   llave falsa (*f.*), ganzúa (*f.*)
pierced   atravesado(a), 18
pimple   grano (*m.*)
pinstriped   a rayas
pistol   pistola (*f.*), 4
place   lugar (*m.*), 9
   to — nearby   arrimar, 9
plaid   a cuadros
plan (to do something)   pensar (e:ie) (+ *inf.*), 5
please   por favor, P
pocket   bolsillo (*m.*), 6
point (a gun)   apuntar, 20
poison   veneno (*m.*), 19
police (force)   policía (*f.*), 1
   — officer   policía (*m., f.*), 1
   — station   comisaría (*f.*), estación de policía, jefatura de policía (*f.*), P
polka dot   de lunares
pornographic   pornográfico(a)
post office   estación de correos (*f.*), oficina de correos (*f.*)
pound   libra (*f.*), 20
practice   practicar
precaution   precaución (*f.*), 13

pregnant   embarazada
preliminary   preliminar, 16
premium   prima (*f.*), 16
present (*adj.*)   presente, 6
prevent   prevenir
preventive   preventivo(a), 16
print   estampado(a)
prison   cárcel (*f.*), prisión (*f.*)
problem   problema (*m.*), 3
prohibited   prohibido(a)
promise   prometer, 20
property   propiedad (*f.*), 11
prosecutor   fiscal (*m., f.*), 16
prostitute   prostituto(a) (*m., f.*)
prostitution   prostitución (*f.*)
protest   protestar, 3
pull over (a car)   arrimar, 9
punch   trompada (*f.*), puñetazo (*m.*)
purse   cartera (*f.*), bolsa (*f.*), bolso (*m.*), 17
push   empujar, 18
put   poner, 9
   — away   guardado(a), 10
   — on   ponerse, 18
   — one's hands against the wall poner las manos en la pared
   — out (a fire)   apagar, 13

Q

question   interrogar, 6; pregunta (*f.*)
questioning   interrogatorio (*m.*), 6
quick(ly)   rápido, 5
quiet   callado(a), 6; quieto(a), 13
quite   bastante, 8

R

race   raza (*f.*), 18
railroad   ferrocarril (*m.*)
raincoat   impermeable (*m.*)
ransom   rescate (*m.*)
rape   violar, 18; violación (*f.*), 18
rather   más bien, medio, 7; bastante, 8
razor   navaja (*f.*), 8
reach   llegar (a), 2
read   leer, 6
ready   listo(a), 19
realize   darse cuenta (de), 13
reason   por qué (*m.*), 8
receive   recibir, 4
recent   reciente, 17

recite recitar, 9
recklessly imprudentemente, 12
recognize reconocer, 7
recommend recomendar (e:ie), 16
record player tocadiscos (*m.*), 10
recover recobrar, 11
red rojo(a), 12
red-haired pelirrojo(a), 7
refuse to negarse (e:ie) a, 9
register matricularse, 15
registered registrado(a), 11
registration registro (*m.*), 6
relative pariente (*m.*, *f.*)
remain permanecer, 6
remember recordar (o:ue), 6;
  acordarse (o:ue) (de), 10
report reporte (*m.*), informe (*m.*), 1;
  (*of a crime*) denuncia (*f.*); (*a crime*)
  denunciar, 1; avisar de, notificar, 1
represent representar
rescue rescatar
residential residencial, 9
resist hacer resistencia, 18
resisting arrest resistencia a la
  autoridad (*f.*)
respond responder, 15
rest: the — lo demás, 6
restaurant restaurante (*m.*)
return regresar, 2; volver (o:ue), 8
review revisar, 10
revolver revólver (*m.*), 4
rich rico(a)
rifle rifle (*m.*)
right derecho (*m.*), 6; (*adj.*)
  derecho(a), 13
  —? ¿verdad?, 2
  — away enseguida, 1
  — -hand side derecha (*f.*), 16
ring anillo (*m.*), 17
  — finger anular (*m.*)
risk riesgo (*m.*), 11
road camino (*m.*), 13
rob robar, 10
robbery robo (*m.*), 1
rock (*coll.* **crack cocaine**) piedra
  (*f.*), 15
roof techo (*m.*)
room cuarto (*m.*), habitación
  (*f.*), 10
rope soga (*f.*)
run correr, 7
  — away escaparse, fugarse, 17
  — into chocar, 13

S

safe seguro(a)
safety seguridad (*f.*)
  — belt cinturón de seguridad (*m.*)
  — (bike) helmet casco de
  seguridad (*m.*), 2
same mismo(a), 9
sandal sandalia (*f.*), 17
save salvar, 2
saved guardado(a), 10
say decir (e:i), 7
scar cicatriz (*f.*), 17
school escuela (*f.*), 7
  — crossing cruce de niños (*m.*)
scream gritar, 18
sealed sellado(a), 16
seat asiento (*m.*)
secret secreto(a), 15
section sección (*f.*), división (*f.*), 1
sedative calmante (*m.*), sedante
  (*m.*), sedativo (*m.*), 19
see ver, 7
  — you later. Hasta luego., P
seem parecer, 4
seen visto(a)
self-defense: in — en defensa
  propia
sell vender, 7
semiautomatic semiautomático(a),
  20
send mandar, 1
sentence dictar sentencia, sentenciar; sentencia (*f.*), condena (*f.*)
sentimental sentimental, 14
separate separar
sergeant sargento (*m.*, *f.*), 1
serial number número de serie
  (*m.*), 10
series serie (*f.*), 10
serious grave, 1; serio(a), 13
serve servir (e:i)
service servicio (*m.*), 15
set on fire dar fuego, pegar fuego
several varios(as), 5
sex sexo (*m.*), 15
sexual sexual, 18
shake temblar(e:ie), 13
shave afeitarse, 20
shirt camisa (*f.*), 4
shiver temblar (e:ie), 13
shoe zapato (*m.*)
shoelace cordón (del zapato)
  (*m.*), 16

shoot disparar, 3; tirar, dar un tiro, dar un balazo
— **up** pullar (*coll.*) (*Caribe*)
short (*in height*) bajo(a), bajito(a) (*Cuba*), chaparro(a) (*México*), 4; (*in length*) corto(a)
shorts shorts (*m. pl.*)
short-sleeved de mangas cortas
shotgun escopeta (*f.*)
should deber, 2
shoulder hombro (*m.*)
shout gritar, 18
show mostrar (o:ue), enseñar, 9
shower ducharse
Shut up! ¡Cállese!, 20
side lado (*m.*), 13
sidewalk acera (*f.*), banqueta (*f.*) (*México*), 9
silent callado(a), 6
silver plata (*f.*), 11
silverware cubiertos (*m. pl.*), 11
sincerely sinceramente, 14
sir señor (Sr.) (*m.*), P
sister hermana (*f.*)
— **-in-law** cuñada (*f.*)
sit down sentar(se) (e:ie)
Sit down. Siéntese., 8
situation situación (*f.*)
size tamaño (*m.*)
skeleton key llave falsa (*f.*), ganzúa (*f.*)
skin piel (*f.*)
skinny flaco(a)
skirt falda (*f.*), 17
slap bofetada (*f.*), galleta (*f.*) (*Cuba*)
— **on the buttocks** nalgada (*f.*)
sleep dormir (o:ue)
sleeveless sin mangas
slow despacio
slowly despacio, 1
small pequeño(a), 2
smell olor (*m.*), 19
— **of** olor a, 19
smoke humo (*m.*), 5; fumar, 7
smuggle contrabandear
smuggling contrabando (*m.*)
so tan, 12; por lo tanto, 20
— **long.** Hasta luego., P
— **that** para que
sobriety test prueba del alcohol (*f.*), 9
solicit solicitar, 15
some algún, alguno(a), 6

someone alguien, 5
something algo, 8
sometimes a veces, 2
son hijo (*m.*)
—**-in-law** yerno (*m.*)
sorry: I'm —. Lo siento., 6
Spanish (language) español (*m.*), 1
spanking nalgada (*f.*)
sparkplug bujía (*f.*)
speak hablar, 1
speed velocidad (*f.*), 9
— **limit** límite de velocidad (*m.*) velocidad máxima (*f.*), 9
spell deletrear, 1
sports car carro deportivo (*m.*)
spot mancha (*f.*)
spread extender (e:ie), 9
— **one's feet** separar los pies
spreadeagle abrir las piernas y los brazos
stab dar una puñalada
stand pararse, 16
— **up!** ¡Póngase de pie!
standing parado(a), 7
start (a car) arrancar
starter arranque (*m.*), motor de arranque (*m.*)
state estado (*m.*), 2; (*adj.*) estatal, 9
statue estatua (*f.*)
stay permanecer, 6; quedarse, 10
steal (from) robar, 10; llevarse, 11
steering wheel volante (*m.*), timón (*m.*) (*Cuba*)
stenographer taquígrafo(a) (*m., f.*)
stepdaughter hijastra (*f.*)
stepfather padrastro (*m.*), 8
stepmother madrastra (*f.*)
stepson hijastro (*m.*)
still (*adv.*) todavía, 2; (*adj.*) quieto(a), 13
stolen robado(a), 10
stomach estómago (*m.*)
stone piedra (*f.*)
stop suspender, 5; detener, 6; parar, 12
—**!** ¡Alto!, 3; ¡Párese!, ¡Pare!
— **(doing something)** dejar de (+ *inf.*), 6
— **line** línea de parada (*f.*), 12
store tienda (*f.*)
straight (*hair*) lacio(a)
to go — ahead seguir (e:i) derecho, 2
strange extraño(a), 4

stranger extraño(a) (*m., f.*), 18; desconocido(a) (*m., f.*)

street calle (*f.*), 1

stretch out extender (e:ie), 9

stretcher camilla (*f.*)

strike golpear, 18

struggle luchar, 18

student estudiante (*m., f.*), 7

study estudiar, 17

stutter tartamudear

submit (oneself) to someterse a, 9

succeed in (doing something) llegar a (+ *inf.*), 18

such a thing tal cosa, 19

sufficient suficiente, 15

supermarket mercado (*m.*), super-mercado (*m.*)

support apoyo (*m.*)

Sure! ¡Cómo no!, 7

surname apellido (*m.*), P

suspect sospechar, 7

suspicion sospecha (*f.*), 8

suspicious sospechoso(a), 10

swear jurar

sweater suéter (*m.*), 17

swindle estafar, 14; estafa (*f.*), 14

switchblade navaja (*f.*), 8

system sistema (*m.*), 5

T

take llevar, 2; tomar, 6

   — **a seat** tomar asiento, P

   — **away** quitar, 8

   — **drugs** endrogarse

   — **off (clothing)** quitarse, 16

   — **out** sacar, 6

talk hablar, 1; conversar

tall alto(a), 4

tank tanque (*m.*)

tape recorder grabadora (*f.*), 11

tattoo tatuaje (*m.*), 7

teacher maestro(a) (*m., f.*)

technician técnico(a) (*m., f.*), 10

teenager adolescente (*m., f.*), jovencito(a) (*m., f.*), 17

telephone teléfono (*m.*), 1

   — **operator** telefonista (*m., f.*), 1

television set televisor (*m.*), 10

tell decir (e:i), 7; contar (o:ue), 18

tennis shoe zapato de tenis (*m.*)

tenth décimo(a), P

tequila tequila (*f.*), 15

terrace terraza (*f.*)

terrified aterrorizado(a), 18

test prueba (*f.*), 9

Thank you very much. Muchas gracias., P

that que, 3; eso (*m.*), 8; aquel, aquello(a), 18

   — **is to say . . .** es decir... , 18

   — **one** ése(a), 8

then entonces, 4

there para allá, 1; allá, allí, 2; ahí, 16

   — **is (are)** hay, 1

   — **was (were)** hubo, 13

therefore por lo tanto, 20

these estos(as), 6

thief ladrón(ona) (*m., f.*), 3

thin delgado(a), 7; flaco(a)

thing cosa (*f.*), 6; artículo (*m.*), 14

think creer, 4; pensar (e:ie), 17

   to — so creer que sí, 7

third tercero(a), 8

this este(a), 2

   — **one** éste(a) (*m., f.*), 8

   — **time** esta vez, 8

threat amenaza (*f.*), 20

threaten amenazar, 18

through por, 2

throw away tirar, 10

thumb pulgar (*m.*)

ticket multa (*f.*), 6

tie corbata (*f.*)

tile roof techo de tejas (*m.*)

time hora (*f.*), 3; tiempo (*m.*), 6; vez (*f.*), 8

   just in — a tiempo, 13

   on — a tiempo, 13

tip punta (*f.*), 9

tire llanta (*f.*), goma (*f.*) (*Cuba*), neumático (*m.*), 20

tired cansado(a), 8

title título (*m.*)

to a, 2; hacia

   — **the left (right)** a la izquierda (derecha), 2

today hoy, P

toe dedo del pie (*m.*)

together juntos(as), 10

tomorrow mañana

tongue lengua (*f.*)

tonight esta noche, 5

too también, 8

   — **much** demasiado(a), 12

tooth diente (*m.*)

top quality de primera calidad, 14

totally totalmente, 11
touch tocar, 9
toward hacia, 7
town pueblo (*m.*), 10
toy juguete (*m.*)
  — **store** juguetería (*f.*)
traffic tránsito (*m.*)
  — **light** semáforo (*m.*), 12
  — **sign** señal de tránsito (*f.*)
  — **violation** infracción de tránsito (*f.*), 6
trained entrenado(a), 4
trash basura (*f.*), 10
treat tratar, 8
tremble temblar (e:ie), 13
trespassing: no — prohibido pasar
trial juicio (*m.*)
trip viaje (*m.*)
trousers pantalón (*m.*), pantalones (*m. pl.*), 4
truck camión (*m.*), 13
true? ¿verdad?, 2
trunk maletero (*m.*), cajuela (*f.*) (*México*), baúl (*m.*) (*Puerto Rico*), 20; portaequipajes (*m.*)
truth verdad (*f.*), 11
try (to) tratar (de), 4
T-shirt camiseta (*f.*)
turn doblar, 2
  — **around** darse vuelta, voltearse, virarse, 20
  — **off** apagar, 9
  — **on (a light)** prender, 4; encender (e:ie), 5
  — **over (something to someone)** entregarle a, 11
  — **signal** indicador (*m.*)
twice dos veces, 17
two-way traffic doble circulación (*f.*), doble vía (*f.*)
type clase (*f.*), 7

U

uncle tío (*m.*), 9
uncomfortable incómodo(a), 2
under debajo (de), 13
  — **the influence (of)** bajo los efectos (de), 6
undercover police policía secreta (*f.*), 15
underneath debajo de, 13
understand entender (e:ie), 6; comprender, 18

unless a menos que, 19
until hasta, 2; hasta que, 19
up-to-date al día, 11
upholstery tapicería (*f.*)
urgent urgente, 4
urgently urgentemente, 14
urine orina (*f.*), 9
use uso, 2; usar, 4
  can be used puede usarse, 6
  will be used se usará, 6
used usado(a)
usually generalmente, 17

V

vacant desocupado(a), 3
vacation vacaciones (*f. pl.*)
valid válido(a), 12
value valor (*m.*), 11
vandalism vandalismo (*m.*), 6
vehicle vehículo (*m.*), 13
venereal disease enfermedad venérea (*f.*), 18
verb verbo (*m.*)
verdict fallo (*m.*), veredicto (*m.*)
very muy, 1
  — **much** muchísimo, 15
victim víctima (*f.*), 17
video camera cámara de video (*f.*), video-cámara (*f.*), 10
videocassette recorder (VCR) videocasetera (*f.*), videograbadora (*f.*), 11
visible visible, 7
vocabulary vocabulario (*m.*)
voluntarily voluntariamente, 20

W

waist cintura (*f.*)
  — **-high** a nivel de la cintura
wait (for) esperar, 7
walk caminar, 2
wall pared (*f.*), 6
wallet cartera (*f.*), billetera (*f.*), 16
want desear, 1; querer (e:ie), 5
warrant orden (*f.*), 8; permiso (*m.*), 20
wart verruga (*f.*)
waste perder (e:ie), 6
watch reloj (*m.*), 16
watching mirando
water agua (*f. but* el agua)
  — **pump** bomba de agua (*f.*)
watering riego (*m.*), 5

way forma (*f.*), 8
weapon arma (*f. but* el arma), 8
wear llevar, llevar puesto(a), 2;
tener puesto(a), 17
week semana (*f.*), 4
weigh pesar, 20
weight peso (*m.*)
welcome: You're —. De nada., No
hay de qué., P
well bien, P
what lo que, 8
what? ¿qué?, 1; ¿cuál?, 4
— **can I (we) do for you?** ¿En
qué puedo (podemos) servirle?,
¿Qué se le ofrece?, P
— **else?** ¿Qué más?, 7
— **time was (is) it?** ¿Qué hora
era (es)?, 18
—**'s new?** ¿Qué hay de
nuevo?, P
—**'s wrong?** ¿Qué tiene?, 7
wheel rueda (*f.*)
wheelchair silla de ruedas (*f.*)
when cuando, 6
when? ¿cuándo?, 11
where? ¿dónde?, 1
whereabouts paradero (*m.*)
which? ¿cuál?, 4
while mientras, 20
white blanco(a), 4
who? ¿quién?, 1
whole: the —. . . todo(a) el (la)...
whose cuyo(a), 15
why? ¿por qué?, 2
wife esposa (*f.*), mujer (*f.*)
wig peluca (*f.*)
will voluntad (*f.*), 17
willing dispuesto(a), 8
window ventana (*f.*), 10; (*in a car*)
ventanilla
windshield parabrisas (*m.*)
— **wiper** limpiaparabrisas (*m.*)
wine vino (*m.*), 20
wish desear, 1; querer (e:ie), 5

with con, P
— **(black) hair** de pelo
(negro), 17
— **him** con él, 6
— **me** conmigo, 6
— **you** contigo (*informal*), 15;
consigo(a) (*formal*)
within dentro de, 6
without sin, 3, 9
— **fail** sin falta, 19
witness testigo (*m., f.*), 14
woman mujer (*f.*), 1
word palabra (*f.*)
work trabajo (*m.*), 8
working: not — descompuesto(a),
19
wrist muñeca (*f.*)
write escribir, 6
— **down** anotar, 10

X

X-ray radiografía (*f.*), 13

Y

yard patio (*m.*), 3
year año (*m.*)
yellow amarillo(a), 7
yes sí, 1
yesterday ayer, 8
yet todavía, 2
young joven, 4
— **boy (girl)** chico(a) (*m., f.*),
chamaco(a) (*m., f.*) (*México*), 13
— **lady** señorita (Srta.) (*f.*), P
— **man (woman)** joven (*m., f.*), 6
younger menor, 4
your su, 1; tu, 2
yours suyo(a)
yourself sí mismo(a)

Z

zone zona (*f.*), 9